The Bloody Century 2:

More Tales of Murder in 19th Century America

Robert Wilhelm

ISBN: 979-8-9907881-0-7
Night Stick Press
Schroon Lake, New York

Table of Contents

Introduction

When I began compiling nineteenth-century murder stories for the blog Murder by Gaslight in 2009, I thought I would run out of material after a year or so. By 2014, I had posted over 250 stories with no end in sight. At that point, I selected fifty of the best stories and published them in the book *The Bloody Century: True Tales of Murder in 19th Century America.* In 2024, with well over 500 murders to choose from, it was time for this sequel—*The Bloody Century 2: More Tales of Murder in 19th Century America.*

The first volume of *The Bloody Century* focused on the most famous murders and lesser-known cases where the story was complete. These were stories in which the perpetrator was captured, faced one or more trials, and often ended with the killer's execution. *The Bloody Century 2* includes a broader selection of murders. While most end with a trial and punishment for the guilty, others, due to suicide, insanity, or lynch mobs, never make it to the courtroom. A few more have no conclusive endings and will remain forever unsolved.

While these stories are all but forgotten today, they were taken very seriously when they occurred. In daily newspapers, murders dominated the front page, often for weeks at a time. They provoked strong emotions for and against the accused, sometimes turning violent. The stories were picked up by newspapers nationwide, and a daily paper could feature out-of-state murders along with local homicides. Most of the story titles are taken from newspaper headlines.

Each story in *The Bloody Century 2* includes one or more illustrations. Some of the pictures come from murder pamphlets, short booklets sold at a murderer's execution outlining the crime, often including a confession of the condemned man. Weekly and monthly magazines also included murder illustrations. Publications such as the *National Police Gazette, Illustrated Police News*, and Frank *Leslie's Illustrated Newspaper* were famous for publishing portraits of the killers and graphic depictions of the crime. Daily newspapers would also include murder illustrations, especially when recapping the story during a trial or prior to an execution.

The stories in *The Bloody Century 2* are grouped by motive or circumstances of the murder: Crime, Romance, Jealousy, Family, Revenge, Adultery, Insanity, Random Violence, Multiple Murders, Connected Murders, and Unsolved. While most of these categories are obvious, some need further explanation. Multiple Murders include mass murders—multiple victims in one event and serial murders—one killer committing multiple unrelated murders. Connected Murders are a special category where several murders are indirectly connected. In one case, two convicted murderers meet in prison and commit a third murder. In another, two separate murders result in the end of New York City's Whyo gang.

As I said in the first volume, I have avoided any social or psychological analysis of the situations and people involved, opting instead for a concise telling of stories that are fascinating in their own right. The stories are short by design, supplying the relevant facts, profiles of those involved, and public sentiment. Some of these murders have been the subject of books, and many more are worthy of book-length treatments. I have made all of the relevant information easy to find on the page. Those interested in learning more about a particular case can find the sources listed in the chapter notes.

The days of America's distant past, the time of gaslights and horse-drawn carriages, are often viewed as quaint and sentimental, but a closer look reveals passions, fears, and motives that are timeless and universal. A population inured to violence was capable of monstrous acts. A visit to the bloody century may well provide insight into our own.

CRIME

The Long Island Murders

A series of violent home invasions in and around Brookville, Long Island, in November 1883, and the months that followed left two people dead and four more seriously injured. The usually serene farming community was thrown into a state of confusion with at least a dozen false arrests, two perjured eyewitnesses, a false confession, lynch mobs, a jailbreak, and, for a time, two independent and equally valid lines of inquiry that could not be reconciled.

One of the Suspected
National Police Gazette, December 8, 1883.

Date:	November 11, 1883
Location:	Brookville, New York
Victims:	Lydia R. Maybee & Anna E. Maybee
Cause of Death:	Strangulation
Accused:	Charles H. Rugg

Synopsis:

On the evening of November 17, 1883, Israel Baxter was walking past the home of his neighbor, Garret Maybee, in the little farming community of Brookville, Long Island, when he heard cries of distress. Knowing he could not help Maybee by himself, he hurried to alert his other neighbors. Soon, half a dozen sturdy farmers were rushing to the Maybee house, armed with shotguns, spades, and other makeshift weapons in case they confronted an intruder.

Garret Maybee, 73 years old, was paralyzed from the waist down due to a stroke ten years earlier, and for the past two years, he had been totally blind. The men found him sitting in his invalid chair, barely conscious and bleeding from several cuts on his head. He was moaning about his poor wife and daughter. They were not in the house, so some of the men went to the barn to look for them. In a corner of the stable, covered with leaves, they found the bodies of Garret's wife, Lydia Maybee, aged 73, and their daughter, 39-year-old Annie. They had both been strangled.

When he regained his composure, Mr. Maybee explained that his wife had gone to the barn at about half-past four to milk the cows. When she had not returned by five o'clock, Maybee sent his daughter to see what was wrong. About half an hour after she left, Maybee heard footsteps in the house that he knew were not his wife's or daughter's.

Maybee called out, "Who is there?"

A low male voice replied, "Me."

He then heard the stranger go upstairs. When he came down a few minutes later he demanded that Maybee give him his watch. Maybee told him he was blind and did not know where it was.

"Then I will kill you," said the stranger.

He grabbed Maybee's cane and beat him unconscious. When Maybee came to, the stranger was gone.

Maybee raised the window and shouted, "Murder."

The community was shocked by the murders. The Board of Town Officers offered a $500 reward for the arrest of the killers, and the Queens County Board of Supervisors added another $500. Suspicion first fell on a tramp who had been seen in the neighborhood and who often slept in the poorhouse a quarter of a mile from the scene of the murder. A suspicious-looking man who answered the description of the tramp had boarded a train for Brooklyn. The detectives went there to investigate.

Two days after the murder, two suspects were arrested in Brooklyn and two more on Long Island. One of the Long Island suspects, James Doyle, who was born in Brooklyn, was identified by Mr. Maybee's son-in-law as the tramp who had been seen in the area. His shoe matched a footprint found near the barn. Another of the arrested tramps, John Brown, claimed that Doyle had shown him the bodies of the two dead women.

Miraculously, the blows to Garett Maybee's head restored his eyesight, but this did not help in identifying the assailant. He did listen to the voice of James Doyle, who was told to say "Me" and "I will kill you." Maybee identified Doyle's voice as that of the man who had assaulted him. The police showed Doyle the bodies, and although he recognized the women, he swore he had never been in the barn and did not kill them.

An inquest was held, and while a net of circumstantial evidence was tightening around James Doyle, the authorities were not convinced that he was the killer. The thief had gone straight to two drawers containing money and Mrs. Maybee's jewelry. The thief took $100 in cash, a cameo brooch, and Mrs. Maybee's watch. The fact that he knew exactly where to look and that he knew Mr. Maybee had a watch as well made them suspect someone who was familiar with the house and the family. Maybee's son-in-law, William Simonson, together with officials from the Long Island Railroad, contacted the Pinkerton Detective Agency and they sent Detective James Wood to investigate. Meanwhile, James

Doyle was able to prove an alibi and was released from custody. The inquest ruled that Lydia and Ann Maybee were strangled by a person or persons unknown.

Detective Wood believed the attack had been motivated by revenge rather than theft and was making quick progress with his investigation. While he was not ready to give the name of the murderer, on December 6 he told the press that an arrest was imminent. The killer was someone familiar to the household, who visited almost daily and had even attended the funeral of the victims. Local police, however, were still arresting tramps, and at least two more were held until they could prove alibis.

A severe snowstorm hindered the investigation, and a month passed with no announcement from Detective Wood. Then, on January 7, 1884, another attack occurred at a home just three miles from Maybee's farm. Mr. and Mrs. James C. Townsend, a prominent elderly couple from Oyster Bay, Long Island, were found unconscious on the floor of their kitchen, each with severe head wounds. Mrs. Townsend, whose wounds were less severe than her husband's, was able to talk to the police, but her information was withheld from the press. From the neighbors, reporters learned that Mrs. Townsend had said that a black man named Simon Rappelyea had come to collect money for washing his wife had done for the family. When she turned to get it, he hit her on the side of the head. Simon Rappelyea was arrested soon after.

Between the Townsend home and the cottage of Simon Rappelyea, the police found a stonemason's hammer and a pair of bloodstained overalls. The detectives traced the hammer and overalls to John Tappan, and they arrested him on suspicion. John Tappan's brother Edmund was also brought in for questioning. Edmund had been one of the men who responded to Garret Maybee's distress calls and had testified at the inquest – he was also Detective Wood's prime suspect and had been under surveillance for several weeks.

Under questioning, Edmund Tappan admitted that his brother John had murdered the Maybee women. Edmund dictated his story to his friend Halstead Frost to unburden his conscience. It was signed by Edmund and notarized. He claimed that John strangled Mrs. Maybee, and then he told Edmund that he would wait for Annie and strangle her as well. When that was done, he went into the house, took the money and jewelry, and when he came out, he gave Edmund $10.

John Tappan denied involvement in both the Maybee murders and the Townsend assaults. But he had worked for Mr. Maybee and knew the layout of the Maybee house. The Tappans became the prime suspects, and Simon Rappelyea was released from custody.

Unburdening his soul did not have the desired effect for Edmund Tappan. After giving his statement, he went into convulsions and became seriously ill. Unofficially, the police believed that Edmund Tappan was the perpetrator of both crimes with the help of someone other than his brother.

Then, on January 25, another assault changed the game again. Around 7:00 a.m., Mrs. Sealey Sprague was surprised in her kitchen by a masked man demanding money. She tried to rush past him, but he grabbed her by the hair and knocked her down. He demanded money again, and she gave him thirty-eight dollars. Mrs. Sprague could see beneath his improvised mask that the man was black. When he left, she ran for help, and Farmer Petit and his son hurried to her aid. They found Mr. Sprague by his barn unconscious, lying in a pool of frozen blood. He had been hit in the head with a railroad 'strap', a piece of iron used to connect rails.

It was not hard to follow the assailant's footprints in the snow, and they tracked him to the village of Westbury, where he stopped to buy some crackers and cheese. The owner of the store had been notified to be on the lookout and managed to keep him in the store until the police arrived.

The greatest challenge for the police was keeping the man from the hands of a lynch mob. According to the *New Haven Register*, "The colored people were as bitter against him as the white," and the angry crowd was noticeably integrated. The officers were able to wrest him from the mob and took him to Gottert's Hotel in Hicksville, where another angry mob soon gathered. At 8:00 that night, they managed to get him on board a milk train to Long Island City, where he was taken to the Queens County Jail.

The man was Charles H. Rugg of Oyster Bay, Long Island. After a day of denying involvement in any of the crimes, Rugg broke down and confessed to the Sprague assault. He was questioned about the other crimes as well, but the police absolutely refused to release any information given on the interrogations.

Rugg had worked on the Maybee's farm in the past, but Garret Maybee did not think he was the killer. He worked there before Maybee lost his eyesight, and he had never been inside the house. He would not have known about Maybee's blindness or the house's layout. Maybee did not think Rugg was strong enough to overpower his daughter. He now believed the voice he heard had been Edmund Tappan and that Tappan and an accomplice committed the murders.

While Rugg was being questioned, an inquest was held on the Townsend assaults, and the Tappans were still the prime suspects. Edmund Tappan broke down in tears on the witness stand, and it was commonly believed that police questioning had driven him insane.

The police would not say who would be tried for the Maybee murders or the Townsend assaults, and the newspapers became increasingly frustrated by the lack of official information. The *New York Herald* summed up the case:

At present the extraordinary situation exists of two prisoners held for each of two crimes – Rugg and Edmund Tappan in one case and Rugg and John Tappan in the other – against every one of whom sufficient evidence exists to secure convictions, while there is not the slightest evidence and scarcely a possibility that they were accomplices.

When investigators found watches stolen from the Maybees and the Townsends in some New York City pawnshops, the noose began to tighten around Charles Rugg. The pawnbrokers identified Rugg as the man who brought them in. Lance Conkling, a friend of Rugg's, told police they had gone to New York after the murders and Rugg "spent money lavishly in various low resorts."

While in jail, Rugg appeared to be ailing and was under a doctor's care. The night of February 17, he was shaking violently, and his jailer, John Murphy, mixed some medicine prescribed by the doctor and brought it into Rugg's cell. When Murphy turned to leave the cell, Rugg jumped him and knocked him down, then ran through the open cell door. He grabbed Murphy's revolver and club and escaped the building by jumping out of a second-story courtroom window. Rugg was at large for three days before being captured in a church in Woodside, Long Island.

Edmund Tappan told the Grand Jury that he had made up the confession and accusations against his brother. He had lied in hopes of getting the reward money, which had grown to $2,800. There was now little question that Rugg had committed all three crimes, and the Grand Jury handed down seven indictments against him – two for first-degree murder, four for assault and robbery, and one for burglary. Unofficially, he was also being considered as a suspect in the unsolved murder of Rose Ambler in Connecticut.

Trial: April 21, 1884

Charles Rugg was tried for the murder of Anne Maybee first; should he be found not guilty, the prosecution was ready to try him again for Lydia Maybee's murder. Garret Maybe, who had lost his eyesight once more, gave heart-wrenching testimony as to the events of November 17 while his doctor sat by his side, holding his pulse to make sure that he did not become overly excited. He did not give his opinion as to who committed the murders, but under gentle questioning by the defense, he admitted that he had first identified the voice of John Doyle.

Rugg was defended by ex-judge Richard Busteed and John F. Quarles, a black attorney who had also represented both Simon Rappelyea and John Tappan in preliminary hearings. They tried to introduce Edmund Tappan's confession as evidence, but the judge would not allow the confession or any mention of it.

The jury deliberated for just over an hour before returning a verdict of guilty.

Verdict: Guilty of first-degree murder

Aftermath:

There were numerous claimants to the reward money offered for the capture of the Maybee murderer. A score of citizens who ran down Rugg in Westbury the day of the Sprague assault each requested an equal share; detectives from Roslyn, Flushing, Mineola, and Oyster Bay requested shares for working the case; other residents of Oyster Bay and Glen Cove wanted shares for contributing information; detective John S. Wood, who worked hardest on the case was precluded from receiving a reward due to his position with the Pinkerton Agency. The distribution of reward money would be determined in court.

Charles H. Rugg was hanged inside the jail in Long Island City on May 15, 1885. Sheriff Furman limited attendance to a couple of hundred of his friends and relatives, and he excluded members of the press because he felt they had not given him the credit he was due in their reporting of the case. Rugg had converted to Catholicism before the execution and went stoically to the gallows. Reportedly, he was reciting "Hail, Mary" when the sheriff cut the rope to spring the trap.

Professional Poisoners

Dr. and Mrs. Henry Meyer used a dazzling array of aliases to stay one step ahead of detectives as they moved from city to city, engaging in lethal insurance fraud. It was their livelihood; they were professional poisoners.

The Poisoners and their New York Victim
New York World. July 16, 1893.

Date: March 30, 1892
Location: New York, New York
Victim: Ludwig Brant, alias Gustave Baum
Cause of Death: Poisoning
Accused: Dr. Henry Meyer

Synopsis:
On July 12, 1893, New York Police detectives Trainor and Von Gerichten concluded a fifteen-month investigation into the murder of Gustave Baum with the arrest, in Detroit, of Dr. Henry Meyer and his wife, Maria. It was a case of insurance fraud. The couple had taken out several policies against Baum's life in New York, and when Baum suddenly died, they tried to collect. Two insurance companies paid without question, but Mutual Life Insurance Company had suspicions. They began to investigate, prompting the Meyers to take what they could and flee New York.

Gustave Baum had been a willing co-conspirator in the insurance fraud. Meyer had met Baum, whose real name was Ludwig Brant, in Chicago's Joliet Prison. After their release, Meyer and Baum regrouped in New York along with Maria Meyer and a third prisoner, Carl Muller, alias August Wimmers. They worked out a scheme where Maria Meyer, using the alias Emilie Rathier, became Baum's bride in a mock marriage ceremony. Baum took out several life insurance policies with Emilie as beneficiary. Then, with Dr. Meyer's help, Baum was to feign sickness. When it appeared that Baum was on his deathbed, they planned to procure a corpse, say it was Baum, and collect on the policies.

Meyer, who was calling himself Dr. Henry Reuter, prescribed medicine that Baum believed would make him appear sick but would do no lasting damage. However, the Meyers had no intention of splitting the take with Baum, and they saw no point in looking for a corpse when it was so much easier to create their own. To facilitate Baum's fake illness, they kept him under the influence of opiates. As Maria appeared to nurse him lovingly, she fed him the poison that would eventually kill him. It is unclear whether Carl Muller was involved in this part of the plan.

When Gustave Baum died on March 30, 1892, Dr. Simon Minden was called in to examine the body. 'Dr. Reuter' detailed the symptoms for him, and Minden agreed that Baum had died from chronic dysentery. Even before the body was buried, Maria went to the offices of Washington Life and New York Life insurance companies and collected payments. However, Mr. Gillette of Mutual Life Insurance refused to pay. He had listened to gossip from neighbors who criticized the widow's lack of mourning, and he noted how quickly she and Baum's doctor had left the neighborhood.

It took three months, but suspicion surrounding Baum's death grew to the point where the coroner agreed to exhume the corpse for further examination. The stomach was given to a chemist who determined that it contained antimony, a strong mineral poison, in a quantity large enough to kill Baum. The hunt for Dr. Meyer and his wife began.

At the time of their arrests in Detroit, the New York detectives were not the only ones hot on the Meyers' trail; detectives from Chicago and Toledo were also ready to make arrests. For a time, it appeared that there would be a legal battle to decide who would be taking the prisoners back to their home state.

The Meyers had settled in Toledo, where they were known as Dr. and Mrs. Hugo Wheler. Shortly after they arrived, Maria gave birth, and they hired a young woman named Mary Neiss as a domestic servant. Maria told Mary that she wanted to purchase some life insurance but was afraid that since birth, her health was not sound enough to pass the medical examination. She persuaded Mary to go to Detroit, pose as Mrs. Wheler, and purchase an insurance policy. When Mary returned to Toledo with a $5,000 policy from the Equitable Life Assurance Society, the Meyers set to work poisoning her. As Mary's condition continued to deteriorate, Carl Muller took pity on the poor girl and became infatuated with her. He declared his love and told Mary about the wicked plot against her; the couple fled together to Chicago.

Undaunted, the Meyers hired another servant and poisoned her. When they tried to collect the claim, the company investigated and found that the description of the dead woman did not match that of the woman who was insured, and neighbors who had known Mrs. Wehler were positive that the dead woman was not the woman they knew. The Meyers quickly left for Detroit, and the Toledo coroner issued a warrant charging Dr. and Mrs. Meyer, alias Wehler, with the murder of an unknown woman.

Pinkerton detectives also investigated Dr. Meyer for insurance fraud in Chicago. Dr. Meyer began his career as a poisoner in Chicago. After graduating from the Chicago Homeopathic school in 1878, he set up an office on Sedgwick Street and became the family physician of Henry Gelderman, a well-to-do grocer. Gelderman's wife was considerably younger than he was, and although Meyer was already married, he became intimate with Mrs. Gelderman.

About a year later, Meyer's wife died suddenly, and shortly after, Henry Gelderman took sick and died. At the time, foul play was not suspected, but suspicions were aroused when Dr. Meyer married Gelderman's widow. The bodies of Mrs. Meyer and Mr. Gelderman were disinterred, and post-mortem examinations revealed they had both been poisoned. Dr. Meyer and his new wife were arrested, but the evidence was insufficient for conviction.

Not long after this, the Geldermans' young daughter drowned in the bathtub, and Dr. Meyer attempted to poison his second wife. She refused to testify against him, and the charges were dropped, but when she caught him having intimate relations with their domestic servants, she sued for divorce.

Dr. Meyer eventually met and married Mary Dressen, a woman with a passion for poisoning equal to his own. It was estimated that they committed at least six insurance murders together before their arrests.

After the arrests in Detroit, it was agreed that since the New York detectives found him first, they should take him to trial in New York. However, the Toledo detectives requested that should Dr. Meyer be acquitted in New York, he was to be held for them.

First Trial: December 8, 1893

Much of the prosecution's case against Dr. Meyer consisted of expert testimony explaining what was found in the stomach of Gustave Baum and what effects it would have. The star witness, however, was Carl Muller, now married to Mary Neiss, who had come to New York at his own expense to testify against Meyer. On the witness stand, he explained the insurance fraud plot where Baum was to feign illness. They ran into trouble, he said, when Dr. Meyer was unable to secure a corpse to replace Baum. Muller had suggested that they abandon the plan and leave town, but Maria Meyer felt it was easier to kill Baum.

Meyer's defense consisted of testimony from expert witnesses who explained that it was quite possible that someone had added the antimony to Baum's stomach after his death. Meyer's attorney, Charles W. Brooke, questioned only four witnesses, saying that there was no need for more testimony since the prosecution had failed to show that Dr. Meyer killed Baum. It was a bold move but it would not be tested in this trial. As Brooke gave his closing statement and vehemently condemned the testimony of Carl Muller, one of the jurymen, A.B. Low, began to shake and twitch uncontrollably. Low had to be carried out of the courtroom, and he began shouting and frantically making Masonic hand signals. One of the doctors at the scene assessed Low's condition as cerebral congestion, and Low was taken to Bellevue Hospital for examination. The trial was postponed, and two days later, the doctors at Bellevue pronounced Low insane. The judge declared a mistrial.

Second Trial: April 12, 1894

Dr. Meyer's second trial the following April took much the same course as the first one. The defense witnesses were primarily doctors who testified that there was no way to tell if the poison was given to Baum after his death. In his closing argument, Brooke attacked the motives and credibility of Carl Muller. While Brooke did not generate enough doubt to win an acquittal from the jury, he did manage to save Meyer from the state's newly installed electric chair. After fifteen hours of deliberation, the jury returned a verdict of second-degree murder.

Verdict: Guilty of second-degree murder

Aftermath:

Dr. Meyer was sentenced to life in Sing Sing prison. Maria Meyer was never prosecuted for her role in the crime.

A Harum-Scarum Creature

In her hometown of Rockford, Illinois, Nellie C. Bailey was called 'a harum-scarum creature' that would come to no good. After marrying a Kansas banker and a Wisconsin actor, she became the mistress of a Texas rancher and was implicated in his murder in Indian Territory. The hometown prediction had come true.

Nellie C. Bailey
National Police Gazette. December 1, 1883.

Date:	October 7, 1883
Location:	Skeleton Ranch, Indian Territory
Victim:	Clement Bothamley
Cause of Death:	Gunshot
Accused:	Nellie C. Bailey

Synopsis:

William Dodson led a drive of 2,300 head of sheep from Kansas through Indian Territory to their new home in Texas in October 1883. A mile behind them, the owner of the new ranch, a widower named Clement Bothamley (sometimes spelled Bothemly), and his sister Bertha traveled in a wagon outfitted with bedrooms and pulled by two yoke of oxen. The wagon was so large that observers compared it with a railroad car. The night of October 7, Dodson heard Miss Bothamley calling from a distance and ran to see what was wrong. She took him to the wagon and led him inside, where Clement lay dead from a gunshot wound to the head.

He killed himself, she told Dodson. Clement had been suffering from rheumatism, and the pain had become unbearable. He had been taking large doses of morphine, but even that had not alleviated the pain. Bertha had been awakened by the gunshot and found her brother lying dead.

They realized that they would have to dig a grave and bury him on the trail. A wagon heading for Kansas had passed them several hours earlier, and

Dodson rode to them to ask for assistance. The men returned with him, and they buried Clement Bothamley near Skeleton Ranch. After a brief ceremony, Bertha and Dodson continued the drive.

In Kansas, federal marshals heard the story of Bothamley's death and suspected foul play. Marshal Hollister and a group of deputies caught up with sheep drive about nine miles south of the site of the murder. They exhumed the body of Clement Bothamley and took it back to Newton, Kansas, to be buried beside his late wife, and then took Bertha Bothamley to jail in Wichita.

They soon learned the woman was not Bothamley's sister, and she was not named Bertha. She was Nellie C. Bailey, Clement Bothamley's mistress. The marshals suspected that Nellie and William Dodson had murdered Bothamley for his money. Before she and Bothamley left for Texas, he deeded to her $20,000 worth of property in Kansas. After his death, she took possession of his trunk containing $7,000 in jewelry and diamonds and his outfit consisting of sheep and stock worth $10,000. At the time, the average farmworker made a dollar a day for ten hours work.

Clement Bothamley (sometimes spelled Bothamley) was an Englishman who left a wife in London and came to America, where he married again. Nellie said he gave her the property to protect it in case his first wife came looking for him. He and Nellie had planned to marry in Texas and run the sheep ranch together.

Nellie Bailey had been married before as well; in fact, she had two previous husbands and had not bothered to divorce either. She was born Nellie Benthusen in Illinois and spent the first fourteen years of her life in Rockford, Illinois. The residents of Rockford remembered Nellie well; when they learned of her trouble with Bothamley, the *Rockford Daily Gazette* reported, "In youth, she was always a harum-scarum creature, and the prediction then made that she would come to no good, appears to have been fulfilled."

Nellie had long dark hair and dark eyes; she was petite with a fine figure and seemed to have a devastating effect on men. At age seventeen, she was engaged to a boy in Illinois named Alvin Lakeside when she caught the eye of a banker named Shannon Bailey. She broke her engagement to Lakeside and married Bailey in Newton, Kansas. Bailey, who was quite a bit older, provided well for Nellie but was gone most of the time, looking after his mining interests in the Black Hills of Dakota. In his absence, Nellie grew restless, traveling first to New Jersey, then to Wisconsin.

In Waukesha, Wisconsin, Nellie stayed with an aunt and attempted to start a theater company. She and a group of young people spent several weeks rehearsing a play that Nellie wrote entitled The Maniac Lover. The plan was to take the play to the Black Hills, then on to California and fame. During this time, Nellie's life had become so wild that her aunt kicked her out of the house. She would later say that Nellie was always a "witchcat."

The play was never performed, but Nellie became intimate with Robert Reise, one of the players. Though she was still married to Shannon Bailey, she told Reise they had secretly divorced. She and Reise were married in Waukesha, and she stayed with him for a short time, but after realizing that he was not as wealthy as she thought, Nellie took off again. She left Wisconsin, and although she continued to correspond with Robert Reise, she would never see him again.

Nellie returned to Newton, Kansas, where she began a relationship with Clement Bothamley, whom she had met in a previous stay in Newton. In the fall of 1883, they planned to move to Texas and start a sheep ranch together. On October 1, they began the ill-fated journey.

In Wichita, Nellie was indicted for murder and held on $10,000 bail. She spent more than a year in jail waiting for her trial. During that time, she complained about the way she was portrayed in the press. She began working on a novel based on the true story of her life to be called *The Drover's Revenge; or, The Secret of Sunset Trail.*

Trial: January 19, 1885

Nellie's trial began on January 19, 1885. The prosecution attempted to prove that Nellie had conspired with William Dodson to murder Clement Bothamley and take his money and property to Texas. Nellie maintained that Bothamley had shot himself. In the end, there was little hard evidence to contradict Nellie's statement, and on January 20, she was acquitted of all charges.

Verdict: Not guilty

Aftermath:

It was reported that following her acquittal, Nellie was offered a position with a professional theatrical company and she planned to accept.

The Minneapolis Svengali

Harry Hayward was a handsome young playboy from a wealthy Minneapolis family. An inveterate gambler, he would finance his habit through theft, insurance fraud, and counterfeit currency. He was also thought to have hypnotic powers. He persuaded Catherine Ging to make him beneficiary on a life insurance policy, then, on December 3, 1894, he lured her to a meeting with Claus Blixt – also acting under Hayward's spell. As Catherine Ging was being murdered, Harry Hayward sat in a Minneapolis theatre watching a play with another woman. When the sordid details were learned, the press dubbed Hayward 'The Minneapolis Svengali.'

Harry T. Hayward
Harry Hayward: Life. Crimes. Dying Confession and Execution, 1896.

Date:	December 3, 1894
Location:	Minneapolis, Minnesota
Victim:	Catherine M. Ging
Cause of Death:	Gunshot
Accused:	Harry T. Hayward, Claus A. Blixt

Synopsis:

The most popular novel in America in the 1890s was the English translation of George du Maurier's Trilby. Readers were fascinated by the character Svengali and his ability to dominate the innocent milkmaid Trilby through hypnosis, lifting her to great heights as a professional singer but ultimately causing her demise. The Minneapolis press saw a parallel between Svengali and Harry Hayward in the murder of Catherine Ging.

Catherine Ging – known as Kitty to her friends – was a tall, imposing woman, described as handsome rather than beautiful, but she had her share of beaux. Kitty had come to Minnesota from New York State, rumored to be running from an ardent suitor. In Minneapolis, she had been engaged to Frederick I. Reed, a clerk at the Golden Rule Department Store. The engagement was off, but she still carried the ring in a chamois bag around her neck. Kitty worked as a dressmaker and lived in the Ozark Flats apartment building in Minneapolis where she struck up a relationship with Harry Hayward, son of the building's owner.

How close they were is open to interpretation. At one point, Harry Hayward claimed that Kitty Ging had agreed to marry him, but it was well known that they both were seeing other people. There is no question, though, that Kitty Ging was seduced by Harry's plans to acquire wealth. Harry had said more than once, "Money is my god," and Kitty listened intently to his plans to sell stolen jewelry and pass counterfeit currency. And she never hesitated to front Harry money for his gambling ventures.

On the night of December 3, 1893, Catherine Ging hired a horse and buggy from the Goosman livery stable. She even requested the horse by name – a gentle buckskin mare called Lucy. She had it sent to the West Hotel, and there, at 7:08 p.m., she took the reins and drove away.

At 9:10 p.m., Lucy returned to the stable, pulling an empty buggy. Around the same time, the body of a young woman was found on Excelsior Boulevard, on the outskirts of Minneapolis, her skull crushed, lying in a pool of blood. Putting the two events together, police were able to identify the woman as Catherine Ging and assumed she had died accidentally. The body lay in the morgue for over an hour before a doctor noticed a bullet lodged behind her left eye.

While police were questioning residents of Ozark Flats, before the body was positively identified, Harry Hayward arrived to give his opinion.

"My two thousand dollars is gone to hell," he said. "It's nobody but Miss Ging. She has not been hurt in any runaway accident; she has been done up for her money."

Earlier in the day, he had loaned Kitty some money in a restaurant, making sure that the waitress and the other patrons saw the large roll of bills. He now suspected she had been murdered for the money.

Frederick Reed, Kitty's ex-fiancé, was the first suspect. The police brought him into the station and questioned him for several hours before they believed his alibi. Miss Lillian Allen was another suspect. She and Kitty had, for a time, been rivals for Mr. Reed's affections, and she had abruptly left Minneapolis. But she also had an alibi. In Kitty's apartment, police found a torn-up note that read, "I cannot marry you." It had been written by Harvey Axford, a traveling salesman who had known Kitty for seven years. He could not marry her because he already had a wife, and residents of their boarding house heard them talking the night of the murder. The police rejected him as a suspect.

While not above suspicion, Harry Hayward had an alibi as well. He had been with his friend, Thomas A. Waterman, most of the evening, then took Mabel Bartleson to the Minneapolis Grand Opera House to see the musical play A Trip to Chinatown. Hayward was questioned extensively, and his answers had been open and forthcoming. He took an active interest in the investigation and volunteered information about Catherine Ging and his relationship with her.

Despite his cooperation, the police arrested Harry Hayward on December 6, along with his brother Adry, for the murder of Catherine Ging. The following day, they also arrested Claus Blixt, a janitor at Ozark Flats.

Their murder plan had been in the works for several weeks. Harry had agreed to lend Kitty some money and, as collateral, he persuaded her to take out a life insurance policy, with Harry as beneficiary. While not above doing the deed himself, this plan required someone else to pull the trigger. He went first to his older brother Adry and asked him to kill Kitty Ging. Adry absolutely refused. The plan so frightened him that on November 30, Adry went to the family lawyer Levi Stewart and told all. Stewart dismissed the story at the time, but after the murder occurred, he took the information to the police.

The man Harry finally persuaded to do the dirty work was Claus Blixt. He would visit Blixt in the basement of Ozark Flats nearly every day. Through a combination of threats and promises, he convinced Blixt that he had to kill Kitty Ging.

"He fixed me with his eyes." Blixt told the police, "I couldn't say no when he looked at me that way – nobody could."

Harry was adamant that Kitty must die, and he was growing impatient.

He told Blixt, "Every time I go up to her room, she puts her arms around me, and I would like to put a knife in the God damned bitch … if there was a dog and her, I would rather shoot her and let the dog go."

The day of the murder, Harry told Kitty he needed her help in a "green goods" deal – he was going to buy counterfeit currency. She was to take some money and go with Blixt to the outskirts of town. Harry would meet them there with the counterfeiters. That night, he gave Blixt a 38-caliber Colt revolver and a quart of whiskey. He told Blixt to drink it all.

Under intense questioning by the police, Adry broke down and told all. He claimed that he and Blixt had both been hypnotized by Harry.

Trial: January 21, 1895

Claus Blixt was scheduled to be tried first, but the prosecution switched the trial dates. They feared that it would be impossible to convict Hayward if Blixt were tried first and found not guilty.

Harry Hayward's trial lasted forty-six days, ten of which were taken up with finding a jury of men acceptable to both sides. Hayward was defended by W.W. Erwin, who was considered the most distinguished advocate in the Northwest. One hundred and thirty-six witnesses were called, but the most damning testimony came from Claus Blixt and Adry Hayward. The defense tried to have Adry's testimony ruled out on the grounds that he was insane, but the judge disagreed.

The climax of the trial was when Hayward testified in his own defense. He denied everything and placed the blame on Adry and Blixt.

The case went to the jury at 11:30 a.m. They deliberated, had lunch, and returned at 2:15 p.m. with a verdict of first-degree murder.

Verdict: Guilty of first-degree murder

Aftermath:

Hayward's attorney appealed the case, but the verdict was upheld and he was sentenced to hang on December 11, 1895. The death sentence had little effect on Hayward, who continued to joke with reporters about his execution. At first, he was granted privileges in prison and allowed to have callers, but after an escape attempt, he was kept isolated.

Claus Blixt pled guilty and was sentenced to life in prison.

Hayward maintained his innocence almost until the end. The evening before his execution, he agreed to give a complete confession to a reporter and a court stenographer. The confession was a long and rambling tale in which he admitted to committing several murders and other crimes in his travels throughout America and Mexico. He saved discussion of the Catherine Ging murder for the end, on the off chance that his sentence would be commuted before he finished. Ultimately, he admitted to plotting the Ging murder and took back his accusations against Adry. Though Hayward confessed, he showed no sign of remorse for Catherine Ging's murder or any of the others he allegedly committed.

Harry Hayward went to the gallows nattily dressed in a cutaway coat and pinstriped trousers. His last words were, "Pull her tight; I'll stand pat." The trap was sprung at 2:12 a.m., but the fall did not break his neck. Hayward slowly strangled to death; he was pronounced dead at 2:25 a.m.

After his funeral, a rumor persisted that Harry Hayward was not dead, that a secret organization revived him. Some said the Freemasons had resurrected him.

He Knew Too Much

Winfield Scott Goss was a chemical experimenter with a well-known fondness for intoxicating spirits. When his workshop, in a cottage outside Baltimore, exploded in February 1872, no one doubted that the badly charred corpse found inside was his. No one, that is, but the four insurance companies who had sold policies on Goss's life totaling $25,000. They had many questions, and Goss's friend and brother-in-law William Udderzook had all the answers. But rather than quelling their doubts, Udderzook's "plausible stories" only fueled them – he seemed to know too much.

Winfield S. Goss
The Udderzook Mystery! 1873.

Date:	July 1, 1873
Location:	Jennersville, Pennsylvania
Victim:	Winfield Scott Goss
Cause of Death:	Stabbing
Accused:	William Udderzook

Synopsis:

On the afternoon of Friday, February 2, 1872, Winfield Goss and William Udderzook went to the cottage that Goss rented for his chemical experiments, trying to create a substitute for India-rubber. They stopped at a store near Goss's workshop, where they purchased a gallon of kerosene in a wicker-covered demijohn and a bottle of whiskey. They also stopped at the home of a neighbor, Gottlieb Engle, where they borrowed an axe to chop firewood. At dusk, Goss filled an oil lamp with about a quart of kerosene from the demijohn. About six o'clock Udderzook went to Engle's house to return the axe. He stayed for dinner with the Engles, and then he and Gottlieb Engle returned to the cottage to drink whiskey.

The three men drank from the bottle Goss and Udderzook had purchased that afternoon and had been drinking for about an hour when the oil lamp went out. Udderzook tried to relight it using a candle, but the dripping paraffin made the wick harder to light. Engle proposed that they cut off a portion of the wick, and Udderzook suggested going to the store for a new wick. They finally decided it would be most expedient if they went to Engle's house for another lamp.

Engle and Udderzook went to Engle's house, leaving Goss in the cottage. They stayed for fifteen to twenty minutes before starting back with the lamp. When they reached the cottage, they saw that it was on fire, and they watched as flames shot out the window. Goss was still inside but they made no attempt to enter the building. Udderzook sent Engle to Baltimore to tell Goss's family what had happened. Udderzook watched the blaze for about an hour before expressing concerns to Mr. Lowndes, the owner of the building, that Goss was inside the burning building.

Lowndes was amazed that Udderzook had not given the alarm sooner. It was now too late to save Goss if he were inside; the roof and one wall had collapsed. As soon as they were able, spectators at the fire tried to ascertain if Goss had been burned with the building. They were able to pull out a body, but it was burned past recognition. Udderzook said he had visited every room in the cottage that afternoon, and he knew no one else was in the house – the body had to be Goss's. In telling the story, Udderzook mentioned every possible detail and was ready to account for and explain any inconsistencies.

Four days after the fire, Winfield Goss's brother, A.C. Goss, wrote to the insurance companies, relating the story of the fire and giving the coroner's verdict: "That W.S. Gross came to his death by the explosion of an oil-lamp." Four insurance policies were written on Winfield Gross's life, all payable to his wife, Eliza. The first was for $5,000 written by the Mutual Life Insurance Company in 1868, the second for $5,000 by the Continental Life Insurance Company of New York in May 1871, the third $10,000 by the Travelers Insurance Company of Hartford in October 1871, and the fourth for $5,000 by the Knickerbocker Life Insurance Company of New York, in January 1872, less than a month before the fire. The insurance companies smelled a rat right away and began their own investigation.

The investigators were troubled by a number of minor facts, which, when taken together, seemed to indicate fraud. Why, for example, was a strong, athletic man as Goss was known to be, unable to escape the burning building? Mr. J.C. Smith, a junk dealer, searched the ashes of the cottage for a watch and chain that Winfield always wore, raising suspicions when his search was unsuccessful. A week later, A.C. Goss, the deceased's brother, "made a thorougher search" and found the watch, chain and keys. A.C. Goss also testified that he was home the night of the fire, but his landlady said he was not home for dinner and did not return until late. The proprietor of a livery stable identified A.C. Goss as the man who engaged a horse and buggy that night.

The investigators now speculated that A.C. Goss had picked up his brother prior to the fire and taken him by horse and buggy to the railroad station. The person who died in the fire was not Winfield Goss. While they were not ready to charge anyone with fraud, they would not pay any of the claims unless the body could be conclusively proven to be that of Winfield Goss. Reluctantly,

Mrs. Goss agreed to the exhumation of the body so the teeth, the only feature of the body not destroyed past recognition, could be examined. Winfield Goss was known to have had a perfect set of teeth and had never been to the dentist for the smallest cavity. The body from the fire had several decayed or extracted teeth, and the front teeth were irregular.

The insurance companies refused to pay the claims, and Eliza Goss filed a lawsuit against them. In May 1873, the trial lasted ten days and the jury found in favor of the plaintiff – the insurance companies must pay. Mrs. Goss, A.C. Goss, and William Udderzook were delighted with the verdict, but they were far from receiving payment; the companies filed a motion for a new trial, and it would be November before that case would be heard.

In fact, the insurance companies had been correct; Udderzook and the Gosses had conspired to commit fraud. The body in the house had not been Winfield Goss; it was a cadaver that William Udderzook had acquired. Since the fire, Winfield Goss had been living in Newark, New Jersey, under an assumed name. The conspirators worried that with Goss's intemperate habits and exuberant personality, he would not be able to keep the secret much longer.

On June 6, 1873, William Udderzook arrived at the hotel in Jennersville, in Chester County, Pennsylvania, accompanied by Goss, using the alias Wilson. Udderzook was absent from the hotel the next day, returning in the evening with a horse and buggy hired from a neighboring livery stable. He settled the hotel bill and drove away with Wilson. Around midnight, he returned alone to the livery stable.

About a week later, a farmer on a road near Jennersville noticed a number of buzzards circling a spot near the road. He looked closer and found a mutilated body just barely covered with leaves and dirt. The body had been stabbed in the chest, and the arms and legs had been severed and thrown into the woods. There was enough evidence for a coroner's jury to determine "that the same man (name unknown) came to his death between the hours of seven o'clock p.m. July 1, 1873 and July 2, 1873, from wounds inflicted by a dirk-knife or other sharp instrument, in the hands of William E. Udderzook, of Baltimore Md."

The body resembled the descriptions of Winfield Goss, and a ring found in the buggy hired by Udderzook was identified as belonging to Goss. William E. Udderzook was arrested for the murder of Winfield S. Goss.

Trial: October 21, 1873

The prosecution retold the story of the fire at Goss's cottage, and they had been able to trace Goss's movements since the fire. He checked into the Central Hotel in Philadelphia under the name A.C. Wilson. Mr. Wilson's handwriting was identified as identical to that of Winfield Goss. He boarded near Athensville, where he pawned a finger ring that was later identified as Goss's. He then went to Newark, New Jersey, where he stayed until June 25, when he went to Philadelphia to meet the defendant. The two then traveled to Jennersville, Udderzook's hometown.

Gainer P. Moore, the man who discovered the body, testified to its condition and said that though the body had been mutilated…

"I raised the head out from the ground, the face had a natural look. By that I mean I could have recognized it easily if I had known the person in life. I have no doubt of this."

The prosecution then proposed to show Mr. Moore a picture of Winfield Goss to determine if he could recognize him as the man he found. Though the defense strenuously objected, the court allowed the photograph to be used. Moore testified that the man in the picture strongly resembled the man he found by the road.

The jury began deliberation on the afternoon of Friday, November 7, and returned a verdict at two o'clock on Sunday – guilty of first-degree murder.

Verdict: Guilty of first-degree murder

Aftermath:

The defense appealed the verdict on several grounds, most importantly that the court should not have allowed photographic identification, arguing that a photograph was twice removed from reality – the photograph is a copy of the negative which in turn is a copy of the subject – and therefore unreliable. The argument went as far as the Pennsylvania Supreme Court, setting legal precedent by allowing the photograph as evidence.

William Udderzook was hanged shortly after noon on November 12, 1874. He maintained his innocence to the end.

The Nicely Brothers

Joseph & David Nicely
The Umberger Tragedy, 1890.

Brothers Joe and Dave Nicely were the prime suspects in the robbery and murder of Herman Umberger in his home in Jennerstown, Pennsylvania on February 27, 1889. They were arrested, identified by eyewitnesses, convicted and condemned to death. But the Nicelys maintained their innocence and tried every means possible – legal and otherwise – to avoid punishment, including: two legal appeals, two pardon board appearances, a direct appeal to the governor, two jailbreaks, conspiracy to suborn witnesses, framing of other suspects, and feigning insanity. None of it worked.

Date:	February 27, 1889
Location:	Jennerstown, Pennsylvania
Victim:	Herman Umberger
Cause of Death:	Gunshot
Accused:	Joseph and David Nicely

Synopsis:
The Umberger family had settled in for a quiet evening at home on Wednesday night, February 27, 1889. In the sitting room were Herman Umberger, aged 67; his 70-year-old wife, Nancy; Ella Stone, the hired girl; and Mrs. Umberger's 10-year-old granddaughter, Nannie Horner. The night was cold and rainy in Jennerstown, and the family was surprised to hear a knock on the farmhouse door at 7:00 a.m.

Two men were there, one taller than the other. No one in the family recognized them, but the men knew where they were; the shorter man said, "Good evening, Mr. Umberger," and asked if they could come in and get warm. Herman Umberger invited them in, offered them chairs by the stove, and had Ella put more wood in the fire.

The taller man had his face tied up with two handkerchiefs. The shorter man, who did all of the talking, said that he had broken his jaw falling out of a buggy. The shorter one, Mrs. Umberger would comment later, was wearing gray wig and a false gray beard. When they were comfortably seated, he explained the reason for their visit. He said that they were constables from Bedford, and they had a warrant to search all the houses in the area for some jewelry that had been stolen from a peddler.

Mr. Umberger agreed to let them search, and Ella got a candle to light the way to the Umbergers' bedroom. He opened several bureau drawers and showed them the contents. In one drawer were two pocketbooks, Umberger explained that he kept a little cash in the house to pay the hired hands. The man said they were looking for jewels, not money, but to be safe, Umberger took the pocketbooks and put them in his vest. In fact, the pocketbooks contained Umberger's life savings, at least $17,000. He was extremely distrustful of banks and carried the pocketbooks in his bootlegs every day and kept them in the bureau drawer at night.

When they were back in the kitchen, the man drew a revolver and said to Umberger, "Your money or your life."

Ella Stone ran screaming out of the house. Mrs. Umberger went outside and started ringing the 'harvest bell', used in the summer to summon the hired hands. On a February night it would serve as an alarm for the neighbors. Little Nannie stood in the corner and watched as the man fired five shots into her grandfather. The two men fled the house, taking the pocketbooks with them.

A large crowd gathered at the Umberger home that night. Herman Umberger's brother Perry announced that the family would offer a $2,000 reward for the return of the money and $500 for the arrest and conviction of the murderer. While a coroner's inquest was held and a postmortem examination of the body was performed, four constables followed footprints in the snow left by the killers, over the mountain and down the western slope of Laurel Hill toward the town of Ligonier. Around midnight they stopped at the house of Collins Hamilton and there they found two loaded revolvers and twenty dollars under his pillow. They also found the false whiskers the killer had worn. They arrested Hamilton and took him away in handcuffs.

The following day, however, evidence emerged against two other suspects, Joseph and David Nicely. The Nicely brothers were men of bad reputation, who had both served time in the Western Penitentiary and were believed to be the leaders of a gang of desperados operating in the area. The police arrested the Nicelys and took them to the Umbergers for identification.

When they saw David Nicely dressed in overalls and an overcoat, Mrs. Umberger and Miss Stern felt sure he was one of the men, and when they heard Joe Nicely speak, they knew, without question, he was the killer. In David's pocket was a red handkerchief with white spots that Ella Stern instantly recognized it as one that David had been wearing around his face.

Collins Hamilton was also taken to the Umbergers' but none of the women recognized him. After a brief hearing he was released. Dave and Joe Nicely were arraigned and charged with murder.

On March 25, Anthony Nicely, father of Joe and Dave, was arrested as an accessory after the fact in the murder of Herman Umberger. He was found in possession of one of the pocketbooks that had been stolen, identified by a distinctive white spot at one end.

Trial: May 27, 1889

While the Nicely brothers were awaiting trial, they allegedly formulated a conspiracy to try to throw suspicion on two other men. Detective Howard of a local detective agency claimed to have unearthed a plot to plant the gray wig in Collins Hamilton's house and one of the pocketbooks, containing $11,000 in the house of a man named Joseph Hoffman. Detective Charles Beegle was to arrest them the day before the trial and bring the evidence to court, thus proving the Nicelys not guilty.

The story was printed in a Pittsburg newspaper and was picked up by several others. The Nicelys and their attorneys vehemently denied the story, but H.F. Kooser of the prosecution believed that there was a conspiracy afoot. In any case, publication of the story eliminated the possibility of any conspiracy being carried out.

When the trial of the Nicely brothers began, hundreds of people came from all over Pennsylvania to watch; most had to stand outside the courtroom and wait for news. Inside the courtroom, more than a hundred witnesses would give testimony. The most important of these were the women at the Umbergers' house the night of February 27, and of these, the most persuasive was young Nannie Horner. She remembered detailed descriptions of the men's clothing, such as a brown patch on the right side of a grey overcoat, two buttons missing, and three frayed buttonholes. The coat itself, taken from the Nicelys' home and kept in isolation until the trial, matched the description perfectly. On cross examination, the defense attorney tried to confuse her into giving conflicting testimony, but Nannie's testimony remained constant. She also picked out both Nicelys, from a row of men, and identified them as the strangers she saw that night.

The Nicelys were well represented at their trial. Their attorneys, W.H. Koontz and Alexander Coffroth were both former congressmen. They tried to prove the footprints in the snow could not have been made by the boots the Nicelys wore. They introduced more than a dozen witnesses who saw the brothers elsewhere that night.

After nine days of trial, the jury deliberated for only a short time before returning a verdict of guilty. However, not understanding the technicalities of the court, the jury did not specifically express the crime of which the defendants were guilty. The judge sent them back to rewrite their verdict, and the defense objected, saying the verdict had already been read. The jury came back with a verdict of guilty of murder in the first degree. The defense asked that the jury be polled, and each man declared the Nicelys guilty.

Verdict: Guilty of first-degree murder

Aftermath:

On the grounds of the irregularity in the jury's rendering of the verdict, Attorney Koontz filed a motion for a new trial. He argued the motion on

August 13 and 14. On August 18 the judge ruled against the Nicelys and refused a new trial. The same day, Joseph and David Nicely were sentenced to hang, "on such day and time as may be appointed by the Governor of the Commonwealth." The following day their attorneys filed an appeal to the Pennsylvania Supreme Court, to be heard the following October.

While Koontz was hard at work on gaining the Nicelys' release by legal means, Joe and Dave were working on means of their own. At noon on September 16, the brothers made a bold dash for liberty and during the scuffle Joe Nicely shot and killed Deputy Sheriff Milton R. McMillen. The Nicelys ran out of the front door, scaled the iron fence around the jail and fled into the woods.

The town mobilized immediately and a well-armed posse, estimated to be 500 strong, took to the woods to find the escaped prisoners. The Nicelys were soon recaptured and ropes were procured for lynching. Cooler heads prevailed and the Nicelys were taken back to jail.

The appeal was argued before the Pennsylvania Supreme court, citing some technical errors with the testimony as well as the irregularities regarding the verdict. On November 11, the court ruled that there were no errors in the trial and upheld the verdict.

On April 15, 1890, Mr. Koonz represented the Nicelys before the Board of Pardons, attempting to have their sentences commuted to life in prison. The Board denied the request. On November 12, they appeared before the Appeals Board again, this time with some new evidence against another man, including a suit of clothes, a double-barreled shotgun, and some revolvers. This request was denied as well.

The brothers were being held in a new jail in Somerset, Pennsylvania, reputed to be one of the strongest in the country. On November 29, the Nicelys and two other men proved this to be untrue when they broke out of the jail, sliding down a rope to the ground fifty feet below. A fifth prisoner attempted the escape but was fatally injured in the fall. The sheriff offered a $200 reward for the Nicelys' capture and a posse of 100 men scoured the countryside. Two days later Dave Nicely was found under some hay in a stable, an arm and a leg broken from the fall, and nearly dead from exposure. The following day, a local farmer, Jonathan Barclay, found Joe Nicely hiding in his barn. With the help of two neighbors, he brought Joe back to jail.

On January 10, the Nicely brothers and their attorneys took their case directly to Pennsylvania Governor James A. Beaver, appealing to him to withhold the death warrant. They presented the Governor with a number of new pieces of evidence. They had affidavits stating that some of the witnesses who identified them had since stated that they were mistaken. Joseph Nicely's physician declared that he suffered from heart disease and could not have gone so far from home in such a storm without becoming seriously ill. Mrs. Nicely swore that David took supper and spent the evening with her. A blacksmith swore he saw David late on the night of the murder. The governor and Board of Pardons received anonymous letters protesting that the Nicelys were innocent. They had an affidavit from a man named Beech who confessed to the murder of Herman Umberger and a chain of facts to substantiate the confession. But the governor was not moved. On January 21, the day before the expiration of his term, Governor Beaver signed the death warrant. The Nicely brothers were scheduled to hang on April 2, 1891.

As they awaited execution, the Nicelys continued their quest for freedom. In early March, a dozen steel saws, nine inches in length, were found in the cells of Joe and Dave Nicely. The sheriff was greatly disturbed over the discovery, saying that no one was allowed to see or speak to the condemned men but their attorneys and relatives, the latter in the presence of an officer.

In the weeks leading up to the execution they attempted to place the blame for the Umberger murder on someone else. Mrs. Nicely charged local constables and private detectives with conspiring to pin the murder on her boys. John Myers, "a reputable citizen of homestead" claimed that a desperado named Fitzsimmons, arrested for murdering Detective Gilkeson, was the real killer of Umberger.

Dr. H.L. Orth examined Joseph Nicely at the request of his father and his attorney, to determine Joseph's sanity. Since his recapture Joseph has suffered fits of depression and when the Board of Pardons refused to rehear his case, "his present imbecility followed" he had not spoken a word since that date.

Dr. Orth was skeptical, but after examining Joe he reported to the new governor that, "I undoubtedly believe him to be insane, and a proper person to be committed to the care of an insane hospital."

The governor issued no reply.

On April 1, the day before the execution, Elder Calvin W. Granger, of the Somerset Disciple Church visited David Nicely and convinced him that it was time to worry about his soul. At 11:00 a.m. Elder Granger baptized David Nicely in a bathtub in the exercise corridor of the jail, in the presence of members of Granger's church, lawmen, prisoners, reporters and a court stenographer. Then David Nicely had his first and last communion.

After the ceremony, he said, "It seems like a mockery, to have reveled in sin through a life, and to ask the Lord to take me; but O! I'll lean on His mercy."

The following morning, Joe Nicely snapped out of his abnormal mental state (or, as the *Somerset Herald* put it, "Joe Abandons the Insanity Dodge"). As if waking from a dream, he asked, "How did I get into this cell?" and "What day is it?"

Elder Granger went to work on his soul as well, but with less success than he had with Dave. However, by 10:00 a.m., Joe came around, and amid hymn singing and deep prayer, Joe took communion with Rev. A.J. Beal of the Evangelical Association Church.

The gallows were built into the Somerset Jail, with traps in the floor, allowing the condemned men to fall into the room below. In the yard outside of the jail, thousands of people stood and waited for the execution. At 12:45 p.m.

the prisoners were transferred from their cells to the west corridor and after another service of prayer and singing, the Nicelys said their last goodbyes. At 1:37 p.m. the traps were sprung; fourteen minutes later they were both pronounced dead.

Publicly, the Nicely brothers and their attorneys maintained their innocence to the end. However, following the execution, Elder Granger produced David Nicely's written confession. In it, transcribed by Granger and signed by David Niceley, he admitted that contrary to all of his previous testimony, he was at the house of Herman Umberger on the night of January 27, 1889. He was there to rob him, not murder him. He fired his pistol once into the ceiling to frighten Umberger, but did not fire any shot that hit him. Though he did not say it explicitly, everyone assumed that he meant the shots that killed Umberger were fired by his brother Joe. Many believed that Joe had also confessed, prior to receiving communion from Rev. Beal, but this was never confirmed.

The Blue Eyed Six

It was a foolproof plan. Six men in Lebanon County, Pennsylvania, bought insurance policies on the life of Joseph Raber, an elderly recluse living in a hut in the Blue Mountains. They were sure Raber would die soon and end their financial problems. But the premiums proved costly, and the men grew tired of waiting for Raber to die. In July 1878, they decided to take matters into their own hands. Their plot was common knowledge in Lebanon County, and it was not long before all six were arrested for murder. The conspirators had a number of common characteristics–all six men were illiterate, all six were living in poverty, and all six were of low moral character – but one trait captured the public's imagination – all six had blue eyes.

The Blue Eyed Six
The Blue Eyed Six, 1974

Date:	December 7, 1878
Location:	Lebanon County, Pennsylvania
Victim:	Joseph Raber
Cause of Death:	Drowning
Accused:	Israel Brandt, Henry Wise, George Zechman, Josiah Hummel, Charles Drews, Frank Stichler ("The Blue Eyed Six")

Synopsis:
It began with four men looking for a way to ease the extreme poverty that had befallen Lebanon County, Pennsylvania in 1878. All but one were married with

children to feed – Israel Brandt had six children, Henry Wise had seven, George Zechman had six. Josiah Hummel had no children but was having trouble supporting himself as an unskilled laborer. Wise was a coal miner. Zechman worked as a farm laborer and a coal miner. Brandt, who had lost one arm in a farm accident, ran an inn in a bad section of St. Joseph Springs, consisting of a bar and one bedroom.

Their plan was to take out life insurance policies on Joseph Raber, a reclusive 65-year-old man living in an abandoned charcoal burner's hut in the Blue Mountains. The hut had a dirt floor and ceiling too low for a grown man to stand up. He lived there with Polly Kreiser, referred to as his 'housekeeper', but common-law wife would be more accurate. Raber did farm labor when he could but mainly lived on public charity. The four men had promised to take care of Raber if he would make them beneficiaries of the insurance policies, and Raber was pleased to do so.

The type of policy they bought was called assessment insurance, also known as 'graveyard insurance'. It was primarily sold to guarantee that the insured would have enough money to be buried when he died with a little extra for his survivors. The concept of assessment insurance was simple; the insured paid a premium to join a pool, and then when any of the members died, the rest in the pool were assessed a certain amount that was then given to the beneficiaries. For example, if a thousand people were in the pool and the assessment was $1.00, a beneficiary would be paid $1,000. Josiah Hummel's policy on Joseph Raber was worth $2,000, George Zechman's was worth $2,000, Israel Brandt's was worth $1000, and Henry Wise's was worth in the neighborhood of $3,000.

In practice, assessment insurance was similar to a pyramid scheme, where the member who died first stood to gain the most. As members died, they would have to be replaced to maintain the policy's value. As time went on, living members often chose to opt out of the pool rather than continue paying assessments.

Joe Raber was old, but he was relatively healthy and showed no signs that he would be dying anytime soon. The constant assessments required to stay in the pools were becoming a financial hardship for his insurers. They realized they could not afford to let Joseph Raber live any longer.

They made and abandoned several murder plans, including throwing Raber from a flatboat into a reservoir and poisoning him with chloroform before admitting they were not able to do the killing themselves. Israel Brandt approached his neighbor, Charles Drews, and offered him $300 to murder Raber and promised he would get the same amount from the other conspirators after the job was done. Drews, in turn, sought help from his son-in-law Joseph Peters and Frank Stichler, a local thief. Peters turned him down, but Stichler agreed to help for a price.

Around dusk on Saturday, December 7, 1878, Drews went into the tavern at Brandt's hotel and told the people there that Joe Raber was dead. That afternoon he and Stichler had paid a call on Joseph Raber and offered him some tobacco if he would accompany them to Kreiser's Store. Raber agreed to go with them. The trip to the store had required crossing Indiantown Creek on a crude bridge made of two twelve-inch planks. Drews said Raber had a dizzy spell partway across, fell into the water, and drowned. The following day, a coroner's jury examined the body and declared the death accidental.

The insurance on Joe Raber's life was common knowledge in Lebanon County, and quite a few people knew of the murder plot as well. No one came forward with information, but an article about the death in the Lebanon Courier concluded with, "It is said that persons in the vicinity hold policies of insurance on Raber's life for $13,000 upwards. There is unpleasant talk of the probability of his death not being accidental."

Two months later, the Courier ran a story with the headline: "The Death of Joseph Raber, He is Supposed to Have Been Murdered. Six Men Arrested, Charged with Crime."

At the prompting of one of the insurance companies, Lebanon County constables questioned Joseph Peters regarding Raber's death. At 4:00 a.m. on February 5, 1879, Peters admitted to seeing Drews and Stichler drown Joe Raber. They had walked across the planks in single file with Stichler in the lead and Drews in the rear. About halfway across, Stichler turned around, grabbed Raber by the shoulders and, threw him into the water, then held him under until he drowned. Peters also accused the other four men of planning the murder. That morning Israel Brandt, Henry Wise, Josiah Hummel, George Zachman, Charles Drew, and Frank Stichler were arrested for murder.

Trial: April 7, 1879

The trial generated national and even international attention. It was the first time in the history of English and American law that six men would be tried together for murder. A few reporters from distant cities came to the Lebanon County Courthouse to witness the proceedings. One of them observed that all the defendants had piercing blue eyes; from then on they were referred to as 'The Blue Eyed Six'.

The trial was presided over by Judges Henderson, Rank, and Light. Fifty-eight witnesses testified, many of whom were German immigrants who spoke little or no English and required a translator. Doctors, insurance men, family, and neighbors of the defendants were called, but the outcome of the trial rested on the testimony of Joseph Peters and his wife, Lena. They had both seen Drews and Stichler drown Joe Raber from the second-floor window of the Drews' house where they were staying. The six defendants had five attorneys who did all they could to discredit the Peters' testimony. They claimed it would be impossible to see the murder through the second floor window and actually brought the window into court. It had multiple panes, and all were too dirty to see through clearly. One pane was partially broken and rags were stuffed in the hole.

The defense had witnesses who testified that Joseph Peters had been drinking all that afternoon and was drunk at the time he allegedly saw the murder. They also brought out the fact that Peters was currently absent without leave from the army.

Then there were the personal connections – Joseph Peters was fully aware of rumors that his wife Lena, Charles Drew's daughter, had been cheating with Frank Stichler while Peters was serving with his unit.

In the end, none of it mattered. The jury deliberated for five hours and then returned a verdict of guilty for all the defendants.

Verdict: Guilty of first-degree murder

Aftermath:

All six defendants requested a new trial. While awaiting sentence Henry Wise made a full confession. At the sentencing, Judge Henderson granted George Zechman a new trial. His involvement in the conspiracy was based solely on statements made by other defendants, which would have been inadmissible if he had been tried alone. Drews, Stichler, Hummel, and Brandt were sentenced to hang. Wise would be sentenced later.

It was assumed that Wise had cut a deal – confession in exchange for a life sentence. The other four convicts then issued their own confessions, placing as much blame as possible on Wise. Ultimately, Wise was sentenced to hang as well. The hangings were postponed until the outcome of George Zechman's second trial.

Zechman was retried and found not guilty. Although he had participated in insuring Joseph Raber, the jury determined he had not been party to the conspiracy. He was a known insurance investor and had insured many people in the past without foul play.

Drews and Stichler were hanged on November 14, 1879, the day after Zechman's verdict was read. Brandt, Hummel, and Wise were hanged on May 13, 1880.

The Cannibal of Austerlitz

Oscar Beckwith, a hermit living in the woods near Austerlitz, New York, fled leaving the butchered remains of Simon Vandercook strewn around his cabin. With no facts to report, the newspapers printed rumors about Beckwith – he had killed Vandercook to eat his flesh, he had eaten others and had a fondness for human flesh. In the public mind, Beckwith became 'The Cannibal of Austerlitz'.

A Hermit's Awful Deed
National Police Gazette, January 28, 1882

Date:	January 10, 1882
Location:	Austerlitz, New York
Victim:	Simon Vandercook
Cause of Death:	Unknown
Accused:	Oscar Beckwith

Synopsis:
Simon Vandercook was a 55-year-old 'eccentric wanderer' from Lansingburgh, New York, a fortune seeker who relatives said was always filled with 'utopian schemes'. In 1882, he claimed he had discovered gold outside of Alford, in Berkshire County, Massachusetts. The place had several small iron mines, with marble and other minerals found there as well so a gold discovery was not considered impossible. Vandercook purchased the land for his gold strike from Oscar Beckwith in exchange for shares in the company he formed to mine the gold.

The mine did not pay off as promised and Beckwith earned less than he earned by cutting trees on the property and selling lumber. Beckwith believed he had been swindled and threatened to sue Vandercook.

Oscar Beckwith was a 72-year-old hermit who lived in the woods, just across the border in Austerlitz, New York. He had a small, squalid shack with no furnishings but a stove, a bunk, and two stools, situated in an isolated spot under a ledge of rock. In spite of his age, Beckwith was strong and powerful; described as a desperate man who had served time for stealing horses.

Vandercook boarded at a farm near Alford, Massachusetts owned by Harrison Caulkins. He left there the morning of January 10, 1882, to pay a call on Oscar Beckwith and he never returned. Caulkins went to Beckwith's shack to look for Vandercook, and as he approached, he could smell burning flesh.

When Beckwith came out to meet him, Calkins said, "For God's sake, what are you burning?"

"Nothing but some pork rinds," Beckwith responded. He said Vandercook had left with a man from Green River, New York and would not be back until March.

Caulkins remained suspicious and returned the next day to find that Beckwith had fled and inside the shack were the mutilated remains of Simon Vandercook. The back was split down between the ribs, and the other portions were sawed and cut up. The bowels and intestines were in a basket, strips of flesh were on the bed, and an arm and leg lay on the floor alongside a blood-stained axe. In the stove were the charred bones of his head, feet, and arms.

The coroner ruled that Beckwith had murdered Vandercook, but there were no funds available to pursue the killer. The town of Alford offered a $500 reward for his capture, the governor of New York also offered $500 and the sheriff of Columbia County offered $250. The rewards generated several arrests on suspicion, but Beckwith had already fled to Canada.

With no news on Beckwith's whereabouts, the newspapers began publishing local rumors. It was alleged that Vandercook's liver was found in Beckwith's frying pan, and part of it was missing. It appeared to some that Beckwith had washed Vandercook's flesh and was preparing to salt it down to sustain him during the winter. It was not hard to believe that Beckwith was a cannibal, he was known to have indiscriminate eating habits. A stage driver who knew him said Beckwith had eaten a horse that died of disease.

As rumors of Beckwith's cannibalism became public, the stories became more extravagant. A woman named Mrs. Wollsey Peck had gone to pick berries near Beckworth's shack a few years earlier and had never returned, perhaps Beckwith had murdered and eaten her. It was stated that Beckwith had a fondness for human flesh, especially that of Native American women. He became known as 'The Cannibal of Austerlitz'.

Beckwith remained at large until 1885. Detective J.B. Gildersleeve of Columbia County tracked him throughout Canada and finally captured him in Bracebridge, Ontario. He brought Beckwith back to New York to stand trial.

Trial: November 16, 1885

Oscar Beckwith was tried in Hudson, New York and convicted of the first-degree murder of Simon Vandercook. However, a succession of appeals, retrials, and 'lunacy hearings' led to five more trials before Beckwith was ultimately convicted and sentenced to hang in 1888. Through six trials, Beckwith's alleged cannibalism was never mentioned.

Verdict: Guilty of first-degree murder

Aftermath:

Beckwith was hanged in Hudson, New York, on March 1, 1888. It would be New York's last execution by hanging and, at 78, Beckwith would be the oldest man to hang in New York State. A 'modern' gallows (see page 195) was shipped to Hudson in pieces from New York City. It was guaranteed to break the condemned man's neck quickly and cleanly, but they hadn't factored in the old man's toughness – Beckwith swung for 18 minutes before dying.

The Brooklyn Barber

A farmhand walking through an oat field in Watervliet, New York on August 7, 1873, came across the corpse of a one-armed man at the top of a ravine. Decomposition had set in and the man's facial features were all but obliterated by the sun. A razor found on the ground near the body inclined the coroner to think the death was a suicide, but a closer examination revealed that, in addition to having his throat cut, the man had been shot nine times in the head and chest. There was nothing on the body to indicate the identity of the man except for a business card from a barbershop in Brooklyn, 150 miles south of Watervliet.

Emil Lowenstein
Trial of Emil Lowenstein, 1874.

Date:	August 5, 1873
Location:	Watervliet, New York
Victim:	John D. Weston
Cause of Death:	Shooting, Slashing
Accused:	Emil Lowenstein

Synopsis:
The card read 'Theodore Grunewald, barber and hairdresser, 35 Atlantic Street, South Brooklyn'. At Grunewald's barbershop detectives learned that on August 5, an employee of the shop, Emil Lowenstein, came in early, took all of his tools, left without a word and never came back.

Lowenstein and his wife lived in the upper half of a two-family house in Brooklyn. John D. Weston and his wife lived in the downstairs apartment. The detectives arrived there and found Mrs. Weston distraught; John Weston had disappeared at the same time as Lowenstein. Weston had left the house the morning of August 5, carrying a small satchel that he had recently purchased. He left twenty dollars on the mantelpiece and told his wife, "there is some money to get breakfast with," and hadn't been seen since.

Weston was an ex-soldier who had lost an arm in the Civil War, and he left the army with a sizable pension. He had also managed to save some money from his job selling newspapers. When Weston failed to return home, his wife checked their bank accounts and found that he had withdrawn all their savings, $458, from two accounts on August 4. She recalled that he had gone out with Lowenstein and when he returned that night, he took hold of Lowenstein's arm and said, "Remember now, Emil." To which Lowenstein responded, "Yes." The next morning, both men were gone.

The police had evidence that they had taken the Harlem railroad to Chatham and changed trains for Albany, arriving at about 5:14am. From there, they went to Watervliet where, the authorities believed, Emil Lowenstein murdered John Weston. However, the reason Weston had withdrawn all his money and the purpose of their journey could not be determined.

Emil Lowenstein had not withdrawn any money. His family was exceedingly poor. He worked at the barbershop in a tattered coat and would often have to borrow carfare from his fellow workers. Twenty-three-year-old, Emil Lowenstein – alias Livingston, Levinston, and Lovisstien – was from a Jewish family that emigrated from Prussia when he was a young boy. The family had disowned him after he had been arrested in Philadelphia and sentenced to Moyamensing prison. Lowenstein had spent much of his time in America traveling. In the words of his attorney, he "… has been a sort of Ishmaelite, wandering about the country, following his trade as a barber."

On August 6, Lowenstein returned to Brooklyn and had apparently come into some money. He began buying new furniture for the apartment, new clothes and jewelry for his wife and himself, and he put a down payment on a barbershop of his own in Manhattan. He also made a strange request of his wife. He said John Weston had given him two revolvers and he wanted her to throw one of them into the river. She obliged while traveling on the ferry from Brooklyn to Manhattan.

Soon after, Mrs. Lowenstein read in the newspaper about the one-armed man found murdered in Watervliet. She put two and two together and accused her husband of killing John Weston. He vehemently denied it but realized that if he stayed in New York, he would be accused of Weston's murder. Lowenstein planned to flee to Canada, where he believed he would be safe. His wife refused to take any money from him but finally agreed to join him in Canada when he wrote to her.

The police were convinced that Lowenstein was guilty but had no idea where he was until, sometime later when they searched Mrs. Lowenstein's apartment and found a letter addressed to Hannah Davidson (her maiden name) postmarked St. Catherines, Ontario. They traced him to a barbershop in St. Catherines and found that he owned a set of six razors with the initial 'L' carved in the handle, along with a Roman numeral, I – VI. The razor found at the murder scene had the letter 'L' and the Roman numeral 'VII' carved in the handle. Emil Lowenstein was arrested and brought back to Watervliet, New York.

Trial: January 26, 1874

Lowenstein pleaded not guilty. He claimed he had not traveled with John Weston to Watervliet but had gone to Philadelphia on August 5, to visit his father. In an earlier trip to California, he had accumulated a large sum of money and hidden it behind a loose stone in the wall of Moyamensing prison. After seeing his father, he had gone to the prison and retrieved the money, which was why he was able to spend so freely when he returned to Brooklyn.

The case against Lowenstein was extremely circumstantial and much of the closing arguments had to do with the amount of evidence necessary to convict him of murder. His attorney argued that there was not sufficient evidence even to identify the body as John Weston. He spoke for five hours, saying essentially that it was necessary for the prosecution to prove beyond a reasonable doubt that only Lowenstein could have murdered Weston – a level of certainty that they had not achieved. The jury disagreed and, after only seven minutes of deliberation, found Lowenstein guilty of first-degree murder.

Verdict: Guilty - First-degree murder

Aftermath:

Emil Lowenstein was sentenced to be hanged. There were no appeals, but an application was made to New York Governor Dix to commute the sentence to life in prison. Dix refused to do so. Lowenstein's execution was set for April 10, 1874.

He had apparently converted to Catholicism in prison because on execution day he was accompanied and counseled by the Reverend Father Francis. Lowenstein knelt while Father Francis prayed over him, and after the prayer, Lowenstein kissed the crucifix. Then he addressed the crowd:

I want to say that I am innocent of the crime for which I am dying. I am condemned to die, and am ready to die, but I die innocent, and the time will come when it will be proved. It may be long or it may be a short time before it comes, but it will come, and then you will know that I died innocent. If I were guilty, I would not deny it, but I would not die with a lie on my lips. I call God to witness that I am innocent of the crime for which I die. I believe that God has forgiven all my sins that I have done in this world, and when I say I am innocent, and it is proved I am so, I hope you will remember it. I am as innocent as a new born babe.

New York State, at the time, used a method of hanging in which a falling weight jerked the body upward. Lowenstein's neck was instantly broken, but it took nearly ten minutes for him to die.

Emil Lowenstein's body was buried in St. Mary's burying-ground on Washington Avenue in Albany.

The Notorious Mrs. Clem

The sensational murders of successful businessman, Jacob Young and his wife in Indianapolis, in 1868, exposed a web of financial fraud involving some of the most influential men in the city. Circumstantial evidence soon pointed to Mrs. Nancy E. Clem, mastermind of the fraudulent scheme, as the perpetrator of the murders. The notorious Mrs. Clem, however, proved remarkably hard to convict.

Nancy E. Clem
The Cold Spring Tragedy, 1869.

Date:	September 12, 1868
Location:	Indianapolis, Indiana
Victims:	Jacob and Nancy Jane Young
Cause of Death:	Gunshot
Accused:	Nancy E. Clem, William J. Abrams, Silas Hartman

Synopsis:
Jacob Young was a 'broker upon the streets' – one who loans money and trades notes without a regular office – in Indianapolis in 1868, and in several respects, his business was somewhat peculiar. His clients were among the most prominent in the city, but he insisted on the utmost secrecy. His two partners, Mrs. Nancy E. Clem and William J. Abrams, worked the same way, and the interest rates that they promised were extraordinarily high.

Each member of this 'ring' lived the lifestyle of a successful businessperson, but even when the business was made public, and the books were opened, no one knew for sure how they were making money. Some believed that they were counterfeiters, because Indiana had been a center of counterfeiting before the Civil War, but none of the members had the required skills. More likely, it was a 'rob Peter to pay Paul' system (what would later be known as a Ponzi scheme) where early investors, like Dr. Charles Duzan, were paid off using money from later investors.

Charles Duzan dealt exclusively with Mrs. Clem, an attractive and personable woman, adept at sales, who was the reputed mastermind of the ring. She kept her business a secret, even from her husband, and it was likely that her clients were not aware that she had partners.

Duzan realized a profit of $9,000 in just four months. He made several more loans to Mrs. Clem, in ever increasing amounts, starting at $500, and going as high as $20,000. Others were not so lucky, Ann Hottle, Mrs. Clem's dressmaker, lent her $935 at 20 percent interest, but when she got cold feet and asked for the principal back, Mrs. Clem refused.

The problem with a scheme like this is that it cannot continue forever, and it was important to know when and how to get out. With a $20,000 note overdue at 25 per cent interest, Jacob Young thought the time was right. On September 12, 1868, he took between seven and nine thousand dollars, in thousand dollar and five-hundred-dollar bills, and left town with his wife. Their bodies were found the next day by the river near Cold Spring. He had been shot in the face. She had been shot in the head and severely burned from the chest down. A shotgun was found at the scene.

It was first suspected to be a murder and suicide, but the shotgun was too far from the body for the man to have used it on himself. The woman had been hit on the head with a blunt object and shot with a pistol. A woman's shoeprint, not made by the victim, was found in the mud near the bodies, and a horse's hoof prints nearby were made by a distinctive horseshoe style.

Despite their condition, the bodies were soon identified as Jacob and Nancy Jane Young, respectable citizens of Indianapolis. No motive could be determined until several circumstantial clues pointed to the probable killers. The shotgun, traced to a local pawnshop, had been purchased the morning of the murder by William Abrams. A man named Silas Hartman had rented a buggy that day and the horse wore the distinctive horseshoes that made the prints at the murder scene. Silas Hartman's sister, Nancy Clem, owned a pair of shoes that matched the footprint. The Youngs were seen traveling rapidly toward Cold Spring that morning, with another unidentified woman in the buggy. They were followed closely by William Abrams and Silas Hartman in a second buggy. When the police learned that Clem and Abrams had been in business with Jacob Young and that Young had been carrying a large sum of money that day, the pieces fell together to their satisfaction, and the three were arrested for murder.

First Trial: December 1, 1868 – Nancy Clem

The three defendants were to be tried separately, with Mrs. Clem to be tried first for the murder of Nancy Jane Young. Because of the brutal nature of the crime and the novelty of trying a woman for murder, interest in the trial was intense.

The prosecution was led by District Attorney Benjamin Harrison, who twenty-one years later would become the 23rd President of the United States. More than 100 witnesses were sworn in to testify for the state.

Testimony continued for three weeks, but the evidence against Mrs. Clem was highly circumstantial and not strong enough to convince all twelve jurors. They were unable to reach a verdict, and the trial ended with a hung jury.

Second Trial: February 9, 1869 - Nancy Clem

The second trial ended in a conviction, but, reluctant to execute a woman; the jury found Mrs. Clem guilty of second-degree murder and she was sentenced to life in prison. Her attorneys began an arduous appeal process.

In March 1869, Silas Hartman, awaiting trial in the Indianapolis jail, surprised everyone by issuing a confession, of sorts. He claimed that the Youngs were killed by a man named Fiscus, and a prostitute named Frank Clark – the unidentified woman seen in the Youngs' buggy. He and Mrs. Clem knew of the affair and received part of the money but were not directly involved in the killings. The following day, Hartman committed suicide in his jail cell by cutting his throat with a razor.

Hartman's confession was not taken seriously, much of what he said had already been contradicted by sworn testimony. The names Fiscus, Clark, and Dorsey, however, would come up in future trials.

Third Trial: August 31, 1869 – William Abrams

Abrams' trial covered no new ground; he was found guilty of second-degree murder and sentenced to life in prison.

The Indiana Supreme Court did not rule until December 1870. The court was not happy with the judge's instructions to the jury. The verdict was reversed, and Mrs. Clem was remanded for a new trial.

Her attorneys contended that Mrs. Clem could not be tried for first-degree murder since, even though the case had been thrown out, the former jury had found her guilty of second-degree murder, and she could not be tried a second time for first-degree murder. This controversy led to a continuance until June 1871. The case was postponed again until July, and some believed the defense's strategy was to delay until all the witnesses had died or moved away.

Fourth Trial: September 26, 1871 – Nancy Clem

After more delays, Mrs. Clem's third trial began in September 1871. Rather than challenge the defense's claim that she could not be tried for the first-degree murder of Nancy Jane Young, the prosecution used the other indictment against Mrs. Clem and tried her for the first-degree murder of Jacob Young. The trial lasted nearly a month and ended in a hung jury – six for conviction and six for acquittal.

Fifth Trial: 5. June 3, 1872 - Nancy Clem

Clem's fourth trial lasted twenty-five days. The jury deliberated less than an hour before returning a verdict of guilty of first-degree murder and a sentence for Mrs. Clem of life in prison.

Of course, the defense appealed the verdict. The Indiana Supreme Court agreed, and the case was sent back to the lower court for retrial.

It is sometimes reported that Nancy Clem was tried five times for murder. In fact, the fifth trial never took place. Mrs. Clem remained in jail until April 1874 when the prosecution filed a motion of nolle prosiqui, dropping the charges against her. By that time, most of the prosecution witnesses who were still alive had left the state. The trials had already cost Marion County nearly $20,000, and it could not afford the expense of bringing witnesses back to Indiana. Without them, the prosecution had no case. Mrs. Clem was free.

Aftermath:

"Consciousness of my own innocence has preserved me," Mrs. Clem told reporters when asked how she managed to look so well after such a long confinement. Despite being a social outcast in Indianapolis, Mrs. Clem was determined to return to business, this time with the help of her husband.

In succeeding years, Mrs. Clem had a few more brushes with the law. In 1878, theft of a $1,500 note led to a charge of grand larceny, and ultimately a four-year prison sentence for perjury. Her husband divorced her while she was in prison, and on her release, she sued to have the divorce annulled. In 1892, an Indianapolis man named John Martin died while under treatment from a female physician, named Mrs. Dr. Patterson. Police discovered that Mrs. Dr. Patterson was Mrs. Nancy Clem and sought her in connection with Martin's death. It was believed that she had fled the country.

Mrs. Nancy Clem died in Indianapolis in 1897. Her death prompted newspapers to retell the story of the Cold Spring murders and to speculate again on the still unsolved mystery of how Mrs. Clem made her money.

ROMANCE

A Crime of Passion

In June 1831, Joel Clough moved into a boarding house in Bordentown, New Jersey, and soon fell in love with his landlady's daughter, a young widow named Mary Hamilton. He made his affections known to Mary and began giving her gifts and writing her letters. Joel thought his efforts succeeded and even believed she had agreed to marry him. But Mary was seeing other men, and this drove Joel Clough violently insane.

The Murder of Mary Hamiton
The Authentic Confession of Joel Clough, 1833

Date:	April 6, 1833
Location:	Bordentown, New Jersey
Victim:	Mrs. Mary W. Hamilton
Cause of Death:	Stabbing
Accused:	Joel Clough

Synopsis:
Joel Clough was a 27-year-old mechanical contractor when he moved into the boarding house run by Elizabeth Longstreth. His business associates considered him intelligent and successful, and all who knew him thought of Clough as a mild and pleasant man.

Also living in the boarding house was Mrs. Longstreth's daughter, Mrs. Mary W. Hamilton, a young widow with a daughter. Clough became enamored of Mar and ardently desired to marry her. According to Clough, she had not discouraged his advances and, after initial hesitation, had agreed to be his wife. Others, including her mother, claimed that Mary paid no particular attention and was angry when she received letters from him. Clough gave her an album he purchased in Philadelphia, and he gave her his gold watch. But she soon stopped accepting his gifts and began seeing other men. Believing he and Mary were still engaged, Clough would visit the men and ask their intentions toward her. In the spring of 1833 – either at Mary's request or out of jealousy and disappointment – Clough settled his account with Mrs. Longstreth and moved out of the boarding house.

Traveling with a business associate, James Wallace, Clough went to Albany and then to New York City. On the trip, Wallace noticed a dramatic change in Clough's personality; his behavior was erratic, and he began to drink heavily.

Clough was to have control of a contract that Wallace was working on, but his intemperance and unsteadiness convinced him to abandon the plan. He left Clough on the dock in New York City and pursued his business in Burlington. He returned two days later to find Clough in the custody of a police officer. Clough had met a girl in a theater and hired a carriage to take her home. When she jilted him, he stole her jewels and was arrested while trying to leave the city.

Clough returned to Mrs. Longstreth's boarding house on April 4, 1833, noticeably pale and depressed. It is unclear exactly what else happened in New York City, but Clough returned in disgrace with his reputation and money gone. He told Mary Hamilton about his condition. In Clough's words, "She expressed regret and offered me all the money she had and her watch. This I refused: but told her if she would honor her engagement, we might yet be happy. Her reply was, 'What, marry you in your reduced circumstances?'"

After breakfast on April 6, Clough returned to his room, incredibly depressed. He would later claim that Mary came into his room as he was in the act of taking his own life with laudanum. When she put her hand on his shoulder to stop him, he pulled a dirk – a long-bladed dagger – from his pocket and plunged it into her left breast. He stabbed her ten more times, piercing her heart and lungs, then dropped the knife and collapsed onto his bed.

No one witnessed the murder, but several of the boarders heard the scream and saw Mary outside the room. With slight variations in wording, all agreed that her last words were, "Oh! Mother, Mother, I screamed and screamed, and you did not come, and Clough has killed me because I would not marry him. I could not Mother, I could not, you know; I must die, I must die!"

Moments later, Mary Hamilton was dead. Joel Clough was given an emetic to purge him of the laudanum. He calmly accompanied the sheriff to jail.

Trial: June 1833

Joel Clough's trial for the murder of Mrs. Mary W. Hamilton was held in Mount Holly, New Jersey, before Chief Justice Joseph C. Hornblower and four associate judges. Mary Hamilton's mother and sisters testified to the events of April 6, as did several boarders at Mrs. Longstreth's house. They also testified that Mary did not encourage Clough's advances and never promised to marry him.

Mary Hamilton's bloody garments were exhibited to the court. The sight of the clothes, especially her corset, pierced with holes and stiffened with blood, seemed to overwhelm everyone in the courtroom. When this was followed by a physician's description of how the stabbing had broken her ribs and riddled her heart and lungs, the trial had to be briefly suspended while everyone regained their composure.

The defense argued that Clough was innocent due to insanity. He had no recollection of actually stabbing Mary, the woman he loved. Several witnesses testified that Clough was a changed man following his trip to New York. James Wallace told what he knew about Clough's drinking and debauchery there.

The jury deliberated for two hours and then returned their verdict.

Verdict: Guilty of murder

Aftermath:

Joel Clough was sentenced to be hanged on July 26, 1833. He was kept in a room on the third floor of the prison in Mount Holly, New Jersey until it was discovered that he had tried to cut through the wall of the room. He then was placed in a cell in the dungeon of the prison. After two weeks there, Clough complained that it was extremely uncomfortable and unfit for the reception of ministers and friends who came to visit. The sheriff agreed to return him to his original room but put him in irons.

On the morning of July 21, the jailers found that Clough had escaped. He had separated the chain from his ankle and forced himself through a narrow passage between the bar of the window and the wall – he had burned the window casing with a candle he had been allowed for writing at night. He fashioned a rope of pieces of blanket and lowered himself to the ground.

The authorities passed out Handbills offering a reward of $100 for Clough's capture. Around 11:00 p.m., he was captured near the Delaware River, about seven miles from Mount Holly.

He was once again housed in the dungeon, where he continued to receive visits from clergymen worried about his soul. Before his execution, Clough became an Episcopalian. He was baptized and given the Lord's Supper by Bishop Doane.

At 2:00 p.m. on July 26, 1833, Joel Clough was "launched into eternity." After hanging for 30 minutes, his body was cut down and placed in a plain mahogany coffin and buried in the grounds of the prison.

The Six Capsules

Helen Potts, a nineteen-year-old student at Miss Comstock's School in New York City, decided not to join her roommates when they went to hear a concert. Helen felt ill, but she had a remedy prescribed by her boyfriend, Carlyle Harris, a medical student. When the girls returned, Helen told them of the wonderful dreams she had been having about Carlyle. But she also complained of numbness throughout her body; before long, she could not move, and her breathing was labored. The dreams soon vanished, giving way to nightmares, revealing a world filled with deceit, betrayal, and, ultimately, murder.

Carlyle W. Harris
The Trial of Carlyle W. Harris, 1893.

Date:	January 31, 1891
Location:	New York, New York
Victim:	Helen Potts Harris
Cause of Death:	Poisoning
Accused:	Carlyle W. Harris

Synopsis:
After the girls at Miss Comstock's School had gone to bed, the night of January 31, 1891, Helen began moaning and had difficulty breathing. They sent for their principal, Miss Day, who unsuccessfully tried to have Helen sit up. Miss Day sent for the school physician, Dr. Fowler, and his assistant, Dr. Baner. By the time they arrived, Helen had lost all muscle control, her pupils were almost entirely constricted, she was bathed in cold perspiration, and her breathing rate was two breaths per minute. The doctors tried to revive her with whiskey, caffeine, atropine, and digitalis, with little success. Helen rallied briefly, then fell into a more profound stupor. A third doctor, Dr. Kerr, was brought in, and they applied an electric shock treatment, which also failed. As a last resort, they tried artificial respiration to keep Helen breathing, but nothing would revive her. She died before dawn.

From the symptoms, Dr. Fowler was convinced that Helen had died from an overdose of morphine, and he began searching her room for signs of the drug. He only found an empty prescription box with a label that read 'one before retiring' and was signed "C.W.H., student". When he asked C.W.H.'s identity, the girls replied that it was Helen's boyfriend, Carlyle W. Harris, a medical student at Columbia University. Though the hour was late, Dr. Fowler sent for Carlyle Harris and brought him to Helen's room.

Harris's first response upon seeing his dead girlfriend was, "My God, what can they do to me?"

When asked why they would do anything to him, Harris responded that he had made out the prescription but was not yet a physician. Harris told Dr. Fowler that Helen had complained of headaches, and he had prescribed twenty-five grains of sulfate of quinine and one grain of sulfate of morphine. He instructed the pharmacist to put the mixture into six capsules so that each capsule would contain only one-sixth of a grain of morphine. He had given her only four of the capsules to reduce the risk of overdose. Harris knew she had already taken three capsules because Helen had told him they were not working. He had urged her to take the fourth capsule as well.

Dr. Fowler remarked that no one had ever died from one-sixth of a grain of morphine, and even if she had taken an entire grain, it would not have produced the effects he saw. There must have been a terrible mistake. The two capsules Harris had kept were examined, and, just as he had said, each contained only one-sixth grain of morphine.

Upon learning of Helen's death, her mother hurried to New York from her home in Asbury Park, New Jersey. The coroner wanted to perform an autopsy, but Mrs. Potts asserted that Helen had always suffered from heart problems; she was convinced that her daughter had died of natural causes. The body was taken for burial in New Jersey.

Authorities in New York remained unconvinced and managed to get a warrant to exhume the body. Fifty-five days after she was buried, the body of Helen Potts was disinterred and autopsied. The examination revealed that her heart and other internal organs were perfectly healthy, but her brain was in a congested condition, indicative of opiate poisoning. A chemical analysis of her stomach and intestines showed significant amounts of morphine. Harris's prescription called for quinine and morphine in a ratio of 25 to 1. Though quinine is the more stable of the two drugs, not a trace of quinine was found.

When questioned under oath, Mrs. Potts admitted that she had lied about her daughter's heart condition. She knew that an autopsy would bring unwelcome publicity, and she was anxious to get her daughter's body back to New Jersey as soon as possible. Mrs. Potts then made another startling revelation: Helen Potts and Carlyle Harris had been secretly married for nearly a year.

They had met in the summer of 1889 when Helen was eighteen, and Carlyle had just finished his first year of medical school. They were introduced by mutual friends and spent time together in Ocean Grove, New Jersey, where both families stayed. Harris resumed his studies at Columbia in the fall, and the Potts moved to New York. When Carlyle came to call, Mrs. Potts was at first glad to see a familiar friend, but when his visits became more frequent and his attention to Helen more marked, Mrs. Potts became concerned. When her daughter spoke of an engagement, Mrs. Potts put her foot down and tried to separate the two, telling Harris that Helen was too young.

On February 7, 1890, Helen was invited to visit the stock market by Carlyle Harris and his brother McCready, and since both brothers would be present, Mrs. Potts gave her permission. Carlyle picked her up at 10:00 a.m., but they never met with McCready and never went to the stock market. Instead, they went to City Hall and were married by an alderman. At Carlyle's insistence, they used assumed names: she was Helen Neilson (her middle name), and he was Charles Harris (his father's name). They did not reveal the marriage to Helen's mother or anyone else.

Within six weeks of this date, Mrs. Potts noticed that Harris visited her daughter much less frequently. While this pleased her, it greatly distressed Helen. The family had moved back to Ocean Grove, and Harris would make plans to visit, only to break them at the last minute, leaving Helen in constant sorrow. To cheer her up, Mrs. Potts invited a friend of Helen's, Miss Schofield, to spend some time with them at Ocean Grove.

When she next saw Carlyle Harris, Helen insisted he tell Miss Schofield about their marriage. After some argument, he agreed. The reason she was so adamant was that Helen was about to undergo an abortion and wanted someone to know about the marriage first; the reason Harris agreed was that Helen refused to have the abortion if he did not tell. Harris told Miss Schofield about the marriage, and she said he must tell Helen's mother. Harris refused.

Later the same day, Harris attempted to perform an abortion on his secret wife. The operation left Helen weak and pale, and when she did not improve, she went to see her uncle, Dr. Treverton, in Scranton, Pennsylvania. Dr. Treverton had to perform a second operation; Harris's operation had killed the fetus, but he had not removed it.

The marriage could no longer be kept a secret from Mrs. Potts, who became livid on hearing the news. She demanded that they make the marriage public immediately and demanded the couple have a proper church wedding. Harris insisted that revealing the marriage would ruin his career and convinced Mrs. Potts to wait until he graduated before making the announcement. He also suggested that she send Helen to Miss Comstock's school, an elite finishing school in New York, where she could learn how to be a doctor's wife. Mrs. Potts agreed but demanded that Harris give her a copy of the marriage certificate and an affidavit stating that he and Helen were truly married though they had used assumed names.

While still in Scranton, Carlyle Harris had a discussion with one of Dr. Treverton's friends, and after a few drinks, he began bragging about his amorous conquests. He said when he could not overcome a girl's scruples with fast talk, he would use ginger ale, secretly laced with whiskey, to break down her inhibitions. When this did not work, he had been known to go so far as marrying a girl to get her into bed. Helen Potts had not been his first bride, and hers had not been his first abortion.

When this news got back to Mrs. Potts, she wrote to Harris with an ultimatum: either he agreed to a church wedding on February 7, the anniversary of their secret wedding, or she would go public with the story herself. On January 20, 1891, Harris wrote back, saying, "All your wishes shall be complied with, provided no other way can be found to satisfy your scruples."

After Mrs. Potts revealed all this information to the New York authorities, they swore out a warrant against Carlyle W. Harris for the murder of Helen Potts Harris.

Trial: January 14, 1891

In Carlyle Harris's trial, the prosecution proposed that among the four capsules that Harris gave Helen Potts was one capsule filled with as much as five grains of morphine. It would not have mattered what day Helen took the capsule; as long as she followed his instructions and took a capsule every day, one of them would kill her. If it had been one of the first three, the remaining capsule or capsules would indicate that only one-sixth grain of morphine had been in each. If the fourth capsule was the lethal one – as it, in fact, was – then the two capsules still in Harris's possession, though less convincing, would still tend to show that each had only one-sixth grain of morphine.

It came out in the trial that, within ten days before Helen's death, one of the classes Harris took at medical school had been focused on the effects of morphine. A large bottle of morphine had been shown to the class, and the students had unsupervised access to it. There would be no way to know if someone had taken any of the morphine, and it was believed that Harris obtained the drug this way.

Harris handled much of the examination of witnesses himself. He brought out testimony stating that some people were especially susceptible to morphine poisoning and could die from as little as a sixth of a grain. The prosecution countered that taking the first capsule with no ill effect had proven that she was not one of these people.

Carlyle Harris's motive for killing his wife was strong. Though the evidence against him was circumstantial, it was compelling. The jury was convinced that the simple but sophisticated plot by Harris to kill Helen Potts had been uncovered. The jury found him guilty.

Verdict: Guilty of first-degree murder

Aftermath:

The case was appealed, but that failed, and Harris was sentenced to death.

Shortly before his execution, he issued a statement professing his innocence of murder but admitting that his life had been immoral. He hoped his execution would serve as an example to other young men who might fall into evil ways with women.

Carlyle W. Harris died in the electric chair at Sing Sing prison on May 8, 1893, while more than 1,000 people stood on the hill outside waiting for the black flag to be raised, signaling the prisoner's death.

His last words were: "I have no further motive for any concealment whatever. I desire to state that I die absolutely innocent of the crime of which I have been convicted."

Harris's mother remained thoroughly convinced of her son's innocence. On May 9, 1893, she placed the following notice in a New York newspaper: "Harris, Carlyle Wentworth, eldest son of Charles L. and Frances McCready Harris. Judicially murdered May 8, 1893."

She had his tombstone engraved with the words the words:

"Murdered by Twelve Men

If the Jury had Only Known."

The Bessie Little Mystery

When Bessie Little's body was found floating in the Miami River in Dayton, Ohio, her death was called a suicide. Her boyfriend, Albert Frantz, had seduced her and promised marriage. Bessie became despondent when she learned he was engaged to another. But a thorough examination of her body revealed two gunshot wounds in her head, ruling out suicide and pointing the finger at Frantz.

Death, Then the River
National Police Gazette, January 16, 1897

Date:	August 27, 1896
Location:	Dayton, Ohio
Victim:	Bessie Little
Cause of Death:	Gunshots
Accused:	Albert Frantz

Synopsis:
A swimmer in the Miami River outside Dayton, Ohio, discovered the body of a young woman floating in the water on September 3, 1896. The coroner found nothing to indicate violence; the cause of death was believed to be suicide, and the unidentified body was hastily buried.

When he heard of the body in the river, Dayton Police Chief Thomas Farrell believed he knew who she was, and he had reason to believe that she had been murdered. Farrell had the woman's body disinterred and soon after she was identified as 23-year-old Bessie Little by her adopted parents and by her dentist, who kept detailed records of his patients' teeth. The coroner still could not determine the cause of death, and the body was reburied.

Her parents said they did not report Bessie missing because she had left home several weeks earlier to look for work. She was living in a Dayton boarding house run by Mrs. Freese. The full story was, the Littles had kicked

Bessie out of their house when they learned she had been intimate with her boyfriend 20-year-old Albert Frantz. They told her not to return unless he agreed to marry her.

Mrs. Freese verified that Bessie had been staying at her boarding house and that Frantz had been paying her weekly rent. She said that the last time she saw Bessie was on August 27, when Bessie told her she was going for a buggy ride with Frantz. He came to the house the following day asking for Bessie, and Mrs. Freese told him she never returned after the buggy ride. Frantz said she was mistaken about the buggy ride; he had not seen Bessie the night before. He then paid Bessie's next week's rent in advance.

Bessie Little and Albert Frantz were from different economic backgrounds. As a baby, Bessie was an orphan at the Miami County Children's Home; Peter Little and his wife adopted her when she was two. But the Littles were poor, and as soon as she was old enough, they put Bessie to work as a domestic servant. Albert Frantz was a stenographer for the Mathias Planing Mill Co. He came from a wealthy family. As the youngest of five children, his parents and siblings spoiled him. Those who knew Frantz well described him as "cruel and cunning," but Bessie was infatuated with him.

Shortly before her death, she consulted a physician, and some believed that she had been pregnant or had even undergone an abortion. Her parents knew enough about her relations with Frantz to bar her from the house until she either broke them off or married him. Among her belongings, police found an unmailed letter addressed to Albert Frantz's father, begging him to force a marriage. It had been easy for Frantz to seduce Bessie, but he had no intention of marrying her.

Frantz maintained that he had not been with Bessie on the night of her disappearance, but Chief Farrell did not believe him. He kept Frantz in custody pending the outcome of the coroner's investigation. Farrell had been able to identify the body because he knew Bessie Little had been thrown in the river even before the body was found. He learned that Frantz, with a relative, had gone to see Rev. Teeter for advice. He told Teeter that Bessie had killed herself and he had thrown her body into the river. He wanted to know how the law would view the situation, so Teeter referred him to Judge J.W. Kreitzer. They attempted to keep the matter secret, but the story leaked out. Acting as Frantz's legal counsel, Judge Kreitzer would not confirm or deny the story. Chief Farrell heard it, and when the body was discovered in the Miami River, Farrell knew it was Bessie.

Farrell was convinced that Albert Frantz murdered Bessie Little, but Frantz still denied seeing Bessie that night, and there was no evidence to link him to her death directly. Then, on September 5, someone found a freshly dried pool of blood, along with two decorative combs identified as belonging to Bessie, on the Stillwater Bridge about half a mile from the spot where the body was found. There were also buggy tire tracks believed to be connected to the blood pool.

This was enough to justify digging up the body once more. This time the coroner's close examination discovered two gunshot wounds in the right ear and although the bullets had been shattered by bone, enough lead was recovered for two 32-caliber bullets. The head was then severed from the body and preserved in a jar; the body was reburied.

Farrell went to Frantz's home to compare his buggy's tires to the prints left on the bridge, only to find that Frantz's stable had burned down the day after Bessie was last seen. The horse was killed, and the buggy was completely destroyed.

Frantz now changed his story. He and Bessie had been riding in his buggy, and Bessie had been somewhat despondent. When he wasn't looking, she drew a revolver and shot herself. Panicked and afraid the story would not be believed, Frantz threw Bessie's body off the bridge. The obvious flaw in this story was that two shots were fired into her head. The post-mortem examination showed two entry wounds, and people living near the bridge recalled hearing cries of "Murder!" that night, followed by two gunshots.

The revolver was still missing, and Chief Farrell was determined to find it. Believing that it had been thrown off the bridge along with the body, he mounted an all-out search of the river below. He obtained twelve powerful magnets, weighing three pounds each, and using two rowboats, dragged them along the bottom of the river, trying to attract the gun. When this failed, he hired Ben Graham, a professional diver who agreed to work for expenses. A.E. Pate, a champion swimmer, also volunteered his services.

While the river search proved fruitless, Farrell learned that Frantz had purchased a revolver at Dodd's gun shop in Dayton three weeks before Bessie disappeared. He also learned that while courting Bessie, Frantz was also engaged to another woman. With this possible motive, the prosecutors felt they had enough circumstantial evidence to try Albert Frantz for the murder of Bessie Little.

Trial: December 14, 1896

More than 100 witnesses testified at Albert Frantz's murder trial. He still maintained that Bessie had shot herself. The prosecution brought out Bessie's severed head to show the jurors the two entry wounds. Several physicians testified as to the possibility that Bessie had shot herself twice in the head. The defense's doctors said it was possible; the prosecution's said it was not. The defense did not claim that Frantz had been temporarily insane, but just in case, the prosecution had six doctors examine Frantz and testify that he was perfectly sane.

Though the evidence was circumstantial, it was enough for the jury to convict Albert Frantz of first-degree murder. He was sentenced to death.

Verdict: Guilty of first-degree murder

Aftermath:

On November 19, 1897, after all possible appeals failed, Albert Frantz became the fourth man to die in Ohio's electric chair. He professed his innocence to the end.

Kissing Cousins

Lillian Madison's relations with her immediate family in the 1880s were strained, if not outright hostile. Her parents disapproved of her social life and kept her from the education she desired. As soon as she could, Lillian left their home in King William County, Virginia. She found comfort and support among her mother's relatives, but she also began a romantic relationship with her cousin, Thomas Cluverius, that would end in her ruin. When Lillian's body, eight months pregnant, was found floating in Richmond's Old Reservoir, her cousin Thomas was the prime suspect.

Thomas J. Cluverius

Date:	March 13, 1885
Location:	Richmond, Virginia
Victim:	Fannie Lillian Madison
Cause of Death:	Drowning
Accused:	Thomas Judson Cluverius

Synopsis:

On the morning of March 14, 1885, Lysander Rose, keeper of Richmond, Virginia's Old Reservoir, was making his rounds and found furrows in the path and beside them saw a shoestring and a red glove. Looking out over the reservoir, he saw something strange floating in the water, and with the help of his workmen, he pulled ashore what turned out to be the body of a young woman. The coroner examined the body, and though he found some minor signs of assault, it appeared that she had drowned. He also determined that she was eight months pregnant. His initial assessment was suicide.

She had not been in the water long, and there had been no decomposition. The body was placed in the almshouse chapel, and thousands of people passed by trying to identify the girl. Twice during the two days she lay in the chapel, someone identified the body as a missing relative, but in each case, the supposed victim was found alive and well. On March 17, a young Richmond woman identified the body as that of her cousin, Fanny Lillian Madison, and this time, the identification proved true. Over the next two days, the coroner changed his assessment to murder, and a suspect was arrested – Thomas Cluverius, another of Miss Madison's cousins.

Fanny Lillian Madison – who went by Lillian – was an unmarried 23-year-old teacher and governess who worked in the western part of Virginia. The oldest of eight children of Charles and Lucy Madison, she was born while her father was fighting in the Confederate army. The family owned a small farm, but they were too poor to send Lillian to school for as long as she wanted, causing animosity. The trouble between Lillian and her parents was part of a larger conflict between the Madisons and her mother's family, the Tunstalls, Walkers, and Cluveriuses.

Lillian stayed at the house of her great aunt, Jane Tunstall, while she was going to public school. Then her great aunt paid Lillian's tuition for one year at Dr. Garlick's Burlington Academy. When she offered to pay for a second year, Lillian's parents refused, deepening the rift between the Madisons and the Tunstalls and further alienating Lillian from her parents. They forbad any contact between Lillian and the Tunstalls and burned all correspondence between them.

When Lillian turned twenty-one, she left home for good. She lived for a while at the home of an uncle, John Walker, then moved to Bath, Virginia to work as a teacher. Charles Madison was against the move and in a letter to John Walker he blamed his wife's family for ruining their daughter:

> *Several years ago some people who ought to have been myself and Lucy's best friends became our bitter enemies. They took our eldest child for a tool to carry out their Hell Blushing schemes and from that day to this our oldest child banded with them they have done all the human brain could devise to accomplish our ruin and what has been the result!*

Charles Madison believed that Lillian had been intimate with Thomas Cluverius, who had also lived at Walker's house.

Thomas Cluverius's background was similar to his cousin Lillian's. He grew up on a small farm but with only three siblings, his life was not so hard. His family was less reluctant than the Madisons to take help from Jane Tunstall. Thomas and his older brother William went to live with her and she financed their education. In September 1880 he began attending Richmond College (now the University of Richmond) and in 1882 graduated with a Bachelor of Law degree.

Cluverius returned to King and Queen County where he was well known and highly regarded. He began a successful law practice. At the time of his arrest, he was assistant superintendent of Sunday school at Olivet Baptist Church. He was known as a man of temperate habits.

One of his associates summed up his character at his trial, "I look upon him, gentlemen of the jury, as one of the most correct, straightforward, and Christian young men in my whole acquaintance."

Several times in July and August 1884 Cluverius stayed overnight at the home of Thomas Walker where Lillian Madison was living. At the Walkers' home Thomas and Lillian "seemed right smartly attached to each other" even though at the time, Thomas Cluverius was engaged to a woman named Nolie Bray. On January 5, 1885, Lillian and Thomas both stayed at a hotel in Richmond and a hotel maid remembered that Lillian did not sleep in her own bed that night. In March 1885, the week of Lillian's death, they were both in Richmond again.

After the body in the reservoir was identified as Lillian, suicide seemed the most likely cause. Being an unwed mother in 1880s Virginia would have been a terrible disgrace. Lillian was also well known for expressing negative, almost suicidal emotions. But after a coroner's inquest that lasted weeks, the jury declared the case a murder and charged Thomas J. Cluverius.

He was arrested at a jewelry store where he had gone to get a replacement for a lost watch key. The missing key had allegedly been found near the murder scene and would become a crucial piece of evidence at the trial.

Trial: May 5, 1885

The indictment against Cluverius was based entirely on circumstantial evidence, and in the period between the murder and the beginning of the trial, the city of Richmond became bitterly divided between those who believed Cluverius was guilty of murder and those who thought Lillian had committed suicide. Finding a jury of twelve men who had not already decided the matter was a significant hurdle.

The evidence in the case included a watch key found near a hole in the fence between a graveyard and the reservoir. Cluverius was missing his watch key, normally attached to his watch chain, and it was claimed it was torn off when he squeezed through the hole. The hole was well known to Richmond College students, who used it when they wanted to swim in the reservoir.

There was also a note written by Lillian, dated March 14, the day after the murder. It was asserted that Cluverius had her write this to provide him with an alibi – he was back at his home in Centreville on the 14th.

Cluverius' relatives paid for the best attorneys available. They focused on their client's character and on the likelihood that Lillian had committed suicide. Though much testimony focused on the time that Thomas and Lillian were both sleeping at the Walkers' house, very little was said in court about Lillian's behavior or her association with other men. It was as if the attorneys and press of Richmond had an unspoken agreement not to tarnish the reputation of a young woman.

The trial lasted for a month, and Thomas Cluverius was found guilty.

Verdict: Guilty of first-degree murder

Aftermath:

The defense appealed the case, but the Virginia Supreme Court upheld the verdict.

This did nothing to settle the matter among the citizens of Richmond and doubt about Cluverius's guilt remained. Though most thought him guilty, 2,713 citizens of Virginia – 299 of them from Richmond – petitioned the governor for clemency.

William Hatcher, Cluverius's spiritual advisor, summed up the ambivalence, "At one moment I fear that he is guilty and will die with a lie on his lips; the next I think that he may be innocent and I fear that it will be judicial murder."

The police, clergymen, and reporters all tried to convince Cluverius to confess but he maintained his innocence to the end. As his execution approached, Cluverius stated that he had been with another woman the night of the murder, but honor forbade him from identifying her and forcing her into publicity and shame to save his life.

The hanging took place on January 14, 1887. By Virginia law, it was to be private, but thousands of people surrounded the jail yard where the execution would take place. The judge had allowed only twelve spectators, but more than 300 had entered the jail yard, and rather than risk a riot, police allowed them to stay. A book written by Thomas Cluverius entitled Cluverius; My Life, Trial and Conviction was sold at the execution for fifty cents a copy to help defray legal expenses. To the disappointment of the crowd, it was not a confession, but they continued to assert that Lillian committed suicide.

A rope made of red and white silk was used to hang him. The intention was to cut it into pieces to sell as souvenirs after the hanging. They had also intended to sound an electric signal the moment the trap was sprung. Both plans were stopped by a special order from Virginia Governor Lee.

Herbert Tobias Ezekiel, who witnessed the hanging, wrote that the Sheriff had oiled the rope with sweet oil rather than cold grease, which would have facilitated the slipping of the noose and broken Cluverius's neck. When the trap was sprung at 1:09 p.m., the silk rope stretched until his feet were just inches from the ground. The loop extended nearly eighteen inches above his head, and it took ten minutes for him to slowly strangle to death.

Thomas Cluverius was buried in the Tunstall burying ground behind the house where he was arrested. A piece of white marble marks the grave of Lillian

Madison in Richmond's Oakwood Cemetery. The body of her unborn son was buried in the coffin with her.

The Kentucky Tragedy

"Great God, it is Beauchamp"
The Avenger's Doom, 1851.

Jereboam Beauchamp stabbed Colonel Solomon Sharp to avenge the honor of his wife, Anna Cooke Beauchamp. The story of the murder – known from the start as the Kentucky Tragedy – was viewed by the Beauchamps as one of love, treachery, vengeance, and tragic heroism; all the elements of the romantic novels they both so dearly loved. But Jereboam and Anna were enacting another familiar American narrative: two troubled misfits lashing out at a world they both disdained.

Date:	November 6, 1825
Location:	Frankfort, Kentucky
Victim:	Colonel Solomon Porcius Sharp
Cause of Death:	Stabbing
Accused:	Jereboam Orville Beauchamp

Synopsis:

The central figure in the Kentucky Tragedy, Anna Cooke Beauchamp, is also its most mysterious. Most of what is known about her comes from two often conflicting documents, *The Confession of Jereboam O. Beauchamp*, and *Vindication of the Character of the Late Col Soloman P. Sharp*, written by his brother, Dr. Leander Sharp. Both documents agree (though making different points) that Anna Cooke Beauchamp was well-read, unconventional, and disdainful of society and its rules. Though later authors would portray her as a great beauty, to Leander Sharp she was "in no way a handsome or desirable woman." Her husband, though deeply in love with her, had little to say about Anna's appearance.

The Cookes were a family of Virginia aristocrats whose declining fortune after the death of Anna's father drove them to Kentucky for a fresh start. Anna with her mother and at least five brothers set up a new estate, called Retirement, outside of Bowling Green, and among them they owned at least two dozen slaves. As the oldest daughter in a respectable family, Anna would have had many suitors. Even if she was not a beauty, as her later detractors would say, she was vivacious and popular as a young woman. But, in her most obvious defiance of social norms, Anna Cooke remained unmarried by choice. As she grew older, Anna's uncommon beliefs and behaviors became unsettling to Bowling Green society, and she was shunned by her peers. She withdrew from society and found solace in reading, particularly the popular romance novels of the day.

Anna had not completely withdrawn from society, she was still seen in the company of men. Her failure to marry prompted rumors of sexual misbehavior – rumors that proved true in 1820 when thirty-five-year-old Anna became pregnant. The baby was delivered stillborn that June. She declared that she had been seduced and abandoned by Colonel Solomon Sharp, and she even revealed the date of the conception – Sunday, September 18, 1819, while Sharp's wife Eliza was in church.

The Sharp family lived near the Cookes and Anna had known Solomon Sharp for at least twelve years. Though he had come from humble beginnings, Sharp rose quickly to a position of wealth and power. He was the most successful attorney in Bowling Green, held the rank of Colonel in the state militia and owned 3,600 acres of land. At age twenty-four, he became a United States Congressman. Sharp was a rising star in Kentucky politics.

John C. Calhoun said of him, "He has few superiors of his age in any part of our country."

John Quincy Adams called him "The brainiest man that ever came over the Allegheny Mountains."

Solomon Sharp also had bitter enemies in the arena of Kentucky politics and in 1821, they used Anna's accusations to try to derail his bid for State Attorney General. They published a broadside charging Sharp with seducing her. The State Senate formed a committee to investigate the matter which found the charge to be "wholly groundless" and confirmed Sharp as Attorney General.

It can never be known for certain whether Solomon Sharp had sexual relations with Anna Cooke, but he gave the appearance of a man who was happily married. His wife Eliza was expecting their first child in 1819. What can be disputed is the charge of seduction which, in traditional parlance, meant taking a young woman's virtue with the false promise of marriage. No one believed that thirty-five-year-old Anna's virtue was still intact and Anna was well aware that Sharp was already married. Contrary to what would be later asserted in Beauchamp's Confession, Anna was not alone with no family at the time of her pregnancy; at least two of her brothers were still alive. Had it been a true case of seduction, they would have been honor bound to seek retribution from Sharp. While her brothers did nothing to defend her honor, Anna found someone who would: Jereboam Beauchamp.

As a boy, Jereboam Orville Beauchamp was precociously intelligent, though he probably exaggerated when he claimed that he "early showed some indications of genius." He was given a solid education and at age sixteen set off on his own, trying his hand at shopkeeping and teaching before settling on a career in law. Like Anna, Beauchamp was strong-willed and eccentric, viewing himself as above the petty dictates of society. He was violent, unruly and vindictive. One acquaintance asserted that he "...never knew him do an act of any kind which indicated magnanimity of soul or real dignity of sentiment."

Leander Sharp denounced Beauchamp's "wild, lascivious, revengeful, unprincipled and shameless conduct." By age eighteen he had been formally charged with fathering a bastard child and was rumored to have fathered others.

Beauchamp was eighteen years old when the news of Anna Cooke's 'seduction' was made public, and when he learned that she was living nearby in Bowling Green he was determined to meet her. The details of their meeting are known only through Beauchamp's Confession, with skepticism expressed in Leander Sharp's Vindication. On the pretext of using her extensive library, Beauchamp managed to meet the reclusive Miss Cooke. Dr. Sharp believed Beauchamp had been more attracted by her status as a fallen woman. Over the course of several meetings, they found that they had shared interests in romantic novels and the poetry of Byron. Though she was seventeen years older than he, Beauchamp fell madly in love with her.

Though Anna returned his love, when Beauchamp asked for her hand in marriage she told him, "that the hand which should receive hers would have to revenge the injury a villain had done her...her heart could never cease to ache till Col. Sharp should die through her instrumentality."

Beauchamp eagerly took on this task. He claimed that in 1821 he traveled to Frankfort to challenge Sharp to a duel. Sharp refused to fight but Beauchamp continued to pressure him in a threatening manner until Sharp fell on his knees and begged for his life. It is unlikely that this event actually occurred. There were no eyewitnesses, and like the charge of seduction, southern honor would have dictated the outcome. No man could survive in Kentucky politics after declining a duel in such a cowardly fashion. The story was probably made up to justify Beauchamp's later actions.

In 1824, Anna agreed to marry Jereboam Beauchamp though Sharp was still alive, but according to Beauchamp's Confession, they continued to plot his murder. In 1825, after his tenure as Attorney General, Sharp campaigned for General Assembly and his opponents revived the charge that he seduced Anna. By the time the news reached the Beauchamps, it included the additional charge that Sharp had obtained a certificate from the midwife who delivered the stillborn baby, claiming that the infant was mixed race. The charge that his wife had sex with a black man was more than Beauchamp could bear. He set off again for Frankfort, bent on murder.

On the night of November 6, 1825, Jereboam Beauchamp disguised himself and, armed with a large butcher knife, sharpened on both edges and dipped in poison, he paid a call on Sharp. Around 2.00 a.m. he knocked on the door.

Beauchamp wrote that when Sharp came outside to see who it was, he plunged the knife into Sharp's heart saying, "Die you villain."

The wound was actually to the abdomen, but it was fatal, and Col. Sharp died soon after being stabbed.

The first suspects included some of the more vehement of Sharp's political opponents, but when it was learned that Beauchamp, the husband of Anna Cooke, had been in Frankfort that day, he became the sole suspect. Four days later a patrol arrived at Retirement, arrested Beauchamp and took him back to Frankfort.

Trial: May 8, 1826

The trial of Jereboam Beauchamp lasted eleven days and included testimony from dozens of witnesses. Beauchamp pled not guilty, and the evidence against him was almost entirely circumstantial. Neither side mentioned charges of seduction – the defense did not want to raise the possibility that Beauchamp had been seeking revenge; the prosecution did not want the jury to think the murder was justified. Consequently, the prosecution made no attempt to establish a motive for the murder.

It looked like the trial was going Beauchamp's way until John Lowe, a friend and neighbor, testified that the Beauchamps had tried to persuade him to commit perjury. He brought to the stand a letter the Beauchamps had given him outlining what they wanted, as well as a seven-thousand-word document coaching Lowe on what to say. Among other falsehoods, Lowe was to say that Jereboam Beauchamp believed that the seduction story was a lie fabricated by Sharp's enemies, and that he had no quarrel with Sharp, always speaking well of him.

This was the turning point; Beauchamp's attorney could not undo the damage caused by Lowe's testimony. The jury deliberated for less than an hour before returning a guilty verdict.

Verdict: Guilty of murder

Aftermath:

Jereboam Beauchamp was sentenced to hang on June 16. Anna was so distraught that she refused to leave her husband's side and joined him in his jail cell – a windowless dungeon accessible only through a trapdoor. Together in the cell, they wrote The Confession of Jereboam O. Beauchamp, a document which they believed would save Jereboam from the gallows. Working from their shared love of romantic novel's Jereboam and Anna created a romance of their own, describing their love, recounting how Solomon Sharp had seduced and abandoned the "worthy orphan female," revealing how the cowardly Sharp had refused to duel. Though now admitting that Jereboam had committed the murder, the Beauchamps believed that the Confession would convince the governor and people of Kentucky that the act was justified and Jereboam should be released.

The Confession was finished before the execution, but Beauchamp was unable to find a publisher. In desperation he petitioned the governor for a thirty-day respite to complete the publication. The governor refused. With all hope gone, Anna and Jereboam decided to commit suicide together. Anna had smuggled a bottle of laudanum into the cell, concealed in her bosom. After leaving instructions for their burial, they drank the laudanum, but it failed to kill them. On the morning of the hanging they tried again, with a small knife Anna stabbed herself in the abdomen then Jereboam took the knife and did the same.

Anna's wound proved fatal but the jailers were able to save Jereboam for the gallows. Five thousand people were gathered outside Frankfort to witness the execution. As he was taken to the gallows he raised the curtains on the wagon so he could wave at onlookers. At the execution grounds the crowd expected Beauchamp to contritely address them, but he declined to do so. Instead he asked for a glass of water and requested that the band play the lively reel "Bonaparte's Retreat from Moscow." When he had heard enough, Beauchamp stood up and at half past one o'clock he was launched into eternity.

The Confession of Jereboam Beauchamp was published after the execution and laid the foundation or the myth of the Kentucky Tragedy. The story inspired dozens of novels and dramas including Politian, an unfinished play by Edgar Allan Poe, which sets the story in sixteenth-century Rome. None of these adaptations were particularly successful, probably because the story they drew from was already a work of romantic fiction.

Jereboam Beauchamp left behind the following instructions for the couple's burial:

> *Directions for Our Burial*
>
> *We do not wish our faces uncovered after we are shrouded, particularly after we are removed to Bloomfield; we wish to be placed with my wife's head on my right arm, and that confined round upon her bosom.*
>
> *J. O. Beauchamp*

A month before the execution Anna wrote an epitaph for their tombstone and, to gain sympathy, attempted to have it published in a newspaper. Like the Confession, the epitaph was not published until after their deaths:

> *Epitaph to be engraven on the tombstone of Mr. and Mrs. Beauchamp; written by Mrs. Beauchamp*
>
> *Entombed below in other's arms*
> *The husband and the wife repose,*
> *Safe from life's never ending storms,*
> *And safe from all their cruel foes.*

A child of evil fate she lived,
A villain's wiles her peace had crossed,
The husband of her heart revived
The happiness she long had lost.

He heard her tale of matchless woe,
And burning for revenge he rose
And laid her base seducer low,
And struck dismay to virtue's foes.

Reader! if honor's generous blood
Ere warmed thy breast, here drop a tear,
And let the sympathetic flood
Deep in thy mind its treasures bear.

A father or a mother thou,
Thy daughter view in grief's despair,
Then turn and see the villain low,
And here let fall the grateful tear.

A brother or a sister thou,
Dishonored see this sister dear;
Then turn and see the villain low,
And here let fall the grateful tear.

Daughter of virtue, moist thy tear—
This tomb of love and honor claim;
For thy defense the husband here,
Laid down in youth his life and fame.

His wife distained a life forlorn
Without her heart's loved honored lord,
Then, reader, here the fortunes mourn,
Who for their love their life-blood poured.

The burial instructions were followed; Jereboam and Anna Beauchamp were buried together in a single coffin in Maple Grove Cemetery, Bloomfield, Kentucky. Anna's epitaph was engraved on the headstone.

JEALOUSY

Murder By Mail

Mrs. Ida Deane's dinner party turned disastrous when she and four of her guests died of arsenic poisoning. They had all eaten chocolates from a box of candy sent anonymously to her sister, Mary Dunning. Evidence pointed to Cordelia Botkin, a mistress of Mary's husband, who successfully plotted to murder Mary out of jealousy.

Cordelia Botkin
San Francisco Call, August 30, 1898.

Date:	August 11, 1898
Location:	Dover Delaware
Victims:	Ida Deane, Mary Dunning, and three others
Cause of Death:	Poisoning
Accused:	Cordelia Botkin

Synopsis:

On Tuesday, August 9, 1898, Ida Deane held a dinner party for friends and family in Dover, Delaware. Afterwards, they all retired to the front porch and passed around a box of chocolates provided by Ida's sister, Mrs. Mary Dunning. Shortly after retiring, Mrs. Deane complained of feeling sick to the stomach. After the usual household remedies proved ineffective, the family sent for a doctor. Several others complained of stomach illness, which grew steadily worse.

Ida Deane died on Thursday. By Friday, four other members of the party were dead, including Mary Dunning. The cause appeared to be some form of food poisoning, but only those who ate the candy were stricken; the rest experienced no illness. A chemist analyzed the chocolates and found that they contained a large amount of arsenic, with some grains as large as coffee grounds.

Mrs. Dunning received the candy in Tuesday's mail, and she did not know who had sent it at the time. The package also included a handkerchief and a note which read:

"With love to yourself and your baby, Mrs. C"

The postmark was smeared but appeared to say San Francisco, California. This was a useful clue, as Mrs. Dunning had lived for a time in San Francisco.

Both Mary and Ida were daughters of former congressman John B. Penington. He took charge of affairs for the family, and his prominence prompted serious investigations in Delaware and California. The Secret Service joined the search, and the governor of Delaware offered a $2,000 reward for the arrest and conviction of the sender of the poisoned candy.

The San Francisco police began their own investigation, but many in Delaware, including Ida's husband, Joshua, believed that the poison was added after the package arrived in Dover. Though Deane was thoroughly convinced that the crime was the work of someone closer to home, Penington had reason to believe that the poisoner was in San Francisco.

Mary's husband, John P. Dunning, a reporter for the Associated Press, was in Puerto Rico at the time of the murder, reporting on the war in Cuba. He left for Delaware as soon as possible. John and Mary Dunning had lived together in San Francisco, but there appeared to be stress in the marriage. He was away on overseas assignments for long periods. Around 1895, Mary returned to Delaware to live with her parents.

After his wife left, Dunning's fortunes began to falter. He lost his position with Associated Press and began spending time at the racetrack, racking up severe losses. He had been seen in the company of three married women in San Francisco – Mrs. Seely, Mrs. Abrogast, and Mrs. Botkin. He was particularly close to Cordelia Botkin, a former vaudeville actress estranged from her husband. She often accompanied Dunning to the racetrack and gave him a room in her house. His fortunes reversed again. He had regained his position at the Associated Press and planned to return to his wife after covering the war in Cuba.

When Dunning arrived in Dover from Puerto Rico, he had a long meeting with his father-in-law and brother-in-law and later with the Attorney General. Dunning would not talk to the press, but newspapers reported that he identified the handwriting on the note as Cordelia Botkin's, confirming what the state's handwriting experts contended.

John Pennington had a collection of anonymous letters that had been sent to Mary informing her of her husband's connection with Cordelia. One theory of the murder said that Botkin was angry that Dunning planned to return to his wife. Another theory said that two women were in love with Dunning, and one who killed Dunnings's wife threw suspicion on the other.

The San Francisco police uncovered a web of circumstantial evidence against Cordelia. Drug store clerks said they had sold her arsenic. Clerks at Haas's candy store identified Mrs. Botkin as a woman who bought candy there. The poisoned chocolates were Haas's chocolates put into a box of candy from Wave Confections. The clerk at Wave remembered the unusual transaction of adding her own candy to their box and identified Mrs. Botkin as the customer. A clerk at the City of Paris store remembered selling Mrs. Botkin a handkerchief similar to the one in the package.

The grand jury in Delaware indicted Cordelia Botkin for murder in Dover, and Delaware authorities attempted to have her extradited for trial. However, they had trouble drafting a request that the governor of California could agree to, and her attorneys questioned the right of California to extradite her to a state where she had never set foot. Finally, they indicted her for trial in San Francisco.

First Trial: 1. December 5, 1899

Cordelia Botkin's trial for the murder of Mary Dunning began on December 5, 1899, and lasted a month and a half. The jury found her guilty of first-degree murder and sentenced her to life in San Quentin Penitentiary.

Botkin continued to profess innocence and immediately began an appeal. The process took four years and ultimately ended with the US Supreme Court granting her a new trial due to errors in the judge's instructions to the jury.

Second Trial: 2. March 10, 1904

When Cordelia Botkin was tried again in March 1904, the court had trouble finding an impartial jury. Ten days into the trial, it was learned that four of the jurors may have been bribed in favor of the defendant. Reluctantly, the prosecution agreed to continue the case with the original jury. Despite the controversy, the jury once again returned a verdict of guilty.

Verdicts: 1. Guilty of First-degree murder, overturned
2. Guilty of First-degree murder

Aftermath:

It was reported that nine members of the jury at first favored hanging before ultimately agreeing to a life sentence. Cordelia Botkin was imprisoned in the State Prison at San Quentin until her death in 1910.

The Webster Mystery

Alice Hoyle had last seen her sister, Lillie, on the night of September 1, 1887, in the room they shared in Webster, Massachusetts. Lillie had left to use the outhouse, and Alice fell asleep before she returned. The next morning, Alice was late for work and left in a rush, thinking that her sister had already left for her job. That evening, Lillie did not come home, and Alice noticed that her watch and jewelry were still on the nightstand where she had left them the night before. Lillie had gone out and never come back. This is the story Alice told the police the following day. As the investigation progressed, she would change it several times.

Lillie Hoyle
National Police Gazette, Oct. 8, 1887

Date:	September 1, 1887
Location:	Webster, Massachusetts
Victim:	Lillie (Lilla) Hoyle
Cause of Death:	Chloroform
Accused:	Dixon R. Cowie & Thomas B. McQuaid

Synopsis:
Lillie Hoyle, 23, and her sister Alice, 19, were orphans; their father died when they were very young, and their mother died in 1883. Though they took care of themselves, they had the support of several aunts and uncles living in Webster. They shared a room in a 2½ story house rented by their uncle Dixon Cowie, and Lillie worked in a restaurant and ice cream saloon on the first floor, run by Mrs. Sarah Taylor. Alice worked in a mill not far away.

According to Alice, Lillie had been in a good mood the night she disappeared, singing and laughing, joking with her sister. The girls had recently returned from a week's vacation at Camp White on the Providence River in Rhode Island, and Lillie was still in high spirits from the trip. Alice was tired and already in bed when Lillie changed out of her summer dress into a faded blue satin wrapper and then left the room. Uncle Dixon, the last person to see Lillie alive, watched her leave the house and head toward the outhouse.

When Lillie failed to return, the people of Webster began a frantic search. Though she had shown no signs of depression, ponds in the area were dragged in fear that she had committed suicide. There was no trace of Lillie until September 20, when two men on the road to the adjoining town of Oxford noticed a foul stench from an abandoned corn crib. When they investigated further, they found the decomposed body of a woman wedged between the timbers. Her hands and feet were tied, and a shawl and other clothing covered her head.

The body was taken to an undertaker and was very soon identified as Lillie Hoyle. When Alice was notified, she was overcome with grief and reportedly became delirious. An autopsy was performed, and though the authorities tried to keep the results secret, the press soon learned that Lillie had likely been murdered to hide the fact that she was seven months pregnant.

By all accounts, Lillie was a beautiful woman with dark brown hair and bluish-gray eyes. She had a good reputation in Webster, and although she had many male and female friends, she had told no one of her condition and was not known to be on intimate terms with any man. Alice was also highly esteemed in town; the two girls were almost always seen together. They both had lovely singing voices and appeared on stage in an amateur production of The Chimes of Normandy. Alice insisted that she did not know the identity of Lillie's lover and had not even known she was pregnant.

Webster's chief of police knew from the start that the case was beyond his abilities and sent for the Massachusetts State Detective Force to aid in the investigation. The detectives worked in the utmost secrecy, keeping any clues they uncovered away from the press. At the same time, the case had become a national story, and reporters, hungry for news and lacking in official cooperation, began reporting all the local rumors.

It was reported that the Cowie household was not as harmonious as it first appeared. Lillie and her uncle Dixon had not been on speaking terms for several months prior to her disappearance. Fannie Wheeler, a close friend of Lillie's, said Lillie was planning to move out of her uncle's house. She was frightened of his violent behavior when drunk.

It was rumored that Alice not only knew of her sister's condition but also knew the identity of her betrayer. This was vehemently denied by the detectives, who told reporters they believed that Alice did not know that Lillie was pregnant. Reporters trying to uncover the identity of the man who had impregnated Lillie learned that she had been close to Isadore Nickel, a clothing merchant who had opened a temporary store in Webster and had left the town in August. Some other possible suitors were named, but there was no evidence to name anyone as Lillie's seducer.

The police investigation was moving in a different direction. An analysis of the contents of Lillie's intestines showed traces of oil of tansy, a drug used to induce a miscarriage. Lillie had apparently attempted to abort the baby, and the police were looking for the doctor who prescribed the drug. Meanwhile, several witnesses reported seeing a carriage speeding along Oxford Road the night of September 1, near where the body was found. Pat O'Day, a Worcester detective who was not actively working the case, told the *New York Herald* that Worcester County was notorious for its large number of 'lying-in hospitals' – private houses where abortions were performed. O'Day believed that Lillie was taken to one of them and had died from of an overdose of chloroform.

Reporters were looking for a mysterious 'Dr. Smith' who had checked into a Webster hotel the night of Lillie's disappearance and left the following day. They were also seeking information on a Webster stable owner who had sold his establishment and left town shortly after the murder. But in spite of an abundance of speculation, the truth was still out of reach, and by the middle of October, the case had grown cold, and the press was making comparisons of Lillie's murder to those of Jennie Cramer and Rose Ambler – recent New England murders that remained unsolved.

Then on October 31, a clue from El Paso, Texas, began to heat things up again. The Webster postmaster received a letter from an El Paso plantation owner who had recently hired an Irishman from Massachusetts. When the subject of Lillie Hoyle was raised – the story had been front page news throughout the country – the Irishman had betrayed a great deal of knowledge in the matter. In fact, he gave a full account of the crime, laying the blame on her uncle, Dixon Cowie, and claiming that he, himself, had been hired to conceal the body. He was paid $50 and told to go to Little Rock where he would receive $150 more. The Massachusetts detectives believed that the Irishman was the Webster hostler who had left town suddenly after the murder.

Nothing conclusive came from this clue either, and the case went cold again for another six months. Then, on May 4, 1888, the police arrested Dixon R. Cowie for the murder of his niece. Cowie and his wife had moved to Darien, Connecticut, and appeared more prosperous than they had been in Webster. The newspapers speculated that he, too, had been paid for his role in the murder. Cowie agreed to return to Massachusetts without the need for extradition.

On the same day, another arrest was made in New York City. Thomas B. McQuaid, a student at the College of Physicians and Surgeons in New York and a former resident of Webster, Massachusetts, was arrested for the murder of Lillie Hoyle. It was alleged that McQuaid had been intimate with Lillie and killed her to cover up her pregnancy. McQuaid was less cooperative than Cowie and remained in custody in New York while extradition papers were filed.

The detectives were reluctant to reveal the evidence against the two men, but the newspapers correctly surmised that Alice had changed her story. After months of denying any knowledge of the murder or her sister's pregnancy, she now admitted that she had been party to a conspiracy against Lillie that had included Cowin and McQuaid. The plan had been to persuade Lillie to have an abortion, by force if necessary, and the result had been her death.

Tearfully, Alice told the grand jury that her uncle had raped Lillie on numerous occasions and had tried, unsuccessfully, to assault her as well. Lillie had also been consensually intimate with McQuaid, and they did not know who was responsible for her pregnancy. McQuaid's family was powerful and prominent in Worcester County, and he was anxious to avoid scandal. Cowin also wanted to avoid scandal but was also motivated by the large sum of money McQuaid offered for his help. Alice joined the plot because she loved McQuaid and would do anything he asked. The three met in a room above McQuaid's father's wholesale liquor store to make their plans.

The night of September 1, Lillie had not left the house but was in the kitchen of Cowie's house, where McQuaid was trying to convince her to have an abortion. They went over it repeatedly, but Lillie refused to agree. Cowie sent out for some beer, and when it arrived, made sure that Lillie's glass was always full. She became drunk but still would not relent. Then they applied the chloroform – Alice could not remember if she or her uncle had first put the saturated cloth to Lillie's mouth – and while McQuaid held the horse, Cowie and Alice carried her, unconscious, to the wagon.

They planned to take her into the woods and perform the operation there. Lillie sat in the front seat wedged between Cowie and McQuaid, and Alice sat in the back as they drove down Oxford Road. Suddenly, Lillie awoke from her stupor, making a loud, piteous cry. From fear of discovery, both men grabbed at her throat. This action so startled Alice that she screamed and then fainted. When she came to her senses, she saw that her sister was dead. The men carried her body away and hid it in the corn crib. They returned home, and Alice waited until the following day to report Lillie missing.

Several witnesses were able to corroborate Alice's story somewhat. Mrs. Taylor recalled seeing Lillie the night before the murder, conversing with a man she believed was Thomas McQuaid. Their voices were raised, and Mrs. Taylor heard Lillie say, "I'll die before I do it." Several people saw the speeding wagon the night of September 1, and most importantly, Mrs. Wilhelmina Roache heard Alice's scream.

Arraignment: October 1, 1888

Cowie and McQuaid were held in the Worcester House of Correction for another six months before their official arraignment. On October 1, 1888, both men pled not guilty, and while their attorneys pushed for a speedy trial, the government was not ready to proceed. They were having trouble locating one of their witnesses, and though they would not say who it was, the press soon learned that Wilhelmina Roche had left Webster and was living in Providence, Rhode Island. She was now claiming that she recognized Dixon Cowie as one of the men in the wagon, but though she did not recognize the other man, she knew he was not Thomas McQuaid. She also denied being paid to leave town.

Alice's testimony was under attack outside of court. The Worcester Telegram was claiming that their reporters ascertained beyond a doubt that Lillie Hoyle died in a house in Webster where she was undergoing an abortion. Five people were present at the time; none was Dixon Cowie or Thomas McQuaid.

Aftermath:

On November 15, it was announced that Cowie and McQuaid would be released without bail. Though the charges had not been dropped, the government did not have enough evidence to try the men. Alice had changed her story again; she now, once again, claimed that she knew nothing about Lillie's death. The Attorney General would not release the details of Alice's latest version but said it was different from her original story and different from the one she told the grand jury. The Attorney General also included some people not previously mentioned in connection with the case.

Since the murder, Alice had been living with another uncle, Andrew Hoyle, and had not been working. The *Boston Herald* speculated that the story Alice told the grand jury may have been an attempt by Alice and her uncle to claim the $500 reward offered by the town, and her recanting may have been paid for by McQuaid's father.

Cowie and McQuaid were never tried, and no other arrests were made, but that's not quite the end of the story. In March 1891, Mrs. Andrew Hoyle came forward with another version of Lillie's murder as told to her by Alice. Mrs. Hoyle was somewhat bitter at this point because her husband of thirty years had left her to live in sin with his niece, Alice, first in Rhode Island, then "out west," though it was believed they hadn't gone any further west than Worcester County. While Alice lived there, Mrs. Hoyle had caught them together several times. Andrew and Alice had moved out about eighteen months earlier, and more recently, Andrew sold the house and furniture, leaving his wife with nothing.

This fourth Alice Hoyle story was actually her first, told privately to her aunt and uncle shortly after the murder. She told them that she, herself, had chloroformed Lillie, and Cowie and McQuaid had disposed of the body. Both girls, though quite promiscuous, wanted to marry Tom McQuaid. He told Alice he wanted to marry her but could do nothing until Lillie's pregnancy was resolved. Alice resolved it by killing her sister. Andrew Hoyle, desperate to save his niece from the gallows and his family from scandal, coached Alice and helped create the story she would tell the police. In the process, they fell in love.

The *Boston Herald* promised that new arrests were imminent, but they never materialized. The story emerged a couple more times in the years that followed, always with 'imminent arrests', but no one was ever arrested, and eventually, the story of Lillie Hoyle's murder faded away completely.

Cain And Abel

Like the Biblical brothers Cain and Abel, the Sawtell brothers of Boston took divergent paths through life. While Hiram settled down and raised a family, supported by his successful fruit business, Isaac was doing time in Charlestown prison. And as with the Bible's first murderer, Isaac's jealousy of his brother became unbearable. Upon his release from prison, he lured Hiram from his family and killed him in cold blood.

Hiram Sawtell
"The modern Cain and Abel"

Date:	February 5, 1890
Location:	Rochester, New Hampshire
Victim:	Hiram Sawtell
Cause of Death:	Gunshot
Accused:	Isaac Sawtell

Synopsis:

In 1876, Isaac Sawtell was convicted of three counts of rape and sentenced to thirty years at the Massachusetts State Prison in Charlestown. His good behavior in prison led the officials to believe that he had reformed, and after serving thirteen years, he was pardoned and released.

When Isaac returned from prison, he was welcomed by his brother, Hiram, who offered him work in his fruit store and even spoke of forming a business partnership. However, their good relations did not last long. Isaac was upset to learn that property owned by their father, now deceased, was in his mother's name and being managed by Hiram. In December 1889, behind Hiram's back, Isaac persuaded their mother to transfer the property to him. Hiram filed an injunction to prevent his brother from selling the property when he heard of this.

On February 1, 1890, Isaac told Hiram's wife, Jeannette, that he and his mother were taking a trip to Lowell and that Hiram had given permission for his seven-year-old daughter, Marion, to accompany them. Reluctantly, Jeannette let Marion go with Isaac, only to find out that Hiram had not given his permission. Two days later Hiram received a telegram from Isaac, sent from Rochester, New Hampshire, saying that Marion had the flu and to come immediately. The next day, Jeannette received a similar telegram. They decided that Hiram would go alone to care for Marion, and he took a 1 p.m. train from Boston to Rochester. Hiram was never heard from again.

Isaac, his mother, and Marion, now healthy again, returned to Boston on February 6. The next day, Jeannette found Isaac in the fruit store and asked what had happened to her husband. Isaac claimed he had not seen Hiram in Rochester and did not know where he was. Jeannette called him a liar and accused him of murdering Hiram. She waited two more days for Hiram's return, then took the story to the police.

When the Boston police went to question Isaac, they found that he had left the city again. They traced him back to Rochester, New Hampshire, but by the time the detectives arrived, Isaac had left town. After interviewing several people in Rochester, the detectives had reason to believe that Isaac had murdered his brother there. Hiram had purchased a pick, a shovel, and an axe from a Rochester hardware store. He had rented a buggy and had been seen riding with a man who resembled Isaac, with his distinctive side-whiskers and shaved chin. Several people reported hearing three gunshots on February 4 near the road where the two men had been seen. The Boston detectives and local police organized a search of the woods nearby.

Meanwhile, the manager of a hotel in Portland, Maine, was suspicious of a man who had registered as J. Bridge. He feared that the guest planned to skip out on his bill and thought he resembled a published description of Isaac Sawtell. He took his suspicions to the police, who put Mr. Bridge under surveillance. The police recognized the man as Isaac Sawtell and arrested him on board a train preparing to leave for Montreal.

When arrested, Sawtell had two train tickets to Montreal. The detectives speculated that the second ticket was for Dr. Blood, a Boston conman Sawtell met in prison. When Blood's picture was printed in a Boston newspaper, a Dover, New Hampshire hotel keeper recognized him. He said Blood had come in looking for a room, carrying a package "…done up in newspaper, about the size of a man's head." Blood publicly denied any connection to Sawtell. His name came up a few more times in the reporting of the murder, but the police never questioned him.

In Rochester, the search was beginning to bear fruit; they found a bloodstained axe wrapped in newspaper, a shoe identified as Hiram Sawtell's, and a bloody handkerchief with the monogram 'S'. Then, near an abandoned farmhouse, they found the partially buried body of Hiram Sawtell, naked except for his socks. There were three bullet holes in his chest, and his head and arms had been cut off. Apparently, the killer had started to dig a grave but grew tired of the job, so he chopped off the arms and head, allowing the body to fit the hole he dug. The head and arms were nowhere to be found.

To complicate matters, the search had extended beyond the New Hampshire border, and the body was found in the woods outside Berwick, Maine. The question of whether the murder was committed in New Hampshire or Maine would be a significant one since New Hampshire had the death penalty and Maine did not. An inquest was held in York County, Maine, and the jury determined that circumstantial evidence pointed to the murder being committed in New Hampshire.

A coroner's jury was called in Rochester, New Hampshire, with nearly 2,000 people trying to get into the town hall to hear the proceedings. Isaac maintained his innocence, saying that the body was not Hiram's, and that Hiram would show up alive when the time was right. He was indicted for the murder of his brother.

Trial: December 16, 1890

Sawtell's trial was held the following December in Dover, New Hampshire. To cover all bases, he was charged with three counts of murder: the willful murder of his brother Hiram; an accessory before the fact in New Hampshire of the murder committed by persons unknown in Maine; and an accessory before the fact in New Hampshire of the murder committed by persons unknown in New Hampshire.

With between 60 and 70 witnesses, the state presented a case which, while circumstantial, was quite convincing. They pinpointed the precise location of the murder as a barn owned by Jed Morrill between Rochester and East Rochester. Several witnesses testified to hearing three gunshots on the night of February 5. The defense challenged the state's witnesses, questioning the dates and identifications. They also denied that there had been any bad blood between the brothers. But the defense's case was much weaker than the prosecution's.

The verdict was read on Christmas Day, 1890. The judge decided to hold court that day so the jury, who had been sequestered since December 16, could spend at least part of Christmas Day with their families. After deliberating for less than two hours, the jury returned a verdict of guilty.

Verdict: Guilty of first-degree murder.

Aftermath:

Sawtell was sentenced to hang more than a year later, on the first Tuesday in January 1892. During that time, his attorney filed an appeal, but the verdict was upheld. Then, on December 1, 1891, Sawtell confessed to shooting his brother but said that the crime had been committed in the State of Maine. He also drew a map telling the police where they could find Hiram's head. They found the head, now just a skull, and it had a bullet hole. This added another wrinkle; it meant that four shots had been fired and all the state's witnesses heard only three.

But regarding the location of the murder, this affidavit contradicted a previous sworn affidavit by Sawtell, which stated that he had no pistol and did not kill his brother. The State of New Hampshire saw no reason to believe the second over the first, and Sawtell was not granted a new trial.

This was his last hope. On Christmas Eve, 1891, just ten days before his scheduled execution, he suffered a stroke. As usual with death row illnesses, the doctors did all they could to save him for the gallows, but after twenty-four hours, he was still unconscious. Sawtell died on January 26. Rumors spread immediately that he had intentionally cheated the gallows by taking opium in some form, but an autopsy the following day proved conclusively that Isaac Sawtell had died of apoplexy.

FAMILY

Married At 15, Dead At 20

Howard Benham married Florence Tout, a wealthy teenager eight years younger than he was. He soon tired of his young wife and looked for a way to leave Florence without losing her money. He decided on poison.

Florence Benham
Evening Tribune, June 1, 1900

Date:	January 4, 1897
Location:	Batavia, New York
Victim:	Florence Benham
Cause of Death:	Poisoning
Accused:	Howard Benham

Synopsis:

James Tout, a wealthy businessman of Byron Center, New York, died before the birth of his daughter Florence, but before he departed this world, he set up a sizable trust fund for the new baby. The inheritance, which would be hers when she married, was managed by a banker and had grown to a small fortune by the time she was in her teens.

When Florence was 15 years old, she received the attention of Howard Benham, an ambitious young man of 23 who worked as a travel agent, booking trips to the Chicago World's Fair on the installment plan. Florence's mother and stepfather disapproved of the courtship but feared their opposition might drive Florence to run away with Benham. On the night of August 3, 1892, she told them not to worry; she had no intention of running away. The following day, she said she was going to Batavia to consult a dentist, but instead, she traveled through to Rochester, where she met with Benham. The two were married in the private office of Justice White.

The Benhams bought a house in a fashionable neighborhood in Batavia. Howard took over management of Florence's inheritance and engaged in private banking and money-lending. The couple had one son, but after five years together, it was apparent to outsiders that their marriage was not a happy one. Howard mistreated his wife and was said to be leading a fast life outside of marriage.

In the early hours of January 4, 1897, Florence Benham died in her home following a short illness. The cause of death was said to be rheumatism of the heart. At first, the announcement did not attract more than ordinary sympathy for the bereaved family, but soon, rumors began to circulate that Florence's death had not been natural. The rumors grew until the clamor of speculation became too strong for Coroner Barringer to ignore. He began an investigation, calling on Mr. Benham, who agreed that, under the circumstances, an inquest and autopsy were necessary.

The coroner began selecting jurors for the inquest and engaging doctors for the autopsy. He had planned to have Florence's heart, stomach, and other organs removed for chemical analysis, but the four doctors who examined her deemed this unnecessary. They unanimously agreed that she had died of heart failure. Death had been caused by atrophy and degeneration of the muscular heart tissue, probably resulting from a severe injury to pelvic organs during the recent birth of her son. Florence was buried on January 7.

The following day, Sam J. Elliot, a pharmacist at a local drug store, reported that about a week before Mrs. Benham's death, he had made two sales, a few days apart, of an ounce of prussic acid to Howard Benham. At the first sale, Benham told Elliot he wanted the strong poison to kill a dog. Elliot was reluctant at first but finally agreed to sell Benham the poison. Benham asked him not to tell the proprietor of the store about the purchase. A few days later, Benham returned for another ounce of prussic acid. The druggist jokingly asked if he hadn't already killed the dog. Benham said never mind the dog; he wanted the acid. Elliot refused again, but when the argument that followed threatened to come to blows, he relented.

At 3:00 a.m. the next morning, the coroner obtained an arrest warrant against Howard Benham from Justice Dunham. At 5.00am, the Batavia police arrested Benham and took him to jail. Coroner Barringer ordered the body of Florence Benham disinterred for a second autopsy. This time, the heart, liver, stomach, and a pint of blood were turned over for analysis to Dr. Frank P. Vandenbergh, former City Chemist of Buffalo, who was frequently called for poisoning cases in Western New York. Dr. Vandenbergh estimated it would take at least two weeks to determine if the organs contained prussic acid.

The inquest began without waiting for the chemical analysis, and this time, the autopsy doctors were not as positive as they had been. Dr. Morris W. Townsend, who had been involved in both autopsies, said that the first autopsy had been done in haste, and they had not been looking for poison. After the second autopsy, he saw indications that the death might not have been natural.

"I do not believe that death was due to natural causes," he said, "and facts were brought out on the autopsies that showed that it might have been caused by prussic acid."

Dr. Tozier, the family physician who had been treating Mrs. Benham at the time of her illness, said that she had been perfectly healthy, and he had thought it was a simple case but became disturbed when her husband said she was in the habit of taking powders and said she was habitually using morphine.

The inquest stretched on for more than a month. About two weeks in, it was reported that Dr. Vandenbergh had discovered prussic acid in Mrs. Benham's organs, but only in trace amounts. After meeting with Benham's lawyers, District Attorney Le Seur decided not to call Dr. Vandenbergh to testify. He probably wanted to avoid turning the procedure into a battle of experts.

The most damaging testimony of all came at the end of the hearing when Florence's mother took the stand. She was at her daughter's house the night Florence died and was awakened by the Benhams' son. She heard voices from the sick room as she went to quiet him. It seemed to her that Benham was trying to force his wife to take medicine.

She heard her daughter protest and exclaim, "I do not see what you want me to take it for!" and later, she said, "I don't care, Howard; I think you are mean to treat me so."

The inquest closed, and Howard Benham was held for first-degree murder.

First Trial: 1. June 30, 1897

The trial for murder in June followed much the same course as the inquest. This time, Dr. W.B. Hatch, who examined Benham in jail, testified that Benham was suffering from stricture, a disorder that was commonly treated with prussic acid. Dr. Vandenbergh testified for the prosecution that he had found traces of prussic acid in the brain, liver, and blood, but the quantity was not determined. According to the Buffalo Currier, "Dr. Vandenbergh's words, as well as his manner, led listeners to believe that there was even some doubt about the trace." However, the circumstantial evidence proved strong enough; Howard Benham was convicted of first-degree murder.

His attorneys filed a request for a new trial. After two months of deliberation, the request was denied, and Benham was sentenced to the electric chair at Auburn State Prison. The defense then filed an appeal, which the Court of Appeals rejected in October 1899.

Second Trial: 2. May 28, 1900

While at Auburn awaiting execution, Benham hired a new lawyer and converted to Catholicism. One or the other seems to have worked for him because, in February 1900, he was granted a new trial. In his second trial, held in May, Benham was found not guilty.

Verdicts: 1. Guilty of first-degree murder

2. Not guilty

Aftermath:

Following his acquittal, Howard Benham married a wealthy southern widow, but his troubles were far from over. In January 1901, Mary A. Farant, guardian ad litem of Howard's young son, also Howard, sued Benham to recover his wife's estate. The suit was filed on the grounds that Benham killed his wife and should not inherit her estate. Though he could not be sent to prison, Howard would be tried once again for the murder of his wife.

While his attorneys tried to negotiate a settlement, Howard worked as a traveling salesman in Ohio. He contracted typhoid and died before the lawsuit was resolved.

Little Conestoga Creek

The discovery of the murdered body of Mrs. Mary Dellinger led to the very public airing of her family's dirty laundry. Her husband Calvin was a philanderer, abusive to his wife, and sadistic to his children. But was he a killer as well?

"It is a dead woman"
National Police Gazette, Nov. 3, 1888

Date:	October 4, 1888
Location:	Lancaster, Pennsylvania
Victim:	Mary C. Dellinger
Cause of Death:	Drowning
Accused:	Calvin M. Dellinger

Synopsis:
A team of railroad men heading to work on a handcar on Friday, October 5, 1888, spotted something strange under a bridge across Little Conestoga Creek near Lancaster, Pennsylvania. One of the men climbed down the steep bank for a closer look and found the body of a young woman. Her clothing was torn, her hair disheveled, and the ground around her showed signs of struggle. Strewn around the body was a white straw hat trimmed with ribbon and bunting, a lady's brown handkerchief, seven buttons torn from her jersey and a horseshoe-shaped breastpin.

The woman was just over five feet tall, with a slender but shapely form. The upper portion of her clothing was wet while the lower was dry, suggesting someone had held her head under the water. She was found on land farmed by

John Gamber, and he took her body by wagon to the dead house of the County Hospital. An examination of the body revealed that she had drowned.

Inside the hat found at the scene was written the name C.M. Dellinger. From this, the body was identified as Mary Dellinger, the 18-year-old wife of Calvin M. Dellinger, a tenant farmer. They lived on Fruitville Pike with their 13-month-old daughter. When he heard the news, Mr. Dellinger hurried to the County Hospital and wept bitterly over his wife's body.

Dellinger explained to the police that he had not seen his wife since Tuesday. She left the house to go shopping and did not return. She was still missing on Thursday, and Dellinger went into Lancaster to see if she had gone to see her father, Isaac Aston. Aston told him that Mary stayed there Wednesday night but had left that morning. Dellinger returned home only to find that Mary had been home, taken some clothing for the baby and her watch, and left again. Once more, Dellinger went into Lancaster and searched for his wife, unsuccessfully, until 11:00 p.m. on Thursday. Mary was reportedly seen on Thursday evening in the company of an unknown man.

When Mary's friends and family were questioned, the police learned that there was more to the story of her disappearance. Calvin Dellinger was known to be a wife-beater who took any opportunity to abuse his Mary. He also tortured their baby; he hit her when she cried, would press the hot chimney of an oil lamp against the baby's face, and once held out a hot poker for her to grab. When his wife tried to interfere, he would turn his wrath on her. Mary could not take it anymore, and on Tuesday, October 2, she decided to leave her husband.

She told him she was going to the grocery store but went to her brother's house in Conestoga Centre instead. She stayed there Tuesday night, and then on Wednesday, he took her to her father's house in Lancaster. On Thursday, she stopped at a friend's house, then went back home. She entered the house by forcing open the shutters, then gathered some baby clothes and other small items. As she was leaving, she saw her husband approaching. She ran to a neighbor's house and hid until he left again. She told her story at every stop, but it is unclear where she went from there or where the baby was.

Mary Aston was not Calvin Dellinger's first wife. That marriage had ended in divorce the previous summer, just before he married Mary. The first Mrs. Dellinger was reluctant to speak of her ex-husband, saying that her thoughts were now centered on her own family, but when she started talking, she added another dimension to the story. She said their marriage had been happy until Dellinger met Mary Aston, then he became abusive and had once threatened to shoot her. He met Mary at a Sunday school picnic, and she had asked him to take her home; after that, they would meet on the sly. His wife found letters Mary had written to him, proposing that they run off and marry. She also found Mary's picture in Dellinger's hat. When she confronted her husband, he said he loved Mary and was planning to marry her.

Mary became pregnant and threatened to bring a paternity suit against Dellinger. When Mrs. Dellinger learned this, she divorced her husband. However, Dellinger and Mary did not immediately get married, and despite the divorce, he and his ex-wife were trying to settle their differences and live together again. Mary had agreed to drop the suit if she was paid $125. Mrs. Dellinger gave him the money, thinking the matter was resolved. Three days later Dellinger married Mary. He had used the money to buy a stage route between Lancaster and Conestoga.

The first Mrs. Dellinger told the police Mary was a "loose character." After the marriage, she met with Mary who told her that Dellinger was not the father of her child. The real father was a schoolteacher in Conestoga, and she planned to run off with him as soon as she could make the arrangements.

Dellinger was rapidly becoming the prime suspect in Mary's murder. In his house, the police found a suit of clothes saturated with water, as well as several rings believed to have been taken off Mary's body. The breastpin found at the murder scene was known to have belonged to him. That evidence, together with Dellinger's history of abuse, led to his arrest for his wife's murder. However, it could not be proven that Dellinger wore the pin on the day of the murder, and his shoes did not make the footprints at the scene of the murder. Though the police were convinced of his guilt, he was released due to lack of evidence.

Upon his release, Dellinger announced that he was offering a $200 reward for information leading to the arrest of his wife's killer. But most people in town still believed that he was guilty of the murder. Though it was reported that the police were no longer investigating, the county brought in a Pinkerton detective named James Nevins to review the evidence more thoroughly. It was not specified exactly what he found, but on November 7, Calvin Dellinger was re-arrested.

Trial: March 7, 1889

In addition to the somewhat thin circumstantial evidence against Dellinger, the prosecution questioned many of Mary's friends and family, who testified to Dellinger's abuse of his wife and the animosity that existed between them. The testimony of Mary's father succinctly sums up the situation:

> *My daughter's eyes were blackened, and she was bruised several times and Dellinger admitted that he had caused it; frequently when Dellinger had quarrels with his wife she was afraid to go with him and he said she had to go with him, that he feared neither hell, Heaven, or the gallows.*

The most damning testimony concerning the murder came from Mrs. Susan Shrenk who had been riding home from work in a carriage on the evening of October 4 and had passed Dellinger and his wife going down Fruitville pike and had heard them arguing. This contradicted his story that he had not seen his wife after Tuesday and had been in Lancaster on October 4.

Dellinger's attorney reminded the jury that his client was charged with the murder of Mary, not beating or abusing her. He raised the possibility that she had committed suicide, and he challenged Mrs. Shrenk's testimony because it was different from what she testified to at the inquest.

The jury deliberated for twenty-four hours before sending a note to the judge saying that they were hopelessly deadlocked at six for conviction and six for acquittal. The judge would not accept this and told them to continue deliberating until they all agreed. After another twenty-six hours, they reached a compromise and found Dellinger guilty of second-degree murder.

Verdict: Guilty of second-degree murder

Aftermath:

The verdict surprised the public, who generally believed that Dellinger was either guilty of a capital crime or not guilty at all. He was sentenced to ten years at the Eastern Penitentiary.

After serving nearly eight years, he was released from prison in February 1897 and immediately got into trouble again. He was out less than a week before he went to his first wife seeking reconciliation. She refused to have anything to do with him, and he was arrested for threatening to kill her.

Thrown Out of the Window

The body of Mary E. Hill was found lying outside her Philadelphia home by her maid returning from church the night of November 22, 1868. She had been killed in her dining room by blows to the head with a fireplace poker. She was then dragged into the sitting room, and then thrown out of the second-story window. Though two people were tried for this murder, and one was sentenced to be hanged, there would be no execution.

Throwing the Body Out of the Window
Frank Leslie's Illustrated Newspaper, Dec. 12, 1868

Date:	November 22, 1868
Location:	Philadelphia, Pennsylvania
Victim:	Mary E. Hill
Cause of Death:	Beaten with a poker
Accused:	George S. Twitchell

Synopsis:
About four years before Mary Hill's death, her daughter, Camilla, had been hired as a housekeeper for a widower named Twitchell, living on a farm near Carpenter's Landing, New Jersey. Shortly after taking over the farm, Twitchell was joined by his son, George, who had been attending college in Connecticut. Though Camilla Hill was several years older than George Twitchell, the two became romantically entwined and eloped to New York City.

They lived in New York for a short time, then moved to Philadelphia, where George Twitchell was engaged in the produce business in the Spruce Street Market. He was unsuccessful at this, and the couple moved in with Camilla's mother, Mary. Her husband, a wealthy contractor, had recently died, leaving her an estate and an abundance of funds.

George and Camilla Twitchell changed Mrs. Hill from her rather unpretentious mode of living to one of costly ostentation. Meanwhile, Twitchell went into business again, this time manufacturing shingles in Camden, New

Jersey. He also failed at this, and in November 1868, the business went bankrupt, leaving him hard-pressed for money.

In spite of that, the Twitchells appeared to be on the best of terms with Mrs. Hill – the servants who lived in the house attested to this. They continued to live quite well on Mrs. Hill's money. However, a real estate broker named Joseph Gilbert would later say that Twitchell had induced him to put Twitchell's name on a deed he was buying for Mrs. Hill. Gilbert had also told him that whenever in anyone else's presence Twichell acted as if he was on good terms with his mother-in-law, but at other times he referred to her as "an old bitch," and Gilbert remembered him saying he wanted to "kill the old bitch."

Around nine o'clock on the night of Sunday, November 22, 1868, Sarah Campbell, a servant of Mrs. Hill, returned from church. The door was locked, and she had to ring the bell repeatedly before Twitchell came to answer. He was partially dressed as if he had already gone to bed.

Twitchell remarked on what a cold night it was then said, "I wonder where mother is," implying that Mrs. Hill was still outside.

He let Sarah in, then returned to his bedroom.

Sarah opened the door leading to the yard and was horrified to see the dead body of Mrs. Hill on the brick pavement beneath the windows of the sitting room.

She called for Twitchell, who came out, exclaiming, "My God, what is this?"

He and Sarah carried the body into the kitchen. Mrs. Twitchell came downstairs in her nightclothes and found her husband washing her mother's face with a wet cloth. The neighbors were given the alarm, and they sent for a doctor. Mrs. Twitchell met them at the door.

"Mother had been killed," she cried, "she fell out of the second-story window."

An examination of the upstairs room revealed drops of blood on the floor of the dining room and the sitting room and blood on the windowsill of the sitting room. Twitchell's shirt was bloodstained as well. Mrs. Twitchell claimed that her mother always carried a large sum of money – $2,000 - $3,000 – in her bosom and often told people about it. The money was not there when the body was found, and Mrs. Twitchell believed that a burglar had murdered her mother for the money.

It seemed unlikely that a burglar would risk capture by throwing the body out the window. Mr. and Mrs. Twitchell, who were the only occupants of the house at the time, became the prime suspects and were arrested for the murder of Mrs. Hill.

Trial: December 28, 1868

George Twitchell was tried first. The evidence against him was circumstantial but strong. Mrs. Hill was murdered in the dining room, and fresh cigar ash there indicated that her killer was familiar enough to sit and smoke while they talked. They no doubt argued about money, and he became angered and decided to kill her, first going to the kitchen for a larger poker than the one in the dining room. He returned and used the poker to beat Mrs. Hill to death. To confuse the evidence, he threw the body out of the window, then went outside and placed the bloody poker under the body. He removed his bloodstained clothing, went to bed, and waited for Sarah Campbell to return and find the body. The defense argued that George Twitchell's character had been exemplary, with no history of violence or bad behavior. He and his wife did not stand to gain by Mrs. Hill's death; her husband's will had stipulated that the estate would go to his wife until her death, then would be passed on to his relatives, not hers. None of the missing money that Mrs. Hill had allegedly been carrying on her person had been traced to Twitchell.

They claimed that someone outside the family had done the murder. The blood on Twitchell's shirt had come from carrying the body into the house. Charles Altgelt, who lived nearby, testified to seeing two men leave Mrs. Hill's house as he walked by around 9:00 p.m. that night – one nondescript, the other tall, wearing a very long coat. The entryway was dark, not lit, as he would have expected.

The prosecution pointed out that the blood on Twitchell's shirt was not smudged as it would be from carrying the bloody body, by in sprinkles, the same as the walls of the dining room – sprinkles that could only be accounted for "…by an open artery or the dash of a weapon upon a bloody surface." Additionally, witnesses testified that Twitchell was not wearing his shirt when he carried the body into the house. They gave no significance to Mr. Altgelt's testimony about strangers leaving the house.

The jury deliberated for only thirteen minutes before returning with a verdict of guilty of murder in the first degree.

Camilla Twitchell was then tried and found not guilty of the murder of her mother.

Verdict: Guilty of first-degree murder

Aftermath:

George Twitchell was sentenced to be hanged, but the execution was delayed due to appeals. The defense filed a request for a new trial on several technical grounds. The new trial was denied, and the case was appealed to the United States Supreme Court, which upheld the lower court's ruling.

With no more possible appeals, the hanging was scheduled for April 8, 1869. On April 3, Twitchell made a confession of sorts. He claimed that on that night, he had been in bed when his wife came in and said, "I have had a quarrel with my mother and killed her." Twitchell helped Camilla throw her mother's body out of the window, and he made a solemn vow to the Eternal God that he would never reveal what happened. However, after his conviction, he believed his wife would come forward and tell all. But she did not, and with his execution just five days away, Twitchell decided to break his vow and tell the truth.

The general public did not believe the confession. They considered Twitchell untrustworthy, and nothing he said changed the evidence. Even if his wife had wielded the poker, the blood spatter on his shirt indicated that he must have been standing next to her. But even if she did it, Camilla Twitchell had already been acquitted and could not be retried for the murder. The confession settled one matter; it proved that the murder had been committed by one or the other of the Twitchells. Mr. Altgelt's "tall man" with his "long coat" was proven to be a myth. Most Philadelphians were now satisfied that Twitchell's execution would be justified.

The morning of April 8, when George Twitchell was to be hanged, the jailers found him lying dead in his cell. Twitchell had cheated the gallows; he committed suicide by taking prussic acid. It was never determined who had supplied it for him.

The Talbotts

Dr. Perry H. Talbott was among the most well-respected citizens of Nodaway County, Missouri. In addition to being a skilled physician, Talbott was state legislator, a writer and a newspaper editor. He was a civic-minded citizen with strong beliefs, highly admired by friends and neighbors. But towards his family, Dr. Talbott was cold and distant. Miserly and neglectful, he had little interaction with his children beyond the occasional scolding. When Dr. Talbott was shot by an unknown assassin on September 18, 1880, in his dying breath he blamed his political enemies. The Nodaway County authorities, however, believed the killer was someone closer to home.

Dr. Perry Talbott
History of The Assassination of Dr. P.H. Talbott, 1881

Date:	September 18, 1880
Location:	Maryville, Missouri
Victim:	Dr. Perry H. Talbott
Cause of Death:	Gunshot
Accused:	Albert & Charles Talbott

Synopsis:
Perry H. Talbott was born in Illinois and earned a medical degree in Columbus, Ohio. Upon graduation he traveled west, first to the California gold fields, then to Northwest Missouri where he made his fortune as a country doctor. In 1853 he married Belle McFarland and together they had twelve children.

After fighting in the Union Army, he entered the political arena as an Independent Democrat. Then in 1876, opposing both Democrats and Republicans, he identified with the Greenback Labor movement, advocating the continued issuance of currency not backed by gold or silver. Talbott was the editor of the Greenback Standard and in 1880 he made the nomination address for the presidential candidate at the Greenback Party convention.

Tall and strong with black hair and beard and deep-set blue-gray eyes, Talbott was a commanding figure. He was a man of extraordinary ability with an indomitable will. He also had an estimation of his own importance which even his friends conceded was somewhat overblown.

Talbott's home, however, would belie any notion that it was occupied by a successful man. He was tightfisted with money and had no interest in adorning his house. The floors were uncovered, and curtains were old and threadbare. He took no pride in his children – five boys and seven girls – who grew up wild and undisciplined. The house was also an arsenal of small arms, with both the girls and the boys familiar with their use.

On the evening of September 18, 1880, after returning from a visit to a sick child, Dr. Talbott was in the sitting room reading a speech that he planned to publish. A shot rang out and a bullet came through the window passed through the doctor's chest and grazed his wife's calf before embedding in the wall. Talbott's son, Albert, grabbed a shotgun and ran from the house to chase the assassin.

Dr. Talbott managed to stay alive until 2:30 p.m. the following day. Before he died, Talbott said he thought the shooter must have been a paid assassin of the national banks, "some enemy of the great cause which I represent."

A coroner's jury convened to examine the death. They concluded that Dr. Talbott had been assassinated by some unknown person.

The verdict did not satisfy anyone. Sheriff Henry Toel and Prosecuting Attorney W.W. Ramsey remained suspicious and continued the investigation. The family had acted strangely following the murder. Though Albert had run out and fired a shot at a man who he claimed was running from the house, no effort was made to rouse the neighbors or to pursue the assassin. The family had shown little concern as the doctor lay dying.

One witness remarked, "It seemed to us that a dying animal in the barn-yard should have created more sympathy then was shown this murdered husband and father."

The marshal of Maryville, Missouri, hired a detective from Kansas named Jonas V. Brighton to aid the investigation. Brighton took the name Frank Hudson and passed off his wife Virginia as his sister Jennie. In this guise, the detective made the acquaintance of the oldest Talbott boys. He soon gained the confidence of the boys, aided by the fact that Albert had taken a liking to his "sister."

Brighton told them that his true profession was robbery and broached the subject of a partnership. The boys readily agreed and even drew up this contract (verbatim):

Monday, October 25, 1880 – We this day of the Lord eighteen hundred and eighty, go in contract together, Albert P. Talbott, Charles Talbott, Wilfred Mitchell, Frank B., Hudson, for the purpose of bank robbing, train robbin, and staig robbin and safe and each one shall be sworn into the same to stay together until death in every attempt to obtain buty, and in case any of one betrays us of our men deth is his portion at any time the first train and bank is robed any one in the bond can resine if he chooses and if he does resine he must keep al secrets to himself or he shall be killed and their must be a equal division of the bouty and before any train is robed or anyting is dun there is one traitor in the band that must be killed before we can proceed fother.

(Signed)
Jennie Hudson
2nd Wilford Mitchell
1st Albert P Talbott
2nd C E Talbott
1st Frank B Hudson

The traitor who needed to be killed was Henry Wyatt, a hired hand who also lived in the Talbott house. The boys told Brighton that they had murdered their father, and that Wyatt knew about it. They did not trust him and wanted Brighton to take him out of the way before he could betray them. Brighton took this information to the Marshal.

In the meantime, the sheriff had obtained information of his own, including a statement from Wilford Mitchell, one of the signers of the contract, implicating the Talbotts. Albert and Charles Talbott, along with Henry Wyatt were arrested for the murder of Perry Talbott. Mrs. Talbott was held as an accessory.

Trial: January 13, 1881

The Talbott case generated enormous interest in Nodaway County and the trial had to be moved from the county courthouse to Union Hall, a room capable of holding seven or eight hundred people. But those chosen for the jury were from the most remote parts of the county and knew little of the case.

The prosecution presented the testimony of Jonas and Virginia Brighton who claimed the brothers had admitted to killing their father and had offered Jonas fifty dollars to kill Henry Wyatt. Wilford Mitchel and others testified that Albert Talbott had spoken about killing his father before the murder.

Henry Wyatt turned state's evidence and testified that the Talbott brothers had planned several times to kill their father and that Charles had shot him through the window. He also told how the Talbotts made their own bullets by shaping pieces of lead, rifling them with a knife and loading them into cartridges. His description matched the bullet extracted from the wall.

The defense spent much of their time impeaching the character of Mr. and Mrs. Brighton. More than a dozen depositions from Kansas attested to the bad character of Jonas who had spent four years in the state penitentiary and Jennie Hudson, who had a bad reputation for "morality and chastity" and might not have been legally married to Brighton. They also presented evidence that Willford Mitchell had conspired with Frank Wyatt to murder Dr. Talbott and throw the blame on Talbott's sons.

When the testimony ended, attorneys for the prosecution and defense, in alternating order, each delivered three closing arguments. The jury deliberated for two and a half hours and returned with a verdict of guilty.

Verdict: Guilty of first-degree murder

Aftermath:

A motion for a new trial was denied and the Talbott brothers were sentenced to hang on March 25, 1881. The case was appealed to the state Supreme Court who upheld the verdict.

On June 24, 1881, thousands of people gathered in Maryville, Missouri to witness the execution of Albert and Charles Talbott, but at the last minute Governor Crittenden sent a telegram postponing the hanging until July 22.

During that interval, Charles Talbott confessed to murdering his father. After he had gone to bed the night of September 18, he heard his mother crying for help. He came downstairs and found his father kicking his mother as she lay on the floor. Charles grabbed a shotgun and shot his father in the back. His father told the story about the assassin because, facing death, he wanted to forgive and be forgiven, and because he wanted the public to think the national banks had hired an assassin to silence him.

The confession created a great deal of excitement in Maryville and changed quite a few minds regarding the Talbott brothers' guilt. Many believed that the truth had come out at last and thought the boys had defended their mother and should be released. But others thought that the confession was self-serving and false. The governor was not convinced; the execution would go on as scheduled.

The day before the hanging the Talbotts issued another 'confession'. Albert spoke this time. He claimed that it was Wilford Mitchell who murdered his father. Several years before Mitchell's wife had been a patient in the Talbott house where the doctor was treating her for consumption. Dr. Talbott and Mrs. Mitchell had an argument and Talbott sent her home. She got a chill on the way home and died soon after. Mitchell had held a grudge and conspired with Wyatt to murder Dr. Talbott.

This new statement had a negative effect. The boys lost the support of those who had believed Charles's confession. This time the governor did not stay the execution.

On July 22, 1881, between eight and ten thousand men, women and children witnessed the hanging, in Maryville, Missouri, of Albert and Charles Talbott.

An Unfortunate Organization

Phrenology, the theory that a person's character is determined by the size and shape of his head, was quite popular in America during the 1850s. A phrenological analysis of Reuben Dunbar in 1851 found that he had "an unfortunate organization" in which his moral faculties were insufficient to balance his animal propensities. While the phrenologist professed scientific objectivity in the analysis of Dunbar's head, she may have been somewhat influenced by the fact that, at the time, Reuben Dunbar was charged with murdering his two young stepbrothers to protect his inheritance.

Reuben Dunbar
Phrenological Character of Reuben Dunbar, 1851

Date:	November 23, 1850
Location:	Westerlo, New York
Victims:	David and Stephen Lester
Cause of Death:	Strangling and clubbing
Accused:	Reuben Dunbar

Synopsis:
Reuben Dunbar was twenty-one years old in 1850. His wife was expecting their first child, and Reuben was worried about his family's financial security. Reuben's mother owned some property that he had hoped would be his on her death, but Mrs. Dunbar, a widow, had remarried, and by law, all her property transferred to her new husband, David Lester. Lester was raising his two nephews, Stephen, aged 8, and David, aged 10 – sons of his dead brother – and the two boys were in line to inherit the bulk of the property that Reuben Dunbar felt should go to him.

On November 23, 1850, David Lester traveled from his home in Westerlo, New York, to spend the day in Stephensville, leaving Reuben Dunbar in charge of young Stephen and David. When Lester returned from his trip, the boys were missing. Reuben said the boys had wanted to pick butternuts or go fishing, and he had advised against it but did not know where they were.

The following day they still had not returned and the men of Westerlo began a search of the surrounding woods. During the search, Dunbar made some unusual statements.

Before there was any talk of foul play, he said, "If they were men, people might think they had money, and had been murdered for money; but anyone might know that they had no money, and what man under heaven would murder those innocent children?"

During the search, one of the men said, "Boys, look in the trees, on the ground, and around the trees."

Dunbar responded, "There is no use looking in the trees; such boys as them won't be found there."

They found David Lester dead, hanging by a rope from a tree limb. The body of his brother Stephen was not far away. He had been clubbed to death.

Though there was no way to directly connect Dunbar to the deaths, his conflicting stories, suspicious behavior, and known animosity towards his two brothers made him the prime suspect. He was arrested for the murders of David and Stephen Lester.

Trial: January 31, 1851

The trial lasted twelve days and was quite a sensation in the city of Albany, where it was held. Two indictments were filed against Dunbar – he would be tried first for the murder of Stephen Lester, and the state was prepared to try him again for the murder of David should their first prosecution fail.

The defense stressed the circumstantial nature of the evidence against Dunbar and begged the jury to have sympathy for the prisoner's wife and his mother. But District Attorney H. A. Hammond made a powerful plea for conviction. He spoke so eloquently that the text of his closing argument was published several times as an example of excellent legal oratory. The jury deliberated for two hours before returning a guilty verdict. After it was read, Reuben Dunbar made this statement in court:

> *All I have to say is that I am not guilty of the charge brought against me. I hope those who have testified against me will, when they return to their firesides, look over the testimony and see whether they have given my words, or words which they have made up themselves. I am about bidding a final farewell to all I hold dear on earth. I shall leave this world in conscious innocence, relying for mercy upon that Being whom I have long professed to serve. I hope, my dying friends, that you will look well to your situation, as this is the last opportunity I shall have to speak to you this side of the spirit world, I hope you will prepare to meet me where we are all hastening.*

Verdict: Guilty of murder

Aftermath:

Reuben Dunbar continued to assert his innocence until shortly before his execution on January 31, 1851, at the Howard Street Jail in Albany, New York. At the last minute, when he could see there was no hope of executive clemency, Dunbar was persuaded by his spiritual advisor, the Reverend Dr. Beecher of the Baptist Church, to confess to both murders.

Before he was even convicted, a pamphlet entitled Phrenological Character of Reuben Dunbar, With a Short Treatise on The Causes and Prevention of Crime, by Mrs. Margaret Thompson was published in Albany. Mrs. Thompson explained Dunbar's character flaws based on the sizes of various regions of his head:

> *If the prisoner has committed the crime with which he is charged, his large Destructiveness, Combativeness, Acquisitiveness, Secretiveness and Firmness, with small Philoprogenitiveness, have been the cause. The size of these organs, as combined with other faculties, especially if perverted, indicate an unfortunate organization; one in which the animal propensities govern, because the moral faculties are not sufficiently large to balance and control them.*

The Lester brothers are buried in the Wickham Farm Burial Ground in Dormansville, New York. They share a single tombstone.

The Walton Matthews Tragedy

John Walton had the misfortune of marrying into a particularly unsavory family. After an argument with her husband, Mrs. Walton paid her son, Charles, to murder John. It appeared that Charles was going to get away with murder, but ultimately, he did not escape justice.

The Assassination of John Walton
Frank Leslie's Illustrated Newspaper,
July 14, 1860

Date:	June 30, 1860
Location:	New York, New York
Victims:	John Walton, John W. Matthews
Cause of Death:	Gunshot
Accused:	Charles Jefferds

Synopsis:

John Walton walked home from work with his cousin Richard Pascall down 18th Street in New York City at 11:30 p.m. on June 30, 1860. Walton owned a distillery on 18th Street and a store on 25th Street. At the time, Walton and Pascall shared a room over the store. At 3rd Avenue, they noticed a man leaning against a tree in the shadows but paid little attention as they walked past him. A few seconds later, the man darted up behind Walton and shot him in the head.

The shooter ran down 3rd Avenue, and Pascall followed, raising the alarm, shouting, "murder!" Several men heard the call and joined the chase. At the front of the pack was John W. Matthews, a well-known railroad contractor. Matthews was closing in as they neared 16th Street. The killer turned, drew his pistol, and fired, hitting Matthews in the chest. In the confusion that followed, the killer dropped the pistol and made his escape.

The men lifted Matthews and carried him to a nearby drugstore, but he died in their arms before they reached it. Walton was still breathing and was taken to Bellevue Hospital, but he died at 8:30 a.m. the next day.

None of the witnesses recognized the shooter, but Pascall was convinced it was John Walton's stepson, Charles Jefferds. About a year earlier, Walton's wife died, leaving him with two daughters. Six months later, Walton married a widow named Ellen M. Russell. She told him she had been married twice before, but both of her husbands were dead. She had two sons from the first marriage, Charles and Edwin Jefferds, aged 22 and 19, respectively. She had one son, Frank Russell, 12, from her second marriage. She also said she had adopted her sister's four-month-old daughter. After the wedding, they all lived together in a house on 23rd Street.

Ellen Russell was an attractive woman and Walton believed her to be a fine, upstanding person. This opinion would soon change. He "observed transactions of a suspicious character on the part of his wife" and decided to make some inquiries. He learned that at least one of her former marriages had ended in divorce, and the husband was still living. Additionally, she had a third husband, a Mr. Morrison, between Jefferds and Russell, who was living in Ohio, and it was doubtful that they ever had a legal separation. Walton also learned that the four-month-old was not the daughter of Ellen's sister but her own illegitimate offspring.

The New York Atlas called Mrs. Walton, "a woman fond of money, luxury and intrigue." Comparing her to Emma Cunningham, who murdered Dr. Harvey Burdell three years earlier, they called her "…one of those smart, intriguing adventurers of the Mrs. Cunningham school, who are constantly laying in wait to trap wealthy middle-aged bachelors and widowers."

Soon after the marriage, Mrs. Walton's eldest son, Charles Jefferds, began misbehaving. He drank heavily and brought unsavory people back to the house. Walton objected, scolding both mother and son. This only made them angrier, and several times Charles threatened Walton's life.

After several months of this, Walton decided the marriage was over and resolved that they separate. He rented a smaller house on 23rd Street for Ellen and her children, and he moved into the room over the store. He rented the big house to someone else. This angered Ellen and her sons even more since the separation would mean the end of Walton's wealth. Charles and Edwin continued to harass Walton. On one occasion, Charles showed Walton a pistol which he said he had bought to shoot him. At another time, Walton suddenly took sick and believed he had been poisoned. He changed his will, leaving the bulk of his estate to his daughters, to make it less likely that he would be murdered for his money.

The double murder on June 30 created quite a sensation in New York City. The mayor offered a $500 reward for the arrest and conviction of the killer. Walton's estate added another $1,000 to the reward. The police began a manhunt for Charles Jefferds, who fled to Long Island. He learned they were looking for him and decided it was safer to turn himself in. The Monday after the murder, Jefferds surrendered to the police but declared his innocence.

The coroner began an inquest into the murders. Among the many witnesses were Richard Pascall, who positively identified the pistol found at the scene as the one Charles Jefferds had used to threaten Walton, and Ellen Walton, who testified that there was no animosity between her son and her husband. The inquest lasted two weeks, and although there was little evidence against Jefferds, he was charged with first-degree murder.

Trial: June 10, 1861

The prosecution was reluctant to bring the case to trial because of the lack of evidence. After an eight-month delay, ignoring two regular terms of the Court of Oyer and Terminer, Jefferds's attorney moved, unsuccessfully, for his client's release. The trial for the murder of John Walton finally began on June 10, 1861, and lasted about a month. Though nearly everyone believed that Jefferds was guilty, the evidence against him was so thin that no one was surprised that the jury found him not guilty.

Verdict: Not guilty

After being free for six months, Jefferds began to get cocky. He taunted John Walton's brother William at an impromptu meeting in the 25th Street store.

Jefferds said, "Do you know who I am? I am Charles Jefferds, the man who murdered your brother, and I can shoot you as quick as I shot him."

William Walton asked Jefferds for the details of the murder, assuring him that he had been acquitted and could not be tried again. Police Detective Moore, who was also present, confirmed that Jefferds could not be retried. Jefferds told them that he had gone out that night specifically to kill Walton. It was after Walton had a quarrel with his mother, and she offered Jefferds $2,000 to kill her husband.

They were correct in telling Jefferds he could not be retried for Walton's murder, but Jefferds had forgotten that he was also charged with murdering John Matthews. The new confession was enough for the district attorney to take that case to court.

Trial: December 18, 1861

The trial for the murder of John Matthews began on December 18, 1861. This time the testimony of William Walton and Detective Moore was enough to convince a jury. Jefferds was convicted of first-degree murder and sentenced to death.

Verdict: Guilty of first-degree murder

Aftermath:

The law at the time stated that Jefferds had to serve one year in prison before he could be executed, and after that, the date would be set by the governor. During that time, his attorney tried unsuccessfully to appeal the verdict. But as of May 1868, more than six years later, Jefferds was still on death row at Sing Sing Prison.

On May 15, 1868, Charles Jefferds was found dead in the stable loft of the prison. He had five axe wounds on his body, any one of which could have been fatal. Jefferds had been unwell the day before and was allowed to skip dinner and do some light work at the stable instead. He had been reading a book in the hayloft when he was attacked.

Two inmates who had been chopping wood in the work yard, Thomas Burns and George Whittington, were charged with the murder. Burns and Jefferds had been enemies because Burns had caught Jefferds in the commission of what was called "a beastly crime" and "an infamous crime against nature" and reported it to other inmates. The following December, Burns was found not guilty, and charges were dropped against Whittington.

In February 1869, the *New York World* published a long article saying that a detective using the pseudonym 'Jefferson Jinks' had spoken with Jefferds before his arrest. The detective claimed that, after a few drinks, Jefferds declared that he had murdered Dr. Harvey Burdell three years before and provided intricate details of the crime.

The murder of Dr. Burdell had caused a sensation in New York and was one of the first great murder cases to be followed nationwide. The *World* article was reprinted or summarized in newspapers throughout America. However, Jefferds's confession was not believed, and the matter was soon forgotten.

REVENGE

Tragedy at Vineland

The *Vineland Independent*'s relentless badgering of Vineland, New Jersey's founder, Charles K. Landis, ended in 1875 when Landis murdered the paper's publisher Uri Carruth. The people of Vineland were divided on whether the deed was justified.

The Shooting of Carruth
Daily Graphic, January 26, 1876

Date:	March 19, 1875
Location:	Vineland, New Jersey
Victim:	Uri Carruth
Cause of Death:	Gunshot
Accused:	Charles K. Landis

Synopsis:

On the morning of March 19, 1875, Charles K. Landis went to the office of the *Vineland Independent* and demanded to see the paper's editor and publisher, Uri Carruth. When he entered the room, Landis approached him, waving a newspaper clipping.

"Mr. Carruth, did you write that?" Landis shouted.

"I did, and I will do it again," said Carruth.

"Will you promise not to attack my wife in future?

"No."

"Defend yourself then," said Landis, drawing a revolver. He chased Carruth into the composing room of the newspaper and there shot him in the head. "I've killed him! I've killed him! I was obliged to do it. I killed him in the cause of God and humanity!" said Landis as he surrendered himself to the deputy sheriff.

The offending article seems frivolous on its face:

> *A prominent Vinelander sat down by the side of his loving wife on the sofa, and looked up in her eyes, and called her a duck and a birdie and rabbit, and all the other*

endearing names. Then he told her he wanted she should learn the use of a revolver, so that in his absence, she could protect their home and silver-ware and defend the honor of Vineland.

Then he went off and bought an elegant seven-shooter and a nice target.

Then he set up the target in one end of the parlor, and gave her a first lesson shooting. Then he told her he wanted she should practice every day. Then he went away for a week. When he returned he found the revolver on the other side of the looking-glass; the parlor door resembled a bad case of small-pox, and the furniture looked as though it had been indulging in a wrestle with a Burlington county hail storm. Did he walk up to his wife, and sicken her with the endearing names of all the birds and four-footed beasts? Not much! he marched out into the street in his shirt sleeves; with but one boot on and that patched over the big toe.

Then he went galloping up and down, telling every man he met, confidentially, that his wife was crazy. Then he went off and tried to get her into a private Insane Asylum: yes he did, the wretch!

Though neither Landis nor his wife was mentioned by name, everyone in Vineland knew who Carruth was talking about. Landis and Carruth had a long-standing feud, and the Independent attacked Landis and his family for years. This was the last straw.

Charles Landis was an attorney and land speculator who purchased 50,000 acres of New Jersey wilderness in 1861 and founded the town of Vineland there. Persuasive advertising in America and Europe induced people to settle in the new town. But property deeds included many harsh conditions, most notably a prohibition on selling intoxicating liquors. Violating any of the burdensome restrictions could result in forfeiture of the property; landowners were hardly more than tenants of Landis.

Despite the restrictions, Vineland grew quickly and by 1875 had a population of 15,000. But as the population increased, so did discontent in Vineland. In 1868, the Vineland Independent began publishing the truth about life in the area and "discourage careless investment by poor people in the poor lands." The Independent was in conflict with Charles Landis from the beginning, but the real trouble began in 1870 when Uri Carruth purchased the newspaper.

Uri Carruth, 50 years old in 1875, was an attorney with publishing experience in Michigan who was known to be a vindictive and combative man. Attacks on Landis in the Independent went beyond criticizing his policies and were meant to humiliate Landis and his family.

"He was neither witty nor humorous, nor sarcastic, nor bitter," said the *Massachusetts Spy* of Carruth, "but coarsely and stupidly impertinent, telling in his paper silly, pointless stories of Landis and his family."

In 1869, Landis had eloped with the daughter of Commodore Meade of the US Navy. Mrs. Landis had "a very excitable nature" and had spent some time in an insane asylum. The mental problems of Mrs. Landis were well known in

Vineland, and she was often the butt of Carruth's attempts at humor. Mrs. Landis found these articles so distressing that her husband worked to keep the Independent out of their house. Despite his precautions, copies of these articles were thrust under the door or thrown into windows; Mrs. Landis would read them and become dangerously violent, remaining "insane" for a week at a time.

At the time of the offending article in 1875, Mrs. Landis was pregnant, and her doctor said that her reason would be permanently overthrown if the excitement were not removed. Charles Landis viewed Carruth's article as an attack on his wife's health and well-being. According to Landis's public statement, he became so distraught that he put a pistol to his head and pulled the trigger. When the gun misfired, he realized he was shooting the wrong man; he took his better pistol, an English revolver, and went to see Carruth.

Landis's shot did not kill Carruth. Though doctors continued to probe his skull, looking for the bullet, it appeared that he would recover and could live with the ball still in his head. Landis was released from jail on $50,000 bail and was trying to arrange a financial settlement with Carruth to drop the charges against him. He offered him $5,000 and 380 acres of land, which Carruth indignantly refused.

Carruth seemed to be improving physically for the next four months, but his finances were in shambles. Friends said he and Landis had agreed to a settlement of $12,000 in cash and securities and were waiting for Landis's signature when Carruth took a turn for the worse and died on October 24. Landis was rearrested and charged with first-degree murder.

Trial: January 13, 1876

At his trial the following January, Landis gave a three-point defense: that he was insane when he shot Carruth; that Carruth's death was not caused by the bullet but by unskilled treatment; and that Carruth's provocation was such to reduce the offense to manslaughter.

Evidence of insanity was slim. Witnesses testified to Landis's excited and nervous demeanor. To the second point, an autopsy showed the bullet had become completely encysted and had not caused Carruth's death. The immediate cause of death had been an abscess in the brain caused by physicians probing his head in the wrong area, looking for the bullet. Landis's attorneys were confident of victory and did not seriously address the third point.

Verdict: Not guilty

Aftermath:

The jury acquitted Charles Landis of murder, and the community remained divided over whether the verdict was just. Some saw it as an example of unequal justice, where a rich man could get away with murder.

Most, however, agreed with *Forney's Weekly Press*: "Mr. Carruth's effort to be 'spicy', unbacked by the ability to be anything more than grossly indecorous, brought him to his death – and the verdict of popular opinion already registered is, 'served him right'."

A Weight of Grief

Fanny Windley began working in the factories of Brooklyn at the age of ten. When she was 15, Fanny was 'seduced' by her 45-year-old employer, George W. Watson. Watson's unwanted attention continued for the next two years, even after Fanny's marriage. Then, one day, on the stairway of the factory, she countered Watson's lewd advances with a gunshot to the head. There was no question that Fanny Windley Hyde killed George W. Watson; it would be up to the jury to decide whether this act was first-degree murder or if Fanny was "under a weight of grief that could not be resisted."

Fate of a Seducer
Illustrated Police News, Feb. 8, 1872

Date:	January 23, 1872
Location:	Brooklyn, New York
Victim:	George W. Watson
Cause of Death:	Shooting
Accused:	Fanny Windley Hyde

Synopsis:

John Windley brought his family to America from Nottingham, England in 1864. He was a poor man, and Fanny Windley began working in England when she was eight. She was ten when they arrived in America, and soon after, she began the life of a factory girl in Brooklyn. She was a bright girl, attending school when she could during the evenings and Sundays, and as she approached adolescence, she was also considered quite beautiful.

When she was 15, Fanny went to work at a hairnet factory owned by George W. Watson, a 45-year-old married man with five children. About four months after she started the job, Watson called Fanny into his office and forced his attention on her. To keep from losing her job, Fanny let him have his way. For the rest of her time at the factory, Watson took every opportunity to take advantage of his young employee. When she tried to leave the job, Watson threatened to reveal what they had been doing to her father, knowing he would view Fanny as equally culpable.

Inevitably, Fanny became pregnant, and Watson gave her some medicine to induce an abortion. The medicine did the job but had the additional effect of destroying Fanny's health. During this period, Fanny moved out of her father's house. She came to see him after two months of absence, and both her father and stepmother commented on how much weight she had lost and how pale she was. Her weight had dropped from 125 pounds to 95 pounds.

At her new lodgings, Fanny met a man named Hyde, a widower with a daughter around her own age. He asked her to marry him, and she agreed. George Watson had promised Fanny that if she married, he would leave her alone – in fact, she had him swear to this on a Bible. But the promise did not last long, and soon Watson was up to his old tricks. This time, Fanny told her husband, and Hyde was livid. He went to see Watson himself and threatened to expose the situation to Watson's wife. Once again, Watson promised to leave Fanny alone, and once again, he broke his promise.

In January 1872, Fanny's brother helped her buy a gun – she said she intended to use it only to frighten Watson away from her. The pistol was small enough to conceal in the bosom of her dress, and it was hidden there when she went into the factory on January 23. She met Watson on a landing of the stairway as he was leaving the office for lunch. There, she shot Watson in the head, killing him. Several hours later, Fanny turned herself in to the police.

Trial: April 15, 1872

The prosecution of Fanny Hyde was one of the sensational New York murder trials that dominated headlines in the 1800s. Watson's family hired a prominent criminal attorney to assist the prosecution, ensuring that Fanny was convicted and, as much as possible, mitigating the damage to his reputation. The district attorney declined the offer. He believed it was an open-and-shut case of premeditated murder – Fannie had lain in wait on the stairway landing and shot Watson in cold blood.

The defense argued that it had not been cold-blooded murder; it was a chance meeting on the stairway. Watson accosted her as usual, and Fanny had resisted. There was evidence that she had fought him off – the body was found with scratch marks on the face. When this did not stop him, Fanny pulled the pistol from her bosom and shot. In her own testimony, Fanny recalled that Watson had called her a whore and said she should go with him. She had no recollection of the shot itself.

The defense took a two-pronged attack. First, they argued for justifiable homicide:

Why, gentlemen, the meanest worm that walks the earth in human form, the frailest thing that revels night and day in the meanest dens of infamy, is mistress of her own body, and the man who dares to lay violent hands on that body against her will, and attempts to use it against her will, and she kills him, she is justified in doing so, and so the Court will instruct you.

Then they argued for temporary insanity:

> *We shall demonstrate to you, as clear as sunlight, that the defendant was no more responsible at the time of firing that shot than the pistol from which it was fired. Her mind was stormed in its citadel and laid prostrate under a stroke of frenzy.*

In either case:

> *Don't you see enough in this case to show you what a weight of grief must have borne down upon this frail creature's head and heart, that this act was perpetrated under a weight of grief that could not be resisted.*

The case was given to the jury at 2:30 p.m. on April 19. They seemed somewhat baffled over what direction to take. At 10:30 p.m., they requested that the court provide them with precise definitions of first-degree murder, manslaughter in the third degree, and justifiable homicide. The judge declared that they had already been given those definitions but obliged them anyway. At around midnight, they sent word that they were hopelessly deadlocked. The judge sent them back and told them to work out an agreement. At 7:00 a.m., they tearfully told the judge there was no possibility of agreement.

The *New York Times* reported that the jury had been swayed by sentiment toward a pretty woman. Ten jurors had voted for acquittal while the other two wanted third degree manslaughter. A compromise was proposed in which they would find Mrs. Hyde guilty of fourth-degree manslaughter. The ten jurors favoring acquittal would pay the resulting fine of $1,000. It was not enough to sway the holdouts, and the jury remained deadlocked.

Verdict: Hung jury

Aftermath:

Fanny Hyde was released on $2,500 bail. In January 1873, her case was called again, and Fanny failed to appear, forfeiting her bail. In March, she was arrested and sent to Brooklyn's Raymond Street jail to await trial. There, she met Kate Stoddard, the city's latest sensational defendant. In September 1873, Fanny Hyde was again released on $2,500 bail. She was never heard from again.

Dark Kentucky Politics

Colonels Swope and Goodloe were two prominent Kentucky politicians. They were bitter rivals until a chance encounter turned into a battle with deadly weapons, ending their feud for good.

A Double Murder
National Police Gazette, Nov. 23, 1889

Date:	November 8, 1889
Location:	Lexington, Kentucky
Victim:	Col. A.M. Swope and Col. William Cassius Goodloe
Cause of Death:	Stabbing
Accused:	Col. A.M. Swope and Col. William Cassius Goodloe

Synopsis:
The two men happened to enter the Lexington, Kentucky post office at the same time on the afternoon of November 8, 1889. They greeted each other with icy glares then went about their business. Both men were leaders in the Republican Party in Kentucky, and both had national reputations. Swope was the former Internal Revenue Collector for the district, Goodloe had been Minister to Belgium, a state senator, and was the current Internal Revenue Collector. Both men fought for the Union in the Civil War, and both rose to the rank of Colonel.

The bad blood between them began at the 1888 Kentucky Republican Convention to nominate delegates to the national convention. Swope supported Senator John Sherman as the Republican presidential candidate, and Goodloe supported Benjamin Harrison. Debate at the Kentucky convention became heated, sometimes sinking to the level of personal insult. Animosity between Swope and Goodloe had become so intense that colleagues stepped in and convinced each man to withdraw his insulting statements and persuaded the men to shake hands.

It was not a true peace, however, and the two would not speak to each other. The feud intensified when Goodloe was appointed Internal Revenue

Collector; a job Swope had held under President Hayes and hoped to hold under President Harrison.

In the post office that afternoon, Swope went to his box to pick up his mail, blocking access to Goodloe's box which was next to his. Goodloe waited, but after getting his mail, Swope struck up a conversation with the clerk, still blocking Goodloe's box.

There are differing accounts of what happened next. Goodloe either said politely, "Will you please allow me to get my mail?" or harshly, "You obstruct the way."

In either case, Swope indicated indifference and had no intention of moving. Goodloe replied, "This is the second insult from you."

They confronted each other and drew weapons, Goodloe had a folding clasp knife with a four-inch blade, Swope had a revolver. Swope fired, hitting Goodloe in the abdomen, he fired again grazing his shoulder. Goodloe lunged at Swope, stabbing him in the breast. He stabbed twelve more times until Swope lay dead on the floor.

Goodloe stood up, walked calmly out the door, and headed directly to his physician's office. The wound, however, was not treatable. William Cassius Goodloe died in great pain two days later, surrounded by his loved ones.

"Public sympathy is about evenly divided," wrote one newspaper, "but universal sorrow is expressed."

ADULTERY

The Guttenberg Murder

On May 3, 1881, Mena Muller and Louis Kettler took the ferry from New York City to Hoboken, New Jersey. They were going to be married in Hoboken, although they each had a spouse already. The legality of the marriage did not concern them; they were returning to Germany and would start a new life there. But somehow, their plans went awry; that night, Louis Kettler returned to New York alone, and ten days later, Mena Muller's body was found in New Jersey with a fractured skull.

Murdering Mena Muller
Wedded And Murdered Within an Hour! 1881

Date:	May 3, 1881
Location:	Guttenberg, New Jersey
Victim:	Philomena Muller
Cause of Death:	Blows to the head
Accused:	Martin Kinkowski (aka, Louis Kettler)

Synopsis:
On May 13, 1881, a man gathering leaves in the woods outside Guttenberg, New Jersey, nearly stepped on the body of a young woman lying dead on the ground. He hurried away to inform the police. That afternoon, the coroner of Hoboken visited the spot and made an examination of the body. She had been an attractive woman with small and symmetrical features. He judged her to be around twenty-five years old. Along the top of her head, on the left side, was a deep gash, and beneath it, the skull was fractured. There was another gash over the right eye. Both wounds had apparently been made with the edge of a heavy stone. Her nose was broken, and her left ear had been injured as if an earring had been torn from it.

She remained unidentified for five days, and then a New York City tobacconist named Simon Muller came to see if it was his missing wife, Mena (short for Philomena). He was accompanied by his wife's sister, Maria Schmidt.

Despite the condition of her face, both positively identified her as Mena Muller and recognized her clothing and jewelry as well.

Mena and her husband had been separated for some time, and two weeks earlier, she told her sister that she found a decent man from Alsace who would marry her and take her to Europe. They planned to travel aboard the steamer *L'Amerique*, to set sail on May 4. Miss Schmidt told this to Simon Muller, who went to the docks on May 4 and watched the gangplank as the passengers boarded the ship. His wife was not among them.

This story confirmed some information that the police already had. Mrs. Frinck, the wife of an alehouse keeper in New York, was suspicious of a couple in the saloon on May 3. The woman seemed to have plenty of money, and she talked incessantly. Before she left, she borrowed a corkscrew to open a bottle of Rhine wine she had purchased in Hoboken. The description Mrs. Frinck gave of the woman tallied exactly with the description of the murdered woman, so police detectives set out to trace the couple's movements.

They found that the wine had been purchased at an inn run by Edward Stabel. The woman who bought it had told him that she and her husband had just been married by the Reverend Dr. Mabon at the Grove Reformed Dutch Church, and she wanted to celebrate the event and treat the minister. The man waited outside, and Stabel did not get a good look at him, but his description of the woman matched that of Mrs. Frinck.

The detectives spoke with Dr. Mabon, who remembered performing the ceremony. They identified themselves as Louis Kettler and Mena Schmidt and gave an address on Third Street in New York, but Mabon could not recall anything specific about the couple. His servant, however, remembered that the man had a full face and a dark mustache. Before the service, he paced back and forth in the garden as if his mind was troubled.

The detectives went next to the Third Street address. No one there knew Mena Schmidt, but they found an expressman who had moved four trunks for a Mena Muller from Third Street to Scherrer's Hotel on Christopher Street. There, they were told that Mr. and Mrs. Kettler had checked in on May 2. They went out on the morning of May 3, but late that night Mr. Kettler had returned alone. He said his wife had stayed at her sister's house, and they were to meet on the steamship the next day. He had his trunks delivered to the steamship wharf and checked out.

With Louis Kettler aboard a ship heading to Europe, New Jersey Attorney General Stockton sent a message to authorities at Le Havre, describing Kettler and requesting his arrest on the charge of murder. Two Hoboken detectives were preparing to set sail for Europe.

But a Jersey City reporter named Gustavus Seide did not believe Kettler had left on *L'Amerique*. There was no certainty that the baggage had been delivered to the wharf, and there was no positive evidence that Louis Kettler had boarded the ship. With some difficulty, Siede located C.A. Strang, the expressman who picked up the baggage at Scherrer's Hotel. Strang told him that he had not delivered the trunks to the wharf but to an address on Charles Street. Then, about ten days later he moved three of them to an address on Thirty-sixth Street. At the Charles Street address, Siede was told that Kettler had left for California, leaving behind a trunk full of crockery and cookware. Siede and Strang took the trunk to Thirty-sixth Street, where no one knew Louis Kettler, but a man fitting his description, named Martin Kinkowski lived there with his wife and two children. Kinkowski was not home, but his wife recognized the trunk and paid Strang fifty cents to carry it into the house.

A Hoboken policeman arrested Gustavus Siede and C.A. Strang as they stood outside watching the house and waiting for Kinkowski's return. Following their own line of inquiry, the police had come to Thirty-sixth Street looking for the same man. They had mistaken Siede for Kinkowski. The matter was straightened out at the police station, and the officers went back to Thirty-sixth Street. That night, they arrested Martin Kinkowski, alias Louis Kettler for the murder of Philomena Muller.

Keeping the prisoner alive was the chief concern that night. News that they had captured the Guttenberg killer traveled fast, and a crowd of over 400 people stood on Thirty-sixth Street, calling to lynch Minkowski. They got him safely to the Hoboken ferry, but another crowd seeking vengeance was waiting on the Jersey side. When Kinkowski was safely in his jail cell, he had to be kept under surveillance – he was so despondent that the jailers feared suicide.

Kinkowski denied any connection to Mena Muller's murder. He admitted that he knew her and said they had been together at Scheutzen Park in New Jersey on May 3. They stopped in a saloon for some beer, and when they came out, they saw two men walking down the road.

One of them said, "Hello, Mena! What are you doing over here?"

When Kinkowski heard this, he turned to Mena and said, "If you are that kind of a woman, I'll have nothing to do with you."

He left her with the two men and never saw her again.

Trial: October 5, 1881

The trial of Martin Kinkowski for the murder of Philomena Muller was held in the Hudson County Court of Oyer and Terminer, prosecuted by Attorney General Stockton. The evidence against Kinkowski was entirely circumstantial but compelling. The prosecution presented a parade of witnesses who testified to seeing Martin Kinkowski and Mena Muller together at various times on May 3 and to the movement of his trunks after the murder. At one point, the courtroom was shocked when a medical examiner produced Mena Muller's skull to illustrate the wounds she received, but there was no physical evidence to link Kinkowski to the wounds.

Kinkowski's defense was little more than his testimony contradicting or explaining away the testimony against him. He held to the story of the two men who she left with that day and wanted to take the court to the spot where it happened. The judge disallowed this. Kinkowski said he had not taken the trunks to Charles Street to conceal them but to hold them for Mena's return.

Throughout the trial, Kinkowski was emotionally charged. In his closing argument, when the Attorney General declared Kinkowski to be the murderer, he jumped to his feet, shouting that God knows he is innocent and will protect him.

He was not protected from the jury, who, after an hour of deliberation, found Kinkowski guilty. When the verdict was read, Kinkowski fainted.

Verdict: Guilty of first-degree murder

Aftermath:

In the days following his trial, Martin Kinkowski suffered from nervous prostration. His attorney appealed the verdict on technicalities and moved for a new trial but his motion was denied. At his sentencing, Kinkowski was asked if he had anything to say before the death sentence was pronounced.

Kinkowski made a statement in German that was translated by an interpreter, "Since this courthouse has been built, a more innocent man than myself never stood before this Court, and God knows it."

Martin Kinkowski was hanged inside the Hudson County Jail in Jersey City on January 6, 1882. He made no confession, professing his innocence to the end.

Love And Law

The tragic love affair between Charles Kring and Dora Broemser ended in one maddened instant – he asked her to leave her husband, she refused, and he shot her dead. The prosecution of Charles Kring for the crime of murder lasted eight years, included six trials, and required a ruling by the United States Supreme Court.

Charles F. Kring
Love & law, 1882

Date:	December 31, 1874
Location:	St. Louis Missouri
Victim:	Mrs. Dora C. J. Broemser
Cause of Death:	Gunshot
Accused:	Charles F. Kring

Synopsis:
Charles Kring came to America from Germany in 1866. He had studied pharmacy, and with backing from his father, he opened a drug store in De Quoin, Illinois. The business prospered for a time, and Kring married and began raising a family. But before long, the business failed, and the marriage proved to be an unhappy one. Kring moved his family to St. Louis and, with his father's help, opened another drugstore. He never made enough money to offset the losses from the first venture, and the St. Louis store closed as well.

In September 1872, Kring took a position at a drugstore that was run by Jake and Dora Broemser. The job didn't last very long. Broemser had insured the store for more than it was worth, and that October, he burned it down to collect the insurance. He planned to open another store in Rock Spring, Illinois, and asked Kring to be his partner. Kring was reluctant at first, but after Dora

Broemser personally pleaded with him to join them, he agreed, investing more money from his father.

On his first meeting with Dora, Kring was instantly infatuated with her – a feeling that soon grew into obsession. Jake Broemser spent much of his time on the road, leaving Kring and Dora together to mind the store. Dora confessed that she also had feelings for Kring, and although both were married, they became lovers.

They managed to keep the affair secret for more than a year, but Broemser had his suspicions, and one night, he caught them together. Broemser took $10,000 from the store and left Kring with the debt. He also told Kring's wife about the affair; she left her husband and moved the family back to St. Louis. Two households had been destroyed.

Kring and Dora moved to Nashville, Illinois, and lived for a time as husband and wife. But they were unable to make a living. When Broemser returned with a plan for opening a patent medicine concern, they agreed to join him. Once again, Kring went to his father for capital. And once again Dora returned to her legal husband while still seeing Kring on the side.

The business was not doing well; Kring was shouldering the debt but seeing none of the revenue. He confronted Broemser for settlement and was surprised to see Dora take her husband's side. The business was dissolved, and they parted company.

Kring remained hopelessly obsessed with Dora. Now living with her mother-in-law, she was several months pregnant, and everyone knew the baby was Kring's. On December 31, 1873, he went to the house with a message for Dora, and she came outside with her sister-in-law, Amanda. He asked Dora if she would become his wife. Kring later described her response. "'And if I say "No," will your heart break? Oh! I pity you, big fellow!' she answered. Her words tantalized me; her cruel mocking taunts drove me to madness – to fury."

Kring recalled all the shame and financial ruin she had caused him and, in an instant, became convinced that she had only been playing a part. She had feigned love to get his money.

He asked her again if she would become his wife. With a smile, she said "no." Kring pulled out a revolver he had purchased earlier in the day and shot her twice. He then pointed the gun at his own heart and tried to fire, but the gun did not go off.

Kring then went to the police station and turned himself in.

First Trial: 1. December 20, 1875

During the preliminary hearing, when Broemser was on the witness stand, Kring picked up a chair and attempted to assault him. Kring was handcuffed during the proceedings to prevent a similar incident.

At first, Kring wanted to plead guilty and denounce Broemser from the scaffold, but his attorneys convinced him to plead not guilty by reason of insanity. A doctor from Illinois testified that Kring had shown "symptoms of epilepsy and catalepsy," several witnesses testified that Kring acted oddly at times, that his father was eccentric with a violent temper, and that his half-sister "was either an imbecile or subject to melancholia."

The jury did not buy it. They deliberated for 16 hours, then, on December 25, 1875, they found Kring guilty of first-degree murder and sentenced him to hang. Kring's attorneys appealed on the grounds that appearing in handcuffs had unduly prejudiced the jury against Kring. The Supreme Court of Missouri granted him a new trial.

Second Trial: May 20, 1878
A juryman became ill, and no conclusion was reached.

Third Trial: January 29, 1879
This trial ended in a hung jury.

Fourth Trial: November 11, 1879.
There was a delay due to the difficulty in finding a jury of twelve men who had not read the newspapers and had already formed an opinion of the case. Kring's attorneys refused to proceed until they were paid some of what he owed them, but Kring's resources were exhausted. He decided to plead guilty to second-degree murder. He agreed to a deal with the prosecutor and expected to get a sentence of two to five years in prison. The judge accepted his plea but sentenced Kring to twenty-five years in the penitentiary.

When Kring heard the sentence, he entered a motion to withdraw his guilty plea to second-degree murder and reenter his plea of not guilty to first-degree murder. The motion was granted, and Kring was given a new trial in May 1881.

Fifth Trial: May 1881
This time, he was found guilty of first-degree murder and again sentenced to hang. This verdict was appealed and upheld by the Missouri Supreme Court.

The ruling was then appealed to the United States Supreme Court. The issue was that at the time of the sentencing for second-degree murder, under Missouri law, a conviction for second-degree murder meant an acquittal of murder in the first degree. Kring could not be retried on the greater charge. However, before the appeal began, the law was changed so that in cases like Kring's, it would be proper to charge with the greater offense. The Missouri Supreme Court applied the second law and denied the appeal. The U.S. Supreme Court said the second law was ex post facto; Missouri had to use the law that was in effect at the time of sentencing. Therefore, they could not charge Kring with first-degree murder.

Verdicts:

1. Guilty of first-degree murder – successfully appealed
2. Mistrial

3. Hung jury
4. Moved to change plea to not guilty of first-degree murder.
5. Guilty of first-degree murder – successfully appealed to Supreme Court

Aftermath:

There were no more trials. In May 1883, Charles Kring was released on bail. It was believed there would not be enough evidence left to convict him of murder. When Kring had entered prison eight years earlier, he weighed 190 pounds; on his release, he was a "mere skeleton," feeble and consumptive; he did not live much longer.

The Cuban Con Artist

In May 1831, Cuban exile Lino Espos y Mina found himself alone and penniless in the town of Andalusia, Pennsylvania. He stopped at the home of Dr. William Chapman and his wife Lucretia and begged for a place to spend the night. A month later, Lino was still living with the Chapman, and William was on his deathbed. Fifteen days after William Chapman died, Lino and Lucretia were married. Was Lucretia Chapman an accomplice to murder or another victim of the Cuban con artist?

Carolino Amalia Espos y Mina

Date:	June 21, 1831
Location:	Andalusia, PA
Victim:	Dr. William Chapman
Cause of Death:	Poisoning
Accused:	Lucretia Chapman Carolino Amalia Espos y Mina

Synopsis:

Growing up in Cuba, Carolino Estrada Entrealgo, known as Lino, turned to crime at an early age. He was handsome and charismatic, with dark eyes and curly hair. Lino was also short and slender and could easily scale walls, climb through the windows of Cuban aristocrats, and make off with their possessions. In a failed attempt to rob the royal treasury in Havana, Lino shot and killed a guard, and at nineteen, he was sent to jail for murder. His parents begged, cajoled, and bribed the authorities until they agreed to release Lino, provided he left Cuba forever. In 1829, he boarded a sailing ship bound for Boston.

Lino lived on credit, obtaining room and board by promising to pay as soon as he could convert his Spanish gold to American currency. When creditors lost their patience, Lino would skip town. He played this throughout the northeast, and in Philadelphia, he was arrested for theft and served fourteen months of an eighteen-month sentence. He was pardoned after convincing officials of his innocence.

Free from prison, Lino slipped aboard a steamboat heading up the Delaware River to New York. He had not traveled very far before a ship's officer asked to see his ticket. Lino was put ashore in Andalusia in Bucks County, Pennsylvania. Dirty and tattered, Lino stopped at the first house he saw, the home of Dr. William and Lucretia Chapman.

The Chapmans were an odd-looking couple; Lucretia was tall and imposing with auburn hair, and William was several inches shorter and quite stout. He was a successful speech therapist, and she was an educator who founded one of the first schools in America dedicated to educating young women. They met in Philadelphia, and though William was ten years older than Lucretia, they found they had much in common. William and Lucretia married and had five children. Eventually, they moved the school to Andalusia to escape the growing industrialization of Philadelphia.

Lino begged the Chapmans for help, and they agreed to let him stay the night. He gave his name as Carolino Amalia Espos y Mina and regaled them with stories of his life and family. He told them his clothes and money had been stolen in France, and he entered the United States penniless. But his father, the Governor of California, had gold and silver mines and would gladly repay the Chapmans for their kindness. Seeing this as an opportunity, William agreed to let Lino live with them while they taught him English and even allowed Lino to order clothes from William's tailor.

While William's interest in Lino was financial, Lucretia's was personal. She was happy to have someone young and energetic to talk to since her marriage to William had grown cold. He had become fat and lazy, preferring to spend his time alone with his studies. When they spoke at all, Lucretia publicly berated her husband for not helping with domestic chores. Unlike William, Lino was a joy to be around. He and Lucretia had long talks and sang songs together. Before long, they would also share a bed. With little attempt at discretion, Lucretia would go to Lino's room in full view of servants and guests.

On Thursday, June 16, 1831, Lino bought two ounces of arsenic powder, telling the druggist he would be using it for taxidermy. The following day, William took sick with stomach cramps and nausea. A doctor was called who diagnosed Williams's sickness as a mild case of cholera morbus – the term used at the time for gastroenteritis. The symptoms persisted, and Lucretia made him some chicken soup, which only made him sicker. The pain and vomiting continued for several days, and on June 22, William died.

Nine days after William's funeral, Lucretia and Lino were married by an Episcopal bishop in a secret ceremony in New York. They planned to honeymoon in Mexico, and Lucretia went first to Syracuse, New York, to see if her sister, Mercy, would run the school in her absence. She returned to find that Lino had sold William's books and Lucretia's silver spoons. Then Lino took the horse and buggy to Philadelphia, sold them, and took a steamboat to Baltimore, sending word that a friend had died there. In his absence, Lucretia learned that all of Lino's stories about himself and his father were lies. She also found out that while she was in Syracuse he had spent a night in a Philadelphia hotel with two women. The marriage was over.

Philadelphia police constable Willis Blayney received word of a Washington businessman being swindled by a man named Lino Amalia Esposa y Mina. Washington police had a letter indicating the man had also swindled a widow named Lucretia. Blayney questioned Lucretia Chapman, who admitted to being married to Lino but could offer no information as to his whereabouts. Lino was arrested in Boston. When a Philadelphia newspaper printed a story accusing him of murdering Dr. Chapman, Lucretia fled her home.

William Chapman's body was exhumed from his grave at All Saints Church. Though at the time there was no test for arsenic poisoning, the condition of the body and the smell of the stomach and other internal organs convinced the autopsy doctors that William Chapman had been poisoned. Lucretia was arrested in Erie County, Pennsylvania, and both she and Lino were charged with murder.

Trial of Lucretia Chapman Espos y Mina – February 14, 1832

Attorneys for the defendants realized that if Lucretia and Lino were tried together they would end up fighting each other, so they moved to have the cases separated. The request was granted over the objection of the prosecution.

Lucretia's case was taken up first, and it was a major attraction, drawing thousands of spectators to the Doylestown courthouse. The prosecution introduced numerous witnesses who testified to Lucretia berating her husband and to her intimacy with Lino prior to her husband's death. They asserted that Lucretia had made the chicken soup that had killed William. As proof that the soup was poisoned, a neighbor testified that his flock of ducks had eaten something in the Chapman's yard that day, and when they came home, they all fell over dead.

Lucretia's lawyer, David Paul Brown, was a skilled orator and among the most famous attorneys in Philadelphia. He contended that there was no proof of poisoning, that any number of things could have killed the ducks, and that William Chapman had died of natural causes. His star witness was the Chapman's ten-year-old daughter, Lucretia, who testified, "Pa ate only a few spoonsful of the soup, but ate very heartily of the chicken. I ate some of the soup myself."

After two days of summation, the jury deliberated for just over two hours and returned a verdict of not guilty.

Trial of Carolino Amalia Espos y Mina – April 24, 1832

Lino's trial was more straightforward. He did not have Lucretia's high-powered attorney, just two court-appointed lawyers, one of whom had not yet passed the bar. They introduced no witnesses and relied only on the verdict of

Lucretia's case and a deposition from a doctor who asserted there was no way to differentiate between death by arsenic poisoning and death by cholera morbus.

The jury deliberated for three hours and then pronounced Lino guilty of first-degree murder.

Verdicts: 1. Lucretia Chapman Espos y Mina - Not guilty
2. Carolino Amalia Espos y Mina - Guilty of first-degree murder

Aftermath:

On June 21, 1832, in front of a crowd that resembled "Philadelphia on the Fourth of July," Carolino Amalia Espos y Mina was hanged. His last words, called out in English, were: "Farewell, my friends. Farewell, poor Mina, poor Mina. He die innocent. He die innocent."

Lucretia's notoriety prevented her from reopening her school or even finding work as a teacher. She eventually traveled west and tried her hand at acting. But her reputation followed her, and she was booed off stage in Cincinnati. Lucretia died in 1841 at the age of 53.

Illicit Infatuation

To the outside world, George and Fanny Crozier were a well-bred, churchgoing couple in a happy and stable marriage. But beneath the surface, George's "illicit infatuation" with 18-year-old Minerva Dutcher, had long been the subject of rumor in the small town of Benton, New York. With Fanny Crozier's sudden death in the summer of 1875, George's desires became public knowledge, and small-town gossip turned to damning evidence against him.

George E. Crozier
The Trial of Geo. E. Crozier, 1876

Date:	July 29, 1875
Location:	Benton, New York
Victim:	Fanny H. Crozier
Cause of Death:	Poisoning
Accused:	George E. Crozier

Synopsis:
George and Fanny Crozier were prominent, highly regarded citizens of Benton, near the village of Penn Yan in the Finger Lakes region of New York State. Both came from good, moral families and regularly attended Benton Center Baptist Church. In 1875, the couple – he 42 years old, she 39 – had been married for twenty years and were preparing for the marriage of their only son, Frank.

On July 15 of that year, Fanny was suddenly and without warning taken ill. She experienced severe burning pain in her stomach and back, dry throat and mouth, and an intense, nearly constant thirst. She partially recovered, but on the night of July 27, she had another severe attack. The next day, her physician, Dr. Barber, diagnosed her with gastritis and prescribed powders of sub-nitrate of bismuth, which her husband administered. The prescription did not help, and on July 29, Fanny Crozier died.

Mrs. Crozier was buried two days later, and the tragedy would have soon faded into memory, but for nagging suspicions of friends and neighbors. Up to the time she was stricken, Fanny had given no indication of anything but perfect health. Her husband behaved suspiciously and seemed resigned to the fact that Fanny's situation was hopeless. In her dying hours, he had turned away friends and relatives who came to bring help and comfort, and he adamantly refused to let anyone else near the prescribed powders. He told Dr. Barber that he did not want a post-mortem examination done on his wife.

Suspicion went beyond Crozier's deathbed behavior. Those who knew them could see that the Croziers' relationship was strained and that George was not as faithful as he should have been. He was inappropriately familiar with an 18-year-old girl named Minerva Dutcher. In fact, though not arousing suspicion at the time, the familiarity had begun four years earlier when Crozier would stop by her school, and the teacher would give Minerva permission to go outside and chat with him.

Crozier probably met Minerva Dutcher at the Baptist Church, where both sang in the choir. He sat directly behind, and they would pass notes to each other and find opportunities to steal away and chat privately. By 1875, the Croziers did not go to church together. Fanny would ride with her brother-in-law, and George would walk, often meeting up with Minerva. His "illicit infatuation" with a girl twenty-two years younger than he became the talk of the church.

The day after Fanny's burial, Sunday, August 1, Crozier went to church and flirted with Minerva as if nothing had happened. "He went to church," the district attorney would later say, "not to receive consolations of religion, not to join in the worship of God or to gather strength from the sympathy of friends, but to prosecute with greater freedom his intrigues with Minerva Dutcher."

George's son Frank and his wife moved in to help his father through a difficult time. George told them they were not needed, as he had hired Minerva as his maid. They moved out of the house, and the following Saturday Minerva moved in. George and Minerva did not go to church that Sunday.

Suspicion became so widespread in Benton that the officials began an investigation. The coroner ordered the body exhumed and the stomach and liver removed for analysis. John S. Towler, professor of chemistry and toxicology at the Medical College of Geneva, New York, did the analysis and found sixty grains of white arsenic, absorbed and unabsorbed in the stomach – enough arsenic to kill twelve people. The circumstantial evidence was strong enough to indict George Crozier for the murder of his wife.

Trial: March 6, 1876

The indictment caused a schism in the Baptist Church between those who thought Crozier guilty and those who did not believe it was possible. By the time of the trial, the whole town was divided; while most believed Crozier was guilty, a large contingent stood behind him.

The evidence against him was circumstantial but compelling. Witnesses testified to George's behavior before his wife's death, including his relationship with Minerva. There appeared to be no one else with the opportunity or motive to kill Fanny Crozier.

While not disputing the fact that Fanny was poisoned, the defense came up with two possible alternative scenarios. First, they asserted that the powders prescribed by Dr. Barber, sub-nitrate of bismuth, were known to contain small amounts of arsenic. Dr. Barber could have, accidentally or otherwise, given Fanny a prescription that killed her. Second, the defense proposed that Fanny had taken her own life. She was known to have purchased arsenic to kill rats, and the defense claimed that she thought she had stomach cancer and did not want to suffer.

It also came out that George had tried to suborn the testimony of his daughter-in-law, offering her money if she would swear that Fanny had told her she thought she had cancer.

The jury deliberated for two hours and then returned a verdict of murder in the first degree.

Verdict: Guilty of first-degree murder.

Aftermath:

George E. Crozier was sentenced to hang on May 3, 1876. His defense attorneys planned to request a new trial, claiming that the testimony regarding Minerva should not have been admissible unless Mrs. Crozier had known about the relationship and disapproved. Governor Tilden granted Crozier a respite until June 16 to allow further consideration of the case.

As the defense prepared their arguments, 800 of Crozier's supporters signed a petition requesting that the governor commute Crozier's sentence to life in prison. The governor agreed to this, with the understanding that there would be no new trial.

Crozier spent the next twenty years in Auburn State Prison. He sang in the prison choir and reportedly was a model prisoner, except that he deliberately cut off one of his fingers to avoid a work detail that he did not like.

He died in prison in 1896 at the age of 63. He never confessed to killing his wife.

Thus, She Passed Away

In 1872 George Wheeler met and married May Tillson in Boston. He made a home for May and her younger sister Della, first in New York, then in California. Along the way, George fell in love with young Della and when she planned to marry someone else, he faced a dilemma – he could not marry her himself and he could not bear to see her wed to another. The solution he chose pleased no one.

Thus, She Passed Away
National Police Gazette, Nov. 6 ,1880

Date:	October 20, 1880
Location:	San Francisco, California
Victim:	Adella (Della) Tillson
Cause of Death:	Strangulation
Accused:	George A. Wheeler

Synopsis:

Around midnight on October 20, 1880, Wheeler went to the San Francisco police station and confessed to the murder of his sister-in-law, Della Tillson. He said he had packed her body in a trunk and left it in the room they shared in a lodging house at 23 Kearney Street. He was held at the station while the police went to check his story.

The police went to 23 Kearney Street and spoke with the landlady. She said Wheeler and his wife had moved into the room about a month earlier and sometime later his sister-in-law moved in across the hall. All had been quiet until a few days ago when a man named George Peckham moved into the house. He appeared to know the other three, and there was constant arguing among all the lodgers.

The police learned the truth when they interviewed the woman across the hall. She was not Wheeler's sister-in-law; she was his wife May. She told them that Wheeler and her sister were living together, in sin, in the other room. George Peckham came to see Della and planned to marry her, and this upset Wheeler. But Mrs. Wheeler did not believe that her husband murdered her sister. She thought he must have been drunk when he made the confession.

When the police opened the other room, they saw no sign of a struggle. They found the trunk Wheeler had spoken of against the wall near the door. It appeared to be filled with clothing, but after removing several layers they found the body of a murdered woman, still warm, crammed into the trunk. They called May Wheeler into the room to see the body. Sobbing hysterically, she positively identified the body as that of her sister Della. Peckham was equally distraught when he identified the body of his lover.

When the hysteria died down, reporters interviewed Mrs. Wheeler and Peckham and uncovered the events that led to the murder. Mrs. Wheeler, twenty-eight years of age, was born May Tillson in Shrewsbury, Massachusetts. In 1872 she married George Wheeler, and they lived together in her parents' house for a while before moving to New York, taking along May's teenaged sister Della.

May Wheeler was somewhat deaf and had been unaware that her husband had been having sexual relations with her sister until Della became pregnant. Della confessed all but begged her sister not to reveal her shame to their parents. Both sisters agreed that it was best to keep the matter secret. The baby died soon after birth and the situation in the Wheeler household continued as before. When Della became pregnant again, they moved to California, where the second child died as well.

They settled in the town of Cisco where Wheeler got a job running an engine at a silver mine. There they met George Peckham, a miner and a gambler. He became friends with Wheeler and became quite fond of Della. He started taking Della out and, at the time, believed he had Wheeler's blessing.

Wheeler's job at the mine did not work out, and he decided that the family should move to San Francisco. There wasn't enough money for all three to travel, so Wheeler took Della and promised to send for May when they could afford it. After they had been gone a month, May grew tired of waiting and went by herself to San Francisco. She knew where her husband and sister were staying but had been surprised to learn that they were posing as husband and wife. Rather than cause trouble, May took another room there, telling the landlady that she was Wheeler's sister-in-law.

Peckham had fallen in love with Della, and when he realized that she was not coming back to Cisco, he went to San Francisco as well. He hoped to marry her and take her to Sacramento. Della had been writing to Peckham, so when he got to San Francisco he knew where to find her. Peckham took a room there too, and all four were living on the same floor at No. 23 Kearney Street.

Peckham was unhappy about Della and Wheeler sharing a room, but she told him they had done it to save money. She said, she slept on the sofa and he in the bed. Peckham began taking her out nights, bringing her home after midnight, and this angered Wheeler. On the day of the murder, Peckham came looking for Della and Wheeler told her she had left, taking a job as a companion to a lady and her daughter. He told Peckham she had gone where he would never find her.

While May and Peckham were telling their stories, Wheeler, at the police station, was telling a story of his own. He said he had been upset about Peckham following them to San Francisco and keeping his sister-in-law out late.

Wheeler convinced her that it was best that she stay away from Peckham, and he and Della spoke with police officer Moorehouse, asking if she could stay with him for a while to keep her away from the bad man who was perusing her. Officer Moorehouse agreed and so did Della, but when she went back to pack her clothes, she had a change of heart.

Wheeler said she told him "there had been a greater intimacy between her and Peckham than I had any idea of, and that she was going away with him."

This was when he decided he would rather see Della dead than with Peckham. In a statement quoted in several newspapers, Wheeler said:

> *She seemed to feel her disgrace very keenly, and begged me to cut her throat. She did not want to go with Peckham, but such was his influence over her that she must go with him, and she would rather die than do it.*
>
> *Then she again asked me to cut her throat. I told her that I could not do that as I could not bear to see her blood, but I told her that I could choke her. She said very well and sat in my lap.*
>
> *I place one hand on her mouth and with the other grasped her throat, and she, throwing her head back on my shoulder, died like a child. She struggled but little at first. She looked into my eyes and I kissing them, told her to close them, which she did, and thus she passed away.*

Reporters were impressed by the calmness and indifference Wheeler displayed while in custody. He knew that by killing Della he would be throwing his own life away as well, but that mattered little to him. As he would say many times, "I would rather have her blood on my hands than have her associate with that man Peckham."

An inquest was held soon after, and Wheeler was indicted for the murder of Adella Tillson.

First Trial: 1. February 2, 1881

Jury selection for George Wheeler's trial was an arduous process; the case was a sensation in San Francisco, and it was difficult to find anyone who had not already made up his mind on the matter. The number of spectators was limited to the number of available seats, leaving hundreds outside, disappointed.

There was no contention over who killed Della Tillson; the prosecution was straightforward. Wheeler had confessed, and all the relevant witnesses testified as to why he did it.

Wheeler's defense was "hereditary insanity." The defense introduced evidence that there was insanity on both sides of Wheeler's family. Several reporters testified to the statements made by Wheeler after his arrest. Expert witness, Dr. J.J. Kendrick, an Oakland physician, testified to various forms of murderous mania, and examined Wheeler's bald head. He was uncertain whether a large scar on the right side of his head would cause insanity.

The prosecution countered the insanity defense by reading, over defense council's objection, from Brown's Medical Jurisprudence of Insanity.

The jury had little patience for the insanity plea and found Wheeler guilty.

He was sentenced to hang on April 19, but the case was appealed and the hanging postponed. The California Supreme Court agreed that the prosecution should not have been allowed to read from *Brown's Medical Jurisprudence of Insanity* without first establishing it as a standard authority. Wheeler was granted a new trial.

Second Trial: 2. September 7, 1882
The result was the same, guilty of murder.

Verdicts:

1. Guilty of first-degree murder, overturned on appeal
2. Guilty of first-degree murder

Aftermath:

Following the first trial, May Wheeler, after a coolly received goodbye visit to her husband in County Jail, accepted a steamship ticket from the YWCA and returned to her father's home in Shrewsbury, Massachusetts.

Wheeler was sentenced to be hanged on January 23, 1884. His last days in prison were taken up with concerns for his soul. A lady from Oakland had urged him to become a Catholic, and he had been meeting with Father Cottle to discuss conversion. As of the night before the hanging, Wheeler, who had been raised Quaker, was not feeling it.

The lady from Oakland may have been Mrs. Stratton, a divorced woman who had been among the hundreds of people who visited the prisoner before the execution. She frequently visited the cell, and the night before the execution, Mrs. Stratton insisted on being married to Wheeler. Wheeler expressed a willingness, but the sheriff took measures to prevent the ceremony.

On the morning of January 23, 1884, 5,000 people assembled outside the jail to witness the hanging of George Wheeler. Demand for entrance tickets was so great that they were being sold for $10.00 apiece. Father Cottle must have gotten through to Wheeler because he was at the prisoner's side as he mounted the gallows.

Wheeler's last words were, "I forgive the world, may the world forgive me." He kissed a crucifix and said, "Jesus, into thy hands I commend my spirit."

The signal was given, the trap was sprung, and George Wheeler fell. His neck was broken, and death was instantaneous.

INSANITY

A Woman Scorned

William Goodrich paid a visit to the lodgings of his brother Charles on Degraw Street in Brooklyn on March 21, 1873. With no response at the door, he entered the house to search for his brother and found him lying on the basement floor, neatly posed as if laid out by an undertaker. Charles had been shot in the head and lying on the floor near his hand lay a revolver, suggesting suicide. But William Goodrich knew his brother too well to believe this.

"You never did this yourself!" he said, "This is murder! Not suicide!"

Kate Stoddard, The Goodrich Murderess
Canadian Illustrated News, July 26, 1873

Date:	March 21, 1873
Location:	Brooklyn, New York
Victim:	Charles Goodrich
Cause of Death:	Gunshots
Accused:	Lizzie Lloyd King, alias Kate Stoddard

Synopsis:
The Brooklyn police agreed with his brother when they saw the body of Charles Goodrich. Suicide was impossible; he had been shot three times in the head. After his death, someone washed the blood from his face and combed his hair. Whoever cleaned him put a clean shirt on the body and posed it. They made a pillow from a piece of damp cloth over a pair of boots and placed it under his head. Three wet towels were hanging in the basement, one stained with blood. Goodrich's watch was gone, and all of his cash was missing, giving the impression that he was murdered by burglars, but because of the way the body had been cleaned and arranged, the police believed the killer was a woman.

There were other reasons to suspect a woman. Charles Goodrich, who was forty-one years old at the time of his death, was a widower living in a Manhattan boarding house. He and his brother William owned a block of houses on Degraw Street that were under construction. In the spring of 1872, Charles 'rigged up' a bedroom in one of the houses so he could sleep when there to supervise the building. His absences from the boarding house became increasingly frequent, and when he was there, his Degraw Street neighbors would see him sitting on the stoop of his building with an attractive young woman. By autumn, she was no longer seen in public, but neighbors often saw her leaving the house early in the morning.

A second woman had also been seen at Goodrich's house that winter, and she was soon identified as Miss Adeline Pabor, Charles Goodrich's fiancé. A letter found in the house explained the motive of the murder and made the still unidentified first woman the prime suspect. The letter, addressed to Goodrich's father, said that the writer believed herself to be married to Charles and had even had a child with him. He had recently told her that the marriage was a fraud and he was throwing her out to marry another. The letter was signed 'Amy G'.

The Goodrich family offered a reward for the capture of the mystery woman. The police learned that she was known as Kate Stoddard and worked as a straw hat maker. Her real name was Lizzie King, and she was from Plymouth, Massachusetts. Before coming to New York, she had been an inmate at an insane asylum in Taunton, Massachusetts, from which she had escaped. The police now had a description: she was a pale, good-looking woman, about twenty-three years of age, of medium height and graceful figure. But beyond that, they had no leads; Kate Stoddard could be anywhere.

The Brooklyn Chief of Police in 1873 was Patrick Campbell, who had not come up through the ranks of the Brooklyn Police Department. He began work in the printing office of the Brooklyn Eagle newspaper, and after rising to the position of supervisor, he turned to politics. Chief of Police was the latest in an advantageous series of political appointments. His lack of police experience proved to be an advantage, allowing him the freedom to try creative solutions not always endorsed by those under his command.

A woman named Mary Handley volunteered information that she had once been a roommate of Kate Stoddard's in Brooklyn. After a lengthy interview, Chief Campbell hired Mary as a detective in the Goodrich case, reporting directly to him. He sent her to follow leads as they arrived from towns in upstate New York.

The search for Kate continued for several months without success. During this time, several other suspects were considered, and other theories floated regarding the murder. Suspects included an Englishman named Barnet or Barrett, James (alias "Pop") Tighe and two other burglars, and a "dark-visaged Spaniard" named Roscoe. Lucette Meyers, who was known to have been "intimate" with Goodrich, claimed that Roscoe killed Goodrich out of jealousy.

The press took an interest in Roscoe as a suspect, but the police dismissed him as a figment of Lucette's imagination. In any case, the mysterious Roscoe was as elusive as Kate Stoddard.

By chance, as Mary was approaching the ferry from Brooklyn to New York on July 8, 1873, she recognized Kate coming from the boat. She called for a police officer to arrest the fugitive, and the woman was soon before Chief Campbell. She denied it all; she denied that her name was King or Stoddard and that she had ever roomed with or even seen Mary Handley before. But Mary was positive she was not mistaken, so Chief Campbell said to the suspect:

"Madame, we don't want to hold you if you are not Kate Stoddard. Be kind enough to tell us where you reside, and I will at once dispatch an officer and ascertain if you are telling me the truth."

"That I'm sure I won't do," said the woman.

"Then," said the Chief, "you will have to remain in custody; but first you must be searched."

The woman wore a large gold locket on a chain around her neck, which she would not hand over. He took it from her and, with some difficulty, forced it open. Some dark-colored crumbs or lumps fell onto the floor. The woman quickly picked them up and put them into her mouth.

Fearing that she might have taken poison, the chief grabbed her arm and asked her what it was.

"That's blood – dried blood," she replied but would say no more.

She was held for several days but refused to talk. Then Campbell made another bold move; he had his men knock on every door in Brooklyn and inquire if any of the households had been missing a young woman since the previous Tuesday. Within two hours, they had 300 names; by the end of the day, they had narrowed the search and found the house they were looking for. A boarding house on High Street was missing a woman named Minnie Waltham, a hat maker. A latchkey found on the prisoner fit the lock on the missing girl's room.

In that room, they found Charles Goodrich's watch and other personal items, along with a revolver with three empty chambers. His money was there, too; none had been spent. There was now no doubt that the woman in custody was Kate Stoddard.

Inquest: July 12, 1873

Before the coroner's inquest, Kate Stoddard allegedly had confessed to the murder of Charles Goodrich. They had met through a personal advertisement that Goodrich had placed in the newspaper, looking for a wife. Upon meeting, each was impressed by the other, and after a brief courtship, a marriage ceremony was held.

They did not live together; Kate lived in the room on Degraw Street until the spring of 1873. During that time, she became pregnant, and Goodrich persuaded her to have an abortion. Goodrich had also been seeing Adeline

Pabor at the same time and decided that she was the one he wished to keep. He became engaged to Miss Pabor and told Kate that their marriage was a sham. A friend of his performed the ceremony. Goodrich and Kate argued, and she begged him to take her back, but he was unyielding. The next day, she found that all of her belongings had been moved to an unfinished room in one of his buildings on Degraw Street.

She went to see him, and during an argument, she drew a pistol and shot him. Kate left but returned later to clean and dress the body. She had saved some of the dried blood from the body inside the locket Chief Campbell had opened. During the frantic police search, Kate had never left Brooklyn and had even attended Goodrich's funeral.

At the inquest, Lucette Meyers identified the articles in Kate's trunk. She said she knew the defendant under several names: Kate Stoddard, Amy Snow, Amy Stone, and Amy Gilmore. Meyers still accused Roscoe of the murder but said she had seen him in conversation with Kate.

Kate took the stand but, on the advice of counsel, refused to repeat the confession she had given the police, saying she would save any statement for her trial. The coroner called on Chief Campbell to relate to the jury the confession that Miss Stoddard had given to the police.

The coroner's jury deliberated briefly before returning with a verdict.

We find that the said Charles Goodrich came to his death by pistol-shot wounds in the head, inflicted by Lizzie Lloyd King, alias Kate Stoddard, with intent to cause death on the evening of the 20th or morning of the 21st of March, 1873, at his aforesaid house in Degraw Street, Brooklyn.

Aftermath:

Before Kate could be tried for murder, a hearing was held to determine her mental competency. The hearing included testimony from doctors who had cared for her at the Taunton Lunatic Hospital, stating that at times, she had been put into a "camisole" (straitjacket) on account of violence or destructiveness.

The judge committed her to the state insane asylum at Auburn, New York. After his pronouncement, Kate asked the judge if she had been convicted of murder. The judge have not answered, "You been decided here guilty of homicide. What I have decided is that you are not in a mental condition to be tried."

To which Kate responded, "Oh! If I am willing to take that risk, I think the rest ought to be."

But that risk was not taken, and Lizzie King, alias Kate Stoddard, was never tried for murder. She spent the rest of her life in the Auburn Asylum.

Even before arrest, the citizens living on Degraw Street, successfully petitioned to rename the section of Degraw Street between 5th and 6th

Avenues to Lincoln Place, to distance the street from the negative association of the murder.

Murdered At Prayer

Lucy Caldwell's disappointment with her husband's financial state was augmented by her growing mental illness. In January 1879, she snapped and assaulted him with an axe as he knelt in prayer.

Murdered at Prayer
Illustrated Police News. Jan. 11, 1879.

Dates:	January 3, 1879
Locations:	South Byfield, Massachusetts
Victim:	John Caldwell
Cause of Death:	Blows from an Axe
Accused:	Lucy Caldwell

Synopsis:

A.E. Ambrose was working in his yard in South Byfield, Massachusetts, on the morning of January 3, 1879, when he was surprised by two of his neighbors, Mrs. Caldwell and her sister Miss Brown, excitedly running toward him. Mrs. Lucy Caldwell was known for her erratic behavior and always seemed somewhat excited, but he had never seen Miss Brown looking so terrified.

Mrs. Caldwell exclaimed, "Go up and take care of him; he threatened to kill me, and I hit him with an axe, and I don't know, but I have killed him."

Ambrose hurried to the neighbor's house. In the kitchen, he found the warm but lifeless body of John Caldwell, lying on the floor, surrounded by a dark pool of clotted blood. His skull had been split open; the frightful wound was eight inches long and five inches deep. A large axe was leaning on a chair. Ambrose took his wagon into town to notify the deputy sheriff.

Miss Brown told the deputy that Mr. and Mrs. Caldwell had been arguing loudly that morning before coming downstairs to breakfast. It was their custom to eat breakfast at about 8:00 and have family prayers afterward. Mr. Caldwell read a chapter from the Bible, then knelt on the floor to pray. Miss Brown joined him, but Mrs. Caldwell did not. He was almost finished praying when Miss Brown was startled by the sound of a violent blow. She sprang to her feet and was horrified by the sight of her brother-in-law lying on the floor with his skull split open and his wife holding the fatal axe. Miss Brown fled from the house, followed by her sister, and both ran to the home of Mr. Ambrose. Mrs. Caldwell did not attempt to escape as the deputy placed her under arrest.

The Caldwells were well-known and widely respected in South Byfield, but Lucy Caldwell was viewed as "partially deranged." She sometimes needed supervision, which was why her sister was staying with them. Some believed that her insanity stemmed from her disappointment that her husband's prominence in the community had not led to financial success. The family physician, Dr. Huse, confirmed that Mrs. Caldwell had, for some time, suffered from "morbid excitement." Mr. Caldwell had contacted the doctor on the previous Monday to consult him about having her confined and to get an opiate to help her sleep.

At her arraignment, Lucy pleaded not guilty, saying she was justified in killing her husband because of his ill-treatment of her. She claimed he had threatened to kill her. The case never went to trial; Lucy was judged insane and committed to the asylum in Danvers, Massachusetts.

The Veiled Murderess

In 1854, a woman calling herself Henrietta Robinson stood trial in Troy, New York, for poisoning a neighbor and his sister-in-law. Despite the judge's admonitions, she sat through the trial with her face covered by a black veil, hiding her appearance from the crowds of spectators who had come to watch. Everything about the defendant was a mystery – her motive for murder, her behavior before and after the crime, and even her true identity. Many believed that "Henrietta Robinson" was an assumed name, but who she really was has never been determined.

Henrietta Robinson
Henrietta Robinson, 1855.

Date:	May 25, 1853
Location:	Troy, New York
Victims:	Timothy Lanagan & Catherine Lubee
Cause of Death:	Poisoning
Accused:	Henrietta Robinson

Synopsis:
In the early 1850s, Henrietta Robinson was a well-known figure in Troy, New York. At first glance, she was a beautiful, refined young woman of means, but those who had close encounters with her knew Henrietta to be wild and unpredictable. She had an unfounded fear of persecution and was quick to take offense. Henrietta traveled heavily armed, pulling her revolver at the slightest hint of insult. According to biographer David Wilson, writing in 1855:

> *She fancied that a gentleman who resided near her, in addition to his active participation in the general persecution that raged against her, had stopped the navigation of the Hudson River. She was found groping in the dark through the halls of public buildings, inquiring for the police office, and demanding of the authorities assistance to protect her house, which,*

all the time, had remained unmolested and undisturbed. She wandered about the city at night, armed with her revolver, and presented it at the breast of one who had the curiosity to observe her movements. She sallied out at a very early hour in the morning clad only in her night garments, and arousing an acquaintance from sleep, requested the loan of a dress, with the singular apology that she had forgotten her outward apparel on leaving home.

Through these episodes, Henrietta kept her background a secret, or rather, told stories so contradictory that none could be believed. Sometimes, her father was a lord who had driven her from his castle; sometimes, she attributed her misfortunes to a wicked stepmother; sometimes, she was the daughter of a humble Irishman in Vermont. But always, she was the target of a terrible conspiracy and lived in constant fear of its agents.

In 1853, Henrietta lived in a cottage with a servant girl and an elderly gardener. On the corner opposite her cottage was a grocery store run by a man named Timothy Lanagan. He and his family lived in an apartment connected to the store, which sold alcohol and had a bar where the locals would congregate for music and dancing.

Henrietta would send the gardener or the servant girl to Lanagan's store for provisions. Before long, these provisions included beer and sometimes brandy. These orders became so frequent that people in the neighborhood believed she must have been constantly inebriated. Eventually, she would come out herself and join the rowdies drinking at the bar in Lanagan's store. But the alcohol did not improve her disposition, and she would often be provoked by some real or imagined insult to draw her revolver. More than once, she had to be forcibly ejected from the building.

On the morning of May 25, 1853, Henrietta purchased a quart of beer from Lanagan's store. Two hours later, she went back and was drinking at the bar until she got into a heated argument with one of the patrons, and Mrs. Lanagan requested that she leave. At one o'clock, she returned and found Mr. and Mrs. Lanagan having dinner with Catherine Lubee, a sister-in-law of Mr. Lanagan's who had been staying with them. They invited Henrietta to join them.

After dinner, Henrietta offered to repay their kindness by treating them to beer on her account. Mrs. Lanagan declined, but Mr. Lanagan and Miss Lubee agreed, and he went to get the beer. Henrietta also requested some sugar, which, she said, would make the beer taste better. There wasn't enough beer to fill all the tumblers, so Mr. Lanagan went for more. When he returned, he found that Henrietta had added the sugar to their glasses. At this point, Henrietta decided she did not want any beer and left the store. Two hours later, Timothy Lanagan and Catherine Lubee were seized with a mortal sickness.

They had been poisoned with arsenic. There was little doubt as to who was responsible. Mrs. Lanagan told the police what had happened in the store. A local druggist told them he had recently sold some arsenic to Henrietta, and the police found arsenic in Henrietta's cottage. When Lanagan and Lubee died, Henrietta Robinson was arrested for their murders.

Through a series of delays and postponements, she was not officially indicted until February 1854, nine months after the murder. Her trial did not commence until May. The delays left the people of Troy with the impression that powerful forces were at work behind the scenes to protect her. In July, Henrietta tried to commit suicide by drinking vitriol. It was unknown how she obtained the poison, but some speculated that the same mysterious forces would prefer her death in prison to a public hearing.

As the story of Henrietta Robinson spread throughout the United States and Canada, articles appeared in various newspapers claiming to identify her. One said she was actually a Mrs. Campbell, who kept a drinking house in the suburbs of Quebec and had run away with a cab driver. A Troy paper claimed she was the daughter of a Dr. Robinson of Montreal, who had died nine years before in a lunatic asylum. A newspaper in Albany claimed she was the daughter of an Irish gentleman of rank and had been disinherited for marrying the son of her father's steward.

A more probable version of Miss Robinson's history began as a rumor circulating in Troy. Someone who had attended the Troy Female Seminary identified her as a classmate named Emma Wood, daughter of William F. Wood, a prominent citizen of Quebec. When the story was printed by the Troy Times, Mr. Wood sued the paper for libel. The Troy Daily Whig received a card from the Wood family, categorically denying that Henrietta Robinson was their daughter. Though four of Mr. Wood's five daughters had attended the Troy Female Academy, all had since married and were living in England, Ireland, and Scotland.

Trial: May 22, 1854

The case finally came to trial nearly a year after the murder. Henrietta was well represented by attorneys who used her history of erratic behavior and lack of motive in the double murder to try to prove her innocence by reason of insanity. The prosecution argued that drunkenness is not insanity and not a defense against murder. To someone in Henrietta's condition, being thrown out of the bar was motive enough.

But the defendant herself grabbed all the attention at the trial by appearing every day with her face covered by a black veil. When witnesses were called to identify her, she would reluctantly lift the veil for the witness's eyes only. On the third day of the trial, the judge told Henrietta to remove the veil or face contempt of court charges. Through her attorneys, Henrietta responded that she would rather submit to whatever punishment required than remove the veil. The judge relented, and she wore the veil for the rest of the trial.

In the end, the jury agreed that, in spite of her antics, Henrietta was not insane and was responsible for her actions. They found her guilty of first-degree murder.

Upon reading the verdict, Henrietta jumped up and shouted, "Shame on you, judge! Shame on you! There is corruption here! There is corruption in the court!"

Verdict: Guilty of first-degree murder

Aftermath:

Appeals kept the case open for another year, but her attorneys' request for a new trial was denied. On June 14, 1855, Henrietta was brought into court, and at the judge's request, she raised her veil as the sentence was read. She was sentenced to hang on the third of August.

As the execution date approached, the governor of New York received appeals from citizens throughout the state to spare her life. Whether at their urging or due to the influence of the unseen forces that seemed to protect Henrietta, the governor agreed to commute her sentence to life in prison. The news did not please Henrietta; she had made peace with God and was fully prepared to die.

Sometime before the sentencing, she had been recognized again, this time as Charlotte Wood, another of Mr. Wood's daughters who had attended the Troy Female Seminary. Many accepted this as her true identity, but Miss Robinson never confirmed it.

Henrietta Robinson spent eighteen years in Sing Sing prison then was transferred to the prison in Auburn, New York. In 1890 she was transferred again to the Matawan Hospital for the Criminally Insane where she spent the last fifteen years of her life. Hospital records indicated she was 78 at her last birthday, but she said she was 89. Though she was urged to reveal her identity on her deathbed, the veiled murderess took the secret to her grave.

The Worst Woman on Earth

When two bodies were found in a hayloft on Paul Halliday's farm in the town of Mamakating, in New York's Catskill Mountains, his young gypsy wife, Lizzie, became the prime suspect in their murders. It was not the first time Lizzie Halliday had been accused of murder, and it would not be the last. In court, she would tear her clothes and babble incoherently; in captivity, she was a danger to herself and everyone around her. Though she exhibited all the signs of a woman who was violently insane, many believed that Lizzie was merely a gifted actress. But no one disagreed when the press crowned Lizzie Halliday "The Worst woman on earth."

Mrs. Halliday in Handcuffs
National Police Gazette, Sept. 23, 1893.

Date:	August 1893
Location:	Mamakating, New York
Victims:	Margaret McQuillan, Sarah McQuillan, Paul Halliday
Cause of Death:	Gunshot
Accused:	Lizzie Halliday

Synopsis:
Paul Halliday, a Union Army veteran, bought a farm in Sullivan County after the war, and there he and his wife raised five children. By the end of the 1880s, his wife had died, and four of his children had married and moved away, leaving Halliday with no one for company but a mentally handicapped son. He lost all interest in life. His only business was making charcoal, but he spent the small income it generated at the local tavern.

Halliday's life changed drastically when he hired a young Irish girl named Lizzie Brown as a live-in housekeeper. A romance developed between Halliday and Lizzie. They soon married, although Mr. Halliday was at least forty years older than his new bride.

The neighbors laughed at Halliday behind his back, but they grew to fear his young bride. She was a short, stout woman with reddish hair and a pointed nose; her most disturbing features were her dark blue eyes, sunken under heavy brows, giving the appearance of a serpent's eyes. She had an erratic disposition and was known to wander through the woods late at night. The neighbors believed she was a gypsy and studiously avoided her.

About two years after the marriage, the Hallidays' farmhouse caught fire. Mrs. Halliday ran to alert the neighbors, but it was too late. The house burned to the ground, and Halliday's son was burned to death inside it. The neighbors knew that Lizzie hated the son, and they believed that she had deliberately started the fire to kill him or had murdered him in the house and set it ablaze to hide her crime. Lizzie was arrested, but there was not enough evidence to hold her.

A year later, she was arrested again, along with an unnamed man, for stealing horses. This time, the court declared her insane and committed her to the Middletown Asylum. She was transferred to the Auburn Asylum, and on the trip, she turned violent, smashing the windows of the omnibus and attacking the sheriff. She was moved again to the Matteawan Asylum, and she was violent there as well. But when the case against her for horse theft was dismissed, Lizzie showed a marked improvement in her mental health. The doctors declared her cured, and her husband came and took her back to the farm.

Many believed that Lizzie was never insane; she had only faked her behavior to avoid punishment. It was a sentiment that would dog Lizzie for the rest of her life. The New York Herald described it this way. "Hers was a remarkable career, showing that she possessed either a wonderful aptitude for crime or a strangely disturbed mind. Perhaps both of these endowments were hers."

While the neighbors in Mamakating stayed away from the Hallidays, they kept an eye on their movements, expecting more violence from Lizzie. In August 1893, they noticed that Paul Halliday had been absent from his farm for several successive days. When a group of neighbors, including another of Halliday's sons, asked Lizzie where her husband went, she said he had gone to Bloomingburg to do some masonry work. The men did not believe this and went to the justice of the peace for a search warrant.

Inside the house, they found a piece of carpet, freshly stained with blood, a spent cartridge from a revolver, and a piece of blood-stained rope. Lizzie turned violent again and hit one of the men on the head with a board. They managed to calm her down, and she agreed to take her stepson to Bloomingburg and show him that Paul Halliday was not dead.

While they were gone, the search party continued looking for a revolver and any more signs of foul play. In the barn, they found a large amount of hay recently piled against the wall, and they began digging through it, expecting to find the body of Paul Halliday. To their astonishment, what they found were the bodies of two women – one middle-aged, one younger – riddled with bullets and badly decomposed. Their hands were tied across their chests, and their feet and knees were bound with ropes.

They brought Lizzie back to Mamakating and held an inquest on the murders. Throughout the proceedings, she behaved in an insane manner, tearing at her clothes and making irrelevant remarks, oblivious to any questions asked her. The inquest was inconclusive. Lizzie was held as a witness, and the debate continued over whether she was truly insane or merely faking insanity.

The following day, the bodies were positively identified as Mrs. Margaret McQuillan and her daughter, Sarah. They had worked for the Hallidays. The search of the farm continued, uncovering two thirty-eight caliber pistols. Then, under the floorboards of the kitchen, searchers found the body of Paul Halliday, with a fractured skull and three bullet wounds to his chest, and bound as the others had been.

The same day, Lizzie attempted suicide in her jail cell. She removed her garter, broke it, and then twisted it around her neck, pulling with all her strength. The suicide attempt failed, but authorities continued to fear for her safety, both inside and outside the jail. It was reported that a band of gypsies had arrived at the Hallidays' house and declared that they were going to have the woman. Also, a group of local citizens formed a lynch mob and declared their intention to have Lizzie as well. Neither of these groups made good on their plans, and the excitement subsided after Halliday's funeral.

Trial: June 17, 1894

Lizzie Halliday was indicted on three counts of murder, and a trial was planned for the following spring. In the interim, she was still making news as details of her life in Ireland emerged. According to Paul Halliday's son, Robert, Lizzie had come from Ulster, in the north of Ireland. She told him she had killed a man in Belfast, but the murder was so cleverly done that it was never found out. Other accounts said the man she murdered in Ireland was her first husband.

While in jail in Monticello, New York, Lizzie continued her violent outbursts and suicide attempts. She was ultimately shackled to the floor of her cell for the protection of herself and others. Authorities were convinced that she was a psychopathic killer. The sheriff went so far as accusing her of being "Jack the Ripper":

> *… recent investigations show that Mrs. Halliday is in all probability connected with the famous Whitechapel murders. It has been proved that she was in Europe at the time. She frequently refers to the subject, both when she is in possession of her mental faculties and when she is raving. Mrs. Halliday is constantly speaking of these murders.*

Crowds from all over New York State came to Monticello to watch Lizzie's trial that June. Many treated the occasion as a holiday and brought their children along. Judge Edwards had to remind the spectators that a courtroom was not a place of amusement and threatened to clear the courtroom if the levity continued.

The case against Lizzie was circumstantial but strong. Her attorney did little to challenge the testimony of prosecution witnesses, confident that Lizzie would be acquitted by reason of insanity. Several doctors from the asylums where Lizzie had been kept testified that she was insane. The prosecution rebutted with medical experts, testifying that Lizzie was not insane. Many people expressed the opinion that she had been acting the whole time. In the end, the jury believed the prosecution and convicted her of first-degree murder.

Verdict: Guilty of first-degree murder

Aftermath:

Lizzie was sentenced to death by electrocution on August 6. She would have been the first woman to be executed in the electric chair, but New York Governor Flower, on the advice of a commission formed to judge her sanity, commuted her sentence to life in prison.

Lizzie was sent to the Mattawan State Asylum, where she continued causing trouble with attempts at suicide, escape attempts, and assaults on attendants. Eventually, she settled into life at the asylum and even appeared in plays produced by the inmates.

After twelve years in the asylum, Lizzie became one of the most trusted patients there. Her good behavior was attributed to the attention of a young nurse named Nellie Wicks, for whom Lizzie had a great deal of affection. In 1906, Nellie planned to leave the asylum and become a private nurse. This news was devastating for Lizzie Halliday, and she threatened to kill her nurse if she tried to leave. The threat was not taken seriously, but on September 27, 1906, Lizzie followed Nellie into the lavatory, locked the door, and began stabbing her with a pair of scissors. Miss Weeks died two hours later.

When Lizzie died in 1918, the *New York Times* remembered her as the woman who murdered five people and reiterated the description of Lizzie as the "Worst Woman on Earth."

Horrible Murder in Twelfth Street

The brutal murder of Mrs. Sharah Shancks in her millenary store was first thought to be a robbery gone bad. Robbery was not the motive. She was the victim of Alfred Buchanan, a mentally ill man, recently pronounced cured and released from the Lunatic Asylum on Blackwell's Island.

Frightful Murder of Mrs. Shancks
Frank Leslie's Illustrated Newspaper, Dec. 22, 1860.

Dates:	December 7, 1860
Locations:	New York, New York
Victim:	Sarah Shancks
Cause of Death:	Blows to the head, slashing.
Accused:	Alfred Buchanan

Synopsis:

Mrs. Sarah Shancks owned a high-end millinery concern – "a fancy thread and needle store" – at 22 East 12th Street, New York. At around 10:00 a.m. on December 7, 1860, Susan Ferguson, who worked as a seamstress for Sarah, entered the store but could not find her employer. She went to the back room where she lived and found her lying on the floor in a pool of blood. Her throat had been slashed, and she was surrounded by broken glass and crockery. Susan ran out of the store to alert the police.

The police and coroner examined the crime scene and determined that Mrs. Shanks was probably killed by a blow to the head that fractured her skull. Her face had been battered, her nose broken, and on the left side of her face, a deep gash ran from the cheek to the jaw. Her throat had probably been slashed after death, and the cut, from ear to ear, was so deep she was nearly decapitated. Investigators found several possible weapons nearby: a small fire shovel bent and covered with blood, an axe head without a handle, and a kitchen knife. Around the body were shattered fragments of a heavy stone water pitcher and shards of glass from broken bottles.

Marks on the linen where the killer had wiped his hands were so saturated with blood that he must have cut his hands in the attack. The box where Sarah kept her money had been emptied of all but a single nickel. The box was covered with blood.

Sarah had been a widow for nearly twenty years, and until recently, she had a companion living in the store with her. In the days before the murder, she had been ill and incapacitated, and neighbors were cooking meals for her. Elizabeth McMann, daughter of a neighbor, brought her breakfast at around 8:20 a.m. and was the last person to see Sarah alive.

At one point, the store had been quite lucrative, Sarah had been well off, but she had lost much of her money in bad investments. She had also been swindled by someone to whom she was engaged to be married.

"The lady bears an unblemished reputation," said the *New York Tribune*, "but seems to have lent a too willing ear to obsequious flatteries."

At the time of the murder, she was engaged to be married to a man named Chambers. He was briefly a person of interest in the investigation, as was Charles Hardy, a dealer who sold Sarah's embroidery, and an unnamed young carpenter who had done work on the store and continued to hang around, much to Sarah's annoyance. The police determined that robbery was the sole motive, and they had no clear suspects.

On December 11, a young man named Alfred Buchanan was arrested in the town of Susquehanna, about 300 miles west of New York City. He had gone to stay with Theodore Springstein, brother of a friend. Springstein welcomed Buchanan into his house but could not help but notice a bandage on the man's hand covering bloody wounds. That, together with the young man's agitated appearance, aroused Springstein's suspicions, and he took the information to the Justice of the Peace.

Captain Caffrey of the New York Police traveled to Susquehanna to bring Buchanan back to New York. In the city, Buchanan was identified as the "young carpenter" who had been bothering Mrs. Shancks.

At first, Buchanan denied any knowledge of Sarah or her murder. He subsequently admitted he knew her but denied that he killed her, saying his hand was wounded in a fight at a Bowery saloon. A man there had called him a son of a bitch and during the brawl that followed Buchanan drew a knife cutting his hand. Buchanan was unable to give the man's name or the name of the saloon.

For several days after the murder, Buchanan stayed within two blocks of Sarah's store without any concealment. The press criticized the city police force for allowing the perpetrator of such a violent crime to flee the city. The *New York Tribune* asserted that Buchanan's arrest was entirely due to newspaper coverage. The New York Atlas claimed that the police were indifferent to murder cases unless a reward was involved.

"The escape was a disgrace to the detective police force in this city," said the Atlas, "and shows beyond question that that branch of our police department is worse than useless."

19-year-old Alfred Buchanan was tall and slim with a sinister expression on a face that resembled a bulldog. He had a long history of mental illness, having been subject to fits for several years. He behaved erratically, and as symptoms of insanity increased, his parents arranged to have him committed to the Lunatic Asylum on Blackwell's Island. After about four months at the asylum, he was pronounced cured and released. Following his return, he was arrested several times for petty theft and arson.

Alfred Buchanan was indicted for the murder of Sarah Shancks, and he pleaded not guilty. Before he could be tried, he was examined by a jury who pronounced him insane. He was not tried but was committed to a state lunatic asylum.

Salvation Army Tragedy

Nettie Biedler was a Salvation Army private who craved Captain Hattie Smith's attention. When the Army held a muster in Omaha, Captain Smith could not spare Nettie the private time she desired. Private Biedler turned to violence in "…a queer combination of jealousy and semi-religious frenzy."

The Motive Was Jealousy
National Police Gazette, Dec. 5, 1891.

Date:	November 14, 1891
Location:	Omaha, Nebraska
Victim:	Hattie Smith
Cause of Death:	Gunshot
Accused:	Nettie Biedler

Synopsis:
In November 1891, the Northwestern Division of the Salvation Army held a muster in Omaha, Nebraska, to honor 'La Marechale' Catherine Booth-Clibborn, leader of the Salvation Army in France. When the afternoon session ended on November 14, Captain Hattie Smith from Oskaloosa, Iowa, walked down the sidewalk conversing with Captain Wallace of Marshalltown. Nettie, a private in the Army, rushed up to them and, without speaking, drew a revolver from the folds of her dress and fired at Captain Smith who let out a shriek and fled down the sidewalk with Wallace. Biedler followed and fired again. The first shot had wounded Smith and she fell to the ground after running less than a block. Biedler then put the revolver to her own head and fired. She died instantly.

Captain Smith had been stationed at Council Bluffs, Iowa before being transferred to Oskaloosa about a month before. Nettie was also from Council Bluffs and the press first believed jealousy was the motive for the shooting. Hattie was engaged to Lieutenant Berry, of Boone, Iowa, and it was believed that Nettie was trying to steal him from her.

On her deathbed, Captain Smith explained that the motive was jealousy of another kind. Severely wounded, Smith was carried from the sidewalk to a drug store, then to her temporary boarding place. A physician examined her and pronounced the wound to be fatal. While still able to speak, Smith explained that she had known Nettie in Council Bluffs and induced her to join the Salvation Army. When they met again in Omaha, Biedler greeted her with a great show of affection and, on several occasions, sought to occupy Hattie's attention to the exclusion of all others.

"It was a case of jealousy," said Smith, "She was jealous because I didn't talk to her more."

Lieutenant Mary Bannister said she carried a message from Biedler to Smith saying Biedler wanted to talk. Smith replied that she was too busy. After lunch, the two did meet for an extended talk but what was said is unknown. Lieutenant Bannister heard Smith say several times that she must go, and Biedler tried to stop her. Biedler said if Smith went out and left her there, she would be sorry for it.

A reporter went to Nettie's home in Council Bluffs and spoke with her younger sister. She said that Nettie and Hattie had been fast friends and she knew of no trouble between the girls which might account for Nettie's actions. She also had no idea that her sister owned a revolver.

Captain Hattie Smith died later that day. The motive for the murder was never fully explained. The *Chicago Tribune* summed it up as "...a queer combination of jealousy and semi-religious frenzy."

RANDOM VIOLENCE

Rum and The Knife

On November 14, 1877, the Lynches of South Boston were expecting a visit from Mrs. Lynch's sister, Bridget Frances Kenneally. Mr. and Mrs. Lynch were sitting in the kitchen at around 6:30 p.m. when the door suddenly flew open, and Bridget fell flat on her face across the threshold. They thought she had fainted, so they carried her to the sofa and attempted to revive her but were unsuccessful. Bridget appeared to be dying, so the Lynches sent for a physician and a Catholic priest, but she died before either arrived, without uttering a word or giving the slightest clue as to the cause.

Scene of the Tragedy
Illustrated Police News, Nov. 24, 1877

Date:	November 14, 1877
Location:	Boston, Massachusetts
Victim:	Bridget Frances Kenneally
Cause of Death:	Stabbing
Accused:	Peter Mahoney

Synopsis:

Bridget was wearing a thick jacket made of dark material, and they noticed a little blood in it but thought she had cut herself in the fall. When they opened the front of her dress, they discovered that Bridget had been stabbed three times in the base of the sternum, and at least one plunge of the knife had punctured her heart.

When the police arrived about half an hour later, they faced a mystery. Bridget Kenneally was a respectable Irish lady, about 30 years old. She was employed as a coat baster (tacking together pattern pieces) at the Continental

Clothing House. She boarded alone in South Boston and was described by her friends as "an estimable young lady in every way." The crime appeared to be completely random.

The officers arrested, on suspicion, an old rum-drinking junk dealer named Peter Mahoney, who was drinking in John J. Teevan's saloon directly across the street. The day before the murder, the Fitzgerald family, who lived on the floor below the Lynches, were holding a christening party. The Fitzgeralds were known to be rather disorderly, and the party became very noisy. Mahoney, who was married to Mrs. Fitzgerald's sister, attended and became extremely intoxicated. He got into an argument with Mrs. Fitzgerald, and when she hit him on the head with a stove-lifter, he left, swearing he would come back and kill her.

Drunk again the following evening, Mahoney was seen threatening some children with a knife and had gotten into a fight with a man. When arrested, the police found a large, two-bladed jack knife on his person, with a fresh blood spot on one of the blades. Mahoney had served time in the penitentiary as a common drunk. He was a violent man, but there was no indication that Mahoney ever had any difficulty with Bridget Kenneally. He had either mistaken Bridget for his sister-in-law or was so angry and crazed with drink that he did not know what he was doing.

The police took Mahoney to jail on suspicion and waited for him to sober up. In the meantime, they investigated the possibility that Bridget had been keeping company with a man with whom she quarreled and who may have been the murderer. This investigation did not pan out; everything pointed to Mahoney as the killer.

Trial: March 18, 1878

At his arraignment the next day, Peter Mahoney pled not guilty to the murder of Bridget Kenneally. But at his trial, the following March, Mahoney retracted his plea of not guilty and pleaded guilty to murder in the second degree. The court accepted his plea and sentenced him to life in the state prison.

Verdict: Guilty of second-degree murder

Little Mary Mohrman

In 1868, Mrs. Mohrman, a widowed mother, lived with her five daughters on Orkney Street in Philadelphia. The youngest girl, Mary, was a favorite of everyone in the neighborhood. 'Little Mary Mohrman,' as all knew her, was described as "one of those sunny-haired, bright-eyed, sylvan-like children, whose innocence, one would think, could soften the hardest soul." This sentiment would be tested and proven horribly false.

Murderer and Victim
Life, Trial, Confession and Conviction of John Hanlon, 1870.

Date:	September 6, 1868
Location:	Philadelphia, Pennsylvania
Victim:	Mary Mohrman
Cause of Death:	Strangulation
Accused:	John Hanlon

Synopsis:
On the evening of Sunday, September 6, Mrs. Mohrman left her six-year-old daughter Mary in the care of her older sisters and went to church. Mary and her friend, Caroline Dinglacker, were playing on Carolines's front steps, next to John Hanlon's barber shop, when a strange man approached them and asked if either of them knew how to get to Fifth and Dauphin Streets. Mary offered to show him, but her playmate was frightened and ran away. The last thing Caroline saw was the man taking Mary by the hand and leading her into an ally.

When Mrs. Mohrman came home from church, the children told her they had not seen Mary since she went around the corner with the strange man. She alerted the neighbors, and a search began. Soon, Mrs. Mohrman was joined by city policemen and detectives. Two days later, Mary's body was found lying in a pond in a vacant lot some distance away. There were bruises on her arms, neck, and wrists, and her underclothes were stained with blood. An autopsy revealed that strangulation was the cause of death and that "her person had been grossly violated." She had died on the same day she was taken.

The police brought in several men for questioning, but there was no evidence to hold any of them. No further clues developed, and a year later, the case was still unsolved.

In November 1869, a man named Charles C. Harris was arrested in Philadelphia for trying to abduct a ten-year-old girl. He approached her as she was playing in the yard of the Tabernacle M.E. Church. She was frightened and tried to run away, but he grabbed her arm and dragged her behind the church, away from the street. The girl's cries caught the attention of a nearby blacksmith, who ran to the scene and held Harris until the police arrived. He was tried and convicted of assaulting the girl and was sentenced to four years at Moyamensing Prison.

The same man had been arrested in October for assaulting Mrs. Annie Bowers, who was walking down the street with her sixteen-year-old sister, Clara Richie. He hit Mrs. Bowers on the head with a rock, nearly knocking her off her feet. At the time of his arrest for this crime, he gave his name as Charles Hanlon. The Alderman settled the matter out of court.

Following his sentencing to Moyamensing, the police learned that Charles Harris, alias Charles Hanlon, was actually John Hanlon, owner of the barbershop next to the site where Mary Mohrman was abducted and one of the early suspects in the case. They were convinced he was her killer.

At the time of the murder, Hanlon was 22, living on Fifth Street in Philadelphia with his mother, sister, and his new wife, who was barely 17. He had learned to be a barber in the Army and opened a barbershop next to his home. Hanlon was unsuccessful at his business and was not well-liked in the neighborhood. There were allegations that he had taken improper liberties with little girls, and it was not hard for the neighbors to picture him as Little Mary Mohrman's killer.

Police detectives Smith, Tyron, and Taggert met with a Moyamensing prisoner named Michael Dunn and asked if he would share a cell with Hanlon and secretly report back to them all that Hanlon said to him. Dunn was an Englishman, a career criminal who had been transported to Australia for theft. When his sentence was finished, he came to America, where he was arrested for theft again. He agreed to help the police, and Hanlon was moved to Dunn's cell.

Hanlon soon confided in Dunn, telling him several times how he had murdered Mary, whom he described as a girl of thirteen or fourteen, not a six-year-old. He said he had previously tried to entice some of the young girls in his neighborhood but was recognized, so he disguised himself with false whiskers and dark clothing. This time, he got Mary to go with him. He took her to his outhouse and raped her there. In some tellings, the murder took place there as well; in others, he strangled her in the basement of his house to keep her from crying. He kept the body in the cellar until Tuesday morning, before dawn, when he carried it to the vacant lot. He was afraid he may have been seen carrying the body by a man named Charlie Mass.

This was enough for the detectives; they arrested Hanlon for the murder of Mary. Michael Dunn was subsequently pardoned for his crimes.

Trial: October 31, 1870

Empaneling the jury for Hanlon's trial took a considerable amount of time because most of those summoned had already formed or expressed an opinion as to Hanlon's guilt. The trial lasted eighteen days, and the courtroom was filled to capacity with spectators each day.

Chief among the dozens of witnesses were Michael Dunn, who related Hanlon's jailhouse 'confession', and Caroline Dinglacker, who told the circumstances of the abduction. Charlie Mass testified that he saw a man carrying a bundle about 4.00 a.m. the day the body was found.

The defense challenged Dunn's testimony as hearsay and perjury, suborned by police detectives. They cross-examined 9-year-old Caroline for over an hour, trying to catch her in contradictions between her current testimony and what she had previously told the coroner. Moss's testimony did not corroborate Dunn's, they said, because he did not recognize the man carrying the bundle, though he did know John Hanlon.

The jury deliberated for more than a day before returning a verdict of guilty.

Verdict: Guilty of first-degree murder

Aftermath:

Hanlon's attorney filed a motion for a new trial, but it was overruled. On December 11, before pronouncing sentence, the judge asked Hanlon if he had anything to say. While holding a Bible, Hanlon railed against all the perjured witnesses who had testified against him, as well as Detectives Smith and Taggert, who paid for their testimony.

He finished by saying, "If ever another such case should come to light, lay before the jury John Hanlon's last words, and let no more blood be spilt by perjury."

Then he kissed the Bible.

Hanlon was sentenced to hang, but the execution did not take place until February 1871. He maintained his innocence until two weeks prior to the hanging, then sent for Detective Smith to apologize for what he had said at the sentencing and asked him to pass the apology on to Detective Taggert as well. While not actually admitting to the murder of Little Mary Mohrman, he had begun a course of rigorous physical penance. He gave up tobacco, strapped rough blankets next to his skin, wore no shoes, and slept on the cold floor without covering. He fasted for seventeen days, then lived on bread and water. His spiritual advisors, Fathers Barry and Mooney, prepared Hanlon for death and gave him absolution.

The hanging was held inside the walls of Moyamensing prison on February 1, 1871. Except for prison officials, the Sheriff, the District Attorney, the prisoner's counsel, and the press, visitors were not allowed.

Hanlon had intended to die in silence, but on the scaffold, he said, "To those who have ever injured me or have done me any wrong, I forgive them, and ask God to forgive them. And all whom I have injured in any way whatsoever, or against whom I have had any ill-feeling, I ask their forgiveness and God to forgive me."

His last words were, "Jesus, have mercy upon me! Holy Mary, pray for me! St. Joseph intercede!"

As Hanlon uttered his last prayer, the Sheriff pulled the cord to spring the platform, and John Hanlon was soon dead.

The Car-Hook Tragedy

On the night of April 26, 1871, while stepping off a Manhattan horse car, Avery Putnam was struck from behind and killed by William Foster, wielding an iron car hook. This cowardly and unprovoked attack outraged the people of New York, but before its ultimate resolution, anger over "The Car-Hook Tragedy" would be overshadowed by a bitter public debate on the morality of the death penalty and allegations of threat and bribery to prevent Foster's execution.

Car-Hook Murder
Recollections of a New York Chief of Police, 1887.

Date:	April 26, 1871
Location:	New York, New York
Victim:	Avery D. Putnam
Cause of Death:	Blows to the head
Accused:	William Foster

Synopsis:

On the evening of April 26, 1871, Avery Putnam had left his place of business on Pearl Street and stopped for a brief visit with his friend, Madam Duval, of 762 Broadway. Madam Duval told Putnam that her daughter Anna Lillie was presently singing at the Church of the Advent on Forty-Sixth Street. She and her other daughter, sixteen-year-old Jenny, would soon leave to accompany Anna Lillie home. Putnam offered to escort the ladies. They agreed, and the three boarded a Broadway horse-car heading uptown.

As they passed the corner of Twenty-ninth and Broadway, Putnam drew Jenny's attention to the clock on the front of the Gilsey House hotel. Jenny stooped to look through the glass in the door at the front of the car. The motion caught the attention of the driver on the other side of the door, who nudged the arm of the man standing next to him. The other man turned around, pressed his face against the glass and smirked at Jenny in an insulting manner.

The man, William Foster, had recently been fired from his job as conductor with the streetcar line and had been drinking all day. Foster opened the door separating the front platform from the passengers and peered into the car, still leering at Jenny. Madam Duval closed the door, and Foster opened it again.

This angered Putnam, who went onto the platform, closing the door behind him, and remonstrated with Foster. He begged him not to annoy Madam Duval, who was suffering from nervous prostration. But instead of quieting Foster, this had the opposite effect. He followed Putnam into the car and tried to sit next to Jenny. Madam Duval quickly switched seats with her to avoid this. Realizing Foster was drunk, Putnam and the ladies tried to ignore him.

"Say," Foster said, "how far are you going up?" When he received no reply, he repeated it twice more and then said, "Well, I'm going as far as you, and before you get out, I'll give you hell."

Foster went back to the front of the car, and nothing further happened until the car stopped at Forty-Sixth Street at the request of Madam Duval. They left through the rear door. Putnam was standing in the glare of the car lamp, with his right foot on the platform and his hand in that of Madam Duval, when Foster struck him with a car hook – a heavy iron tool used by conductors. According to Madam Duval, Foster struck him again before dropping the car hook and running from the scene. She screamed for help, but the driver whipped the horses and drove down Broadway at breakneck speed.

They reported the incident to the police, and late that night the driver and conductor of the horse-car were arrested. Reluctantly, they revealed that the killer was William Foster. At 3:00 a.m., the police arrested Foster and took him to the Tombs prison to await trial.

Trial: May 22, 1871

Foster had very little to offer in his own defense. There had been several witnesses to the murder in addition to Madam Duval and her daughter, and at the time of his arrest, Foster admitted to the crime. He denied that the murder was premeditated and claimed he was too drunk to know what he was doing. He appealed for mercy for the sake of his wife and children.

The prosecution offered evidence that the murder, though unprovoked, was premeditated. Foster lived on Twenty-Second Street but had stayed in the car well past his stop. He had asked the driver if he had the car-hook four blocks before they reached Forty-Sixth Street. When the driver tried to stop him, Foster turned and threatened the driver before chasing after Putnam.

The case was given to the jury on May 25; the following morning, they returned a verdict of guilty of first-degree murder, but with a recommendation to mercy.

Verdict: Guilty, first-degree murder

Aftermath:

July 14, 1871 was the day set for Foster's execution, but two appeals pushed the hanging into 1872. Both appeals failed, and Foster was rescheduled to hang on March 4.

As the date of the execution approached, public sympathy for Foster began to increase. Clergymen of all faiths and denominations spoke out against capital punishment from the pulpit and in the press. New York Governor John A. Dix received letters and petitions from all over the country begging him to pardon Foster. Seven members of the jury that convicted Foster petitioned Dix to pardon him, saying they had only agreed to the guilty verdict when the recommendation for mercy was added.

But sympathy for Foster was not universal; many in New York and elsewhere were anxious to see him hang. Mainstream newspapers printed just as many letters in support of execution as opposed. More than a dozen merchants of Pearl Street, where Avery Putnam had his business, petitioned the governor to uphold the sentence.

There were also allegations that Foster's family and influential friends were using bribery and threats to win support for a pardon. Madam Duval said she had been approached three times by people seeking her support in winning a pardon for Foster. One said it would be to her advantage if Foster were saved. There would be a great deal of money in it for her.

Another one said to her, "But supposing there was money for you in this thing; or, putting it in another form, supposing this man is hanged: he has friends large in political and money influence. The well-being of yourself and your daughters may be endangered for the next twenty years."

Mrs. Ellen L. Putnam, wife of the murdered man – who had successfully sued the streetcar line for $5,000 – wrote a letter to Governor Dix recommending a commutation of Foster's sentence. William L. Allen, husband of a cousin of Mrs. Putnam, claimed she did so in exchange for money from the friends of William Foster. He said they first offered to pay for her son's education. Allen told her to demand cash instead, to ask for $25,000 and accept no less than $15,000, and to sign nothing until the money was in her hand.

When Allen's statement was published in the newspapers, Mrs. Putnam, now living in Providence, Rhode Island, sent the papers a letter denying there was any bribe; the letter to Dix had expressed her honest feelings. Allen also sent a letter to the press, denying that Mrs. Putnam was bribed and that he had ever made such a statement.

Governor Dix finally granted Foster a two-week reprieve, and crowds gathered at the door of the Tombs, trying to find out what it meant. Many believed that Foster's supporters had been successful and the hanging would not take place, but the governor had not been convinced by their arguments. On Friday, March 21, 1873, in front of a crowd of 300 people, William Foster was hanged in the yard of the Tombs.

Queen of the Demi-Monde

In the years following the Civil War, Basin Street in New Orleans was the center of the most notorious red-light district in America, and the house at No. 40 Basin Street, run by Miss Kate Townsend, was the most elegant brothel in the country. When she was fatally stabbed in her bedroom in 1883, Kate's death was mourned by 'sporting men' from coast to coast, but, in accordance with Miss Kate's wishes, no man was allowed to attend her funeral.

Kate Townsend
National Police Gazette, Nov 24, 1883.

Date:	November 3, 1883
Location:	New Orleans, Louisiana
Victim:	Kate Townsend
Cause of Death:	Stabbing
Accused:	Troisville Egbert Sykes

Synopsis:
Kate Townsend was still in her teens when she became a prostitute in New Orleans. She had left her home in Liverpool, England, after giving birth to twins, and came alone to America. In New Orleans, she worked in a brothel run by Maggie Thompson, and became quite popular with the patrons. Kate was beautiful, but also smart and ambitious. Avoiding the tragic fate of most in her profession, she left Maggie Thompson's in 1863 and rented a house of her own on Customhouse Street. There she prospered, catering to powerful politicians and city officials, who, in 1866, helped to set her up at a more permanent location, the brownstone and marble mansion at 40 Basin Street.

No. 40 was magnificently furnished in black walnut and white marble with a profusion of velvet, damask and gold – it was said that even the chamber pots were gilded. The house and its furnishings were estimated to be worth $200,000 in an age when a skilled carpenter worked for two dollars a day.

The demeanor within the house was equally elegant. The ladies who worked there – referred to as 'boarders' – always received their guests wearing evening gowns and were forbidden to use vulgar language. Only gentlemen were allowed entry and upon arrival were expected to buy champagne for all the boarders. On a man's first visit, he would be interviewed by Miss Kate to determine if he was a man of character, and whether his credit was good, as his pocket money was likely to run out fast. Kate served as her own bouncer and was perfectly capable of refusing entry to anyone who did not meet her standards.

From the beginning Kate Townsend was accompanied in business by Troisville Egbert Sykes (known as Bill) who was referred to as her 'fancy man'. He kept the books and handled official business, as Kate, reportedly, could not read or write. They were not married, though they lived together as husband and wife for the twenty-five years prior to Kate's death.

In the early years, during Reconstruction, the clientele of 40 Basin Street consisted primarily of wealthy carpetbaggers from the north. But as Reconstruction ended, Kate was forced to lower her standards, and although the money continued to flow, she was not happy with the new situation. In 1870 a fight between two drunken gamblers, at No, 40 Basin, left one man dead. The police gave Kate the murder weapon as a souvenir – a nine-inch Bowie knife which she kept under her pillow at night and in her handbag during the day.

Kate took to drink, and her disposition turned irritable. She had also gained an enormous amount of weight, possibly due to a glandular condition, and in the 1880s she weighed more than 300 pounds. A reporter for the Daily States remarked that "her bust was one of the sights of the city."

The relationship between Kate and Troisville Sykes was deteriorating as well. The two were constantly arguing and the fights would sometimes turn violent. Kate would frequently beat Sykes, who was described as a mild, timid man, and once she nearly cut off his nose with her knife. Sykes had also begun to drink heavily and smoke opium. He was continually stealing money from Kate. But he was still committed to her and became jealous when Kate started seeing a younger man named McKern.

On the night of November 2, 1883, Kate and Mollie Johnson, one of the boarders at the house, were out with McKern and another man. They got extremely drunk and during an argument with McKern, Kate drew the Bowie knife and made him apologize. Mollie recalled that on the way home Kate said, "I've got to cut somebody, I'll go home and open Sykes's belly." It was a threat she had heard many times before and did not take it seriously.

Sykes went for a walk the next morning; when he returned, Kate was still sleeping, and he sat down for coffee. Soon after, she rang for the housekeeper, Marie Philomene, who went up to the bedroom and found Kate standing in her chemise and holding the Bowie knife. She said she wanted to see Sykes right away.

According to Sykes, when he entered the room Kate hit him in the head with a goblet. She relaxed for a moment when Marie brought her coffee, but after the housekeeper left, Kate sprang up and attacked him with the Bowie knife. He managed to wrest it from her hand, and she grabbed a pair of pruning shears and continued the attack. Sykes claimed that he could not remember the details of what happened next, only that he murdered Kate.

He had thrown both the knife and the shears out of the window, then emerged from the room, bleeding from his chest and leg. Mollie and Marie ran to the bedroom to find Kate lying on the bed, covered with blood. She had been stabbed eleven times; at least three were mortal wounds to the chest. They summoned the police and Troisville Sykes turned himself in.

Trial: January 30, 1884

Kate's will was found among her belongings. In it she left all her estate to Sykes and named him executor. The matter of the will was taken up before the murder trial. As the man accused of her murder, Sykes could not inherit her estate unless found not-guilty, however, there was no law saying he could not be the will's executor. Sykes's attorneys argued that prohibiting him from being executor and denying him the fees thereof, amounted to punishment before he was found guilty. To further complicate matters, an attorney named Thomas Rozier, on behalf of the 'absent heirs' of Kate Townsend, argued against Sykes becoming executor.

The judge ruled that Rozier could not represent 'absent heirs' until he proved that some actually existed, and that Sykes could become executor of the will. Sykes immediately initiated a fraudulent transaction to sell 40 Basin Street to a third-party for $30,000, who would then rent the house to Mollie Johnson, who would keep the brothel in business. The $30,000 went immediately to Sykes's attorneys to pay for the will litigation and the upcoming murder trial.

At his murder trial, Sykes first pleaded not guilty, but after Mollie testified to the threats Kate had made on his life, his attorneys convinced him to change his plea to self-defense. Sykes testified, admitting that he killed Kate, explaining what he believed happened, but was still unable to recall the details.

The trial lasted only four days and the jury found him not guilty.

Verdict: Not guilty.

Aftermath:

When the Judge, W.T. Huston, learned of Sykes's sale of the house at 40 Basin, he declared it illegal and removed Sykes as executor. He also ordered "all women of lewd life" to vacate the property. Since Sykes was found not guilty, he was eligible to inherit from the estate; however, after a lengthy battle all that remained was slightly more than $43,000. Since Sykes and Kate were not legally married, he was subject to Louisiana's concubinage law which limited the amount he could inherit to $340. The rest went to attorneys.

Kate Townsend had left instructions with Mollie concerning her wake and funeral. There was to be champagne, wine, and refreshments and everyone was to have a good time. No men were allowed to attend the wake and absolutely no men were to view the body. Mollie allowed only forty women to do this, though many more had come to the wake. A hearse took her body to Metairie Cemetery, followed by a procession of twenty carriages, carrying only women.

MULTIPLE MURDERS

Horror!

For several days, there had been no activity on the Deering farm, just south of Philadelphia, so on April 11, 1866, their neighbor, Mr. Ware, went over to see what was wrong. He found the house empty, but in the barn, he saw a human foot protruding from the hay. Ware ran for help, and together they uncovered the brutally mutilated bodies of Christopher Deering, his wife Julia, four of their children – ranging in age from eight years to fourteen months – and Elizabeth Dolan, a visiting cousin. Outside the barn, they found the body of Cornelius Cary, a seventeen-year-old hired hand, similarly mutilated.

The following day, the headline in the *Philadelphia Inquirer* bore the single word: "Horror!"

Antoine Probst
Frank Leslie's Illustrated Newspaper,
May 5, 1866

Date:	April 7, 1866
Location:	Philadelphia, Pennsylvania
Victims:	Six members of the Deering family, Elizabeth Dolan and Cornelius Cary
Cause of Death:	Blows from an axe, blows from a hammer
Accused:	Antoine Probst

Synopsis:
Only two members of the Deering household had been spared from the carnage. Ten-year-old Willie had been away visiting his grandparents that day, and Antoine Probst, a young German immigrant who worked as a hired hand and lived with the Deerings, was nowhere to be found. Probst quickly became the prime suspect, and the mayor of Philadelphia offered a one-thousand-dollar reward for his capture.

At age 20, Antoine Probst came to America from his home in Baden, Germany, in 1863. Within two hours of his arrival in New York, he enlisted in the Union Army, enticed by a $300 bounty offered to recruits. He rode with the Twelfth Pennsylvania Cavalry for six or eight weeks before deserting. Returning to New York, Probst tried the same trick again, enlisting in the Forty-first New York Infantry Regiment for the bounty. Nine months later, he deserted in Washington, traveled to Philadelphia, and enlisted again, this time in the Fifth Cavalry. In May 1865, he was honorably discharged. Probst never saw any action during his time in the military, but during one stint, he accidentally shot off his own thumb.

Though the bounty racket had proven successful, Probst squandered his money on alcohol and women and remained perpetually poor. Looking for work, he stopped at the Deerings' farm on the south end of Philadelphia. Mrs. Deering hired Probst on the spot, knowing that her husband needed a farmhand. They paid him fifteen dollars a month and provided room and board.

But Probst was not cut out for farm work. One rainy day, about three weeks later, Mr. Deering sent him out to work despite the weather. Not wanting to work in the field in the rain, Probst resigned, took his pay, and left the farm. He did some odd jobs in Philadelphia, and then, either sick or feigning sickness, he went to the Philadelphia Almshouse and stayed there for several months.

In February 1866, Probst returned to the Deering farm and asked for his job back. Mr. Deering took pity on the poor German boy and rehired him for ten dollars a month. This time, though, Probst had more on his mind than farm work. During his first stay at the farm, he had seen Deering counting money, and he believed that the Deerings kept large sums of cash in the house. He planned to steal the money at the earliest opportunity, and he did not rule out the possibility of killing Christopher Deering or other members of the family to get it.

Probst saw his opportunity on Saturday, April 7, 1866. Deering had left early in the morning to go into the city and pick up his cousin Elizabeth Dolan. Probst carried a large axe – the one they used on tree roots – as he went into the fields with the other hired hand, Cornelius Cary. It started raining, and they took refuge under a large tree. As Cary sat under the tree talking about the job, Probst stood behind him and, lifting the axe, swung it across the left side of Cary's head. After several more blows, Probst cut his throat, severing his head.

He returned to the barn and set the large axe in the corner next to a small axe and a hammer. He then enticed the Deering family into the barn, one at a time. He told eight-year-old John that he needed his help, and after John entered the barn, Probst hit him on the head with the small axe. As with Cary, he applied several more blows to the head and then chopped at the throat. Then he went to the house and told Julia he needed help with a colt in the barn. After she entered the barn, Probst gave her the same treatment he had given her son. He told six-year-old Thomas that his mother needed his help in the barn and dispatched Thomas. He told four-year-old Annie the same story, and while carrying fourteen-month-old Emma, he led Annie into the barn. Annie saw the axe coming and raised her hand for protection. Probst severed her fingers before landing an axe blow to her head. Finally, he killed the baby as well.

Around half-past one, Christopher Deering returned with his cousin, twenty-five-year-old Elizabeth Dolan. She took her clothes and went into the house, and Deering went into the barn, followed by Probst. Probst killed Deering with the small axe, then went into the house to find Dolan. She asked him where everyone was, and he told her in the barn. He followed her into the barn, killed her with the hammer, and chopped her throat with the small axe. He arranged the bodies in straight rows and covered them with hay.

Then Probst went looking for the money. He found fifteen dollars in Christopher's wallet, though three dollars were counterfeit. He searched the house but did not find the money he believed was there. He took what he could from Mrs. Deering's pocketbook and stole coins from the children's money boxes. The cash he found totaled less than twenty dollars.

Police in Philadelphia were on the lookout for Probst, a "Dutchman" with a missing thumb. Officer James Dorsey was determined to find the killer, questioning so many Dutchmen that his actions became a joke among his fellow officers. On the night of April 23, he was standing on the corner of Twenty-third and Market with two of his comrades when they saw a man, face covered by a slouch hat, leaving a saloon.

"There goes an Irishman, Dorsey," said one of the officers. "Follow him up and arrest him. It may be Probst in disguise. "

They all laughed, but Dorsey followed him anyway. He pulled the hat off the man's head and looked him in the face.

"You're a Dutchman!" said Dorsey.

"No, me Frenchman!" the man replied.

But when Dorsey saw that the man was missing a thumb, he knew he had captured Antoine Probst.

The mayor of Philadelphia questioned Probst through a German interpreter. He admitted to killing Cornelius Cary but claimed that his accomplice, a Mr. Gaunter, had murdered all the rest. After the questioning, as the officers were taking Probst from the Ninth Ward stationhouse to Moyamensing Prison, they were attacked by an unruly mob. The crowd, which included relatives of the murdered family, tried to seize the prisoner, and it was all the officers could do to prevent Probst from being torn to pieces.

Trial: April 19, 1866

Antoine Probst was charged with eight counts of first-degree murder. On the recommendation of his court-appointed attorneys, he pled not guilty to all charges. The defense tried to emphasize the circumstantial nature of the evidence against Probst and stressed the unlikeliness that one man could have committed all the murders. But their argument had little impact on the jury, who returned after only twenty minutes of deliberation with a guilty verdict on all counts.

Verdict: Guilty, first-degree murder

Aftermath:

Following his conviction and death sentence, at the urging of his attorneys and his spiritual advisor, The Reverend P.A.M. Grundtner, Probst agreed to confess to all the murders. Probst, a Roman Catholic, fingered his rosary beads as he dictated, in broken English, the details of all eight murders. He had become obsessed with the money he believed was in the Deering house, and robbery was the sole motive for the murders.

On June 8, 1866, Antoine Probst was hanged in the yard of the county prison. Witnesses, who attended with the permission of the sheriff, included hundreds of distinguished gentlemen from throughout the United States. The execution went smoothly; Probst died quickly without suffering. His last words were, "God will forgive me."

Probst's body was given to Dr. B. Howard Rand. With five assistants, he performed a number of scientific experiments on the corpse. The right eye was removed and carefully examined to test the theory prevalent at the time that the last image seen by a dead person remains impressed on the retina, as with film in a camera. In another experiment, electrodes were attached to the mouth and temple, and a strong electric current was applied, causing the jaw to convulse and the chest to heave. After the experiments, the body was taken to the Jefferson Medical College for a postmortem examination. They removed and preserved Probst's skeleton, and for many years, it was displayed in the college museum.

Andrew Hellman, Alias Adam Horn

Andrew Hellman never enjoyed married life and after 18 unhappy years he ended the marriage by chopping his wife with an axe. After escaping punishment in Ohio, he changed his name, moved to Maryland, and did it all again.

Andrew Hellman Murdering His Wife
Serious Almanac, 1845.

Date:	September 26, 1839; March 16, 1843
Location:	Logan County, Ohio; Reisterstown, Maryland
Victims:	Mary Abel Hellman; Matilda Horn
Cause of Death:	Blows from an axe
Accused:	Andrew Hellman; Adam Horn

Synopsis:

Andrew Hellman was 25 when he traveled from Germany to Baltimore in 1817. He had been apprenticed to a tailor but decided to see the world when his apprenticeship ended. After a few years of wandering around Europe, he set sail for America.

In 1820, he was boarding at the farmhouse of George M. Abel in Loudoun County, Virginia, and working on neighboring farms. Hellman professed a strong dislike of women and was quite outspoken in his belief that their only role in the world was as servants to men. Despite this, he engaged the affections of George Abel's 20-year-old daughter, Mary.

The Baltimore Sun described her as "a blithe, buxom and lighthearted country girl with rosy cheek and sparkling eye, totally unacquainted with the deceitfulness of the world."

Mary and Andrew were married in December 1821. After just a few months of marriage, Hellman gradually lost affection for his new wife. They were still living with her parents, so he kept his fiendish disposition reined and treated Mary with indifference. When their first child, Louisa, was born the following year, he viewed the birth as a severe misfortune.

In 1823, despite his apparent dislike of his wife, he became irrationally jealous, and when Mary became pregnant again, he accused her of infidelity. Henry Hellman was born that September, and Andrew disowned him and denounced Mary as a harlot.

The following spring, they moved out of Mary's father's home and rented a small place nearby. In 1827, their third child, John, was born, and Andrew declared that if she ever had another child, he would kill her. During this period, he would leave home for months and then return home with promises of reformation. When he was home, his wife and children constantly feared his disposition.

Mary's father, wanting to give his children a start in the world, sold a portion of his farm and bought pieces of land in Ohio for Mary and her two brothers. In 1831, Andrew, Mary, and their children moved to Carroll County, Ohio. They lived there for five years, during which Andrew became a prosperous farmer owning two fine farms. In 1836, he sold the farms and moved the family to Logan County, Ohio, where Mary's brother lived.

Andrew became more morose, but his family had become used to his dark moods and expected nothing better. In 1839, all three of the children were suddenly taken sick, and in 48 hours, Louisa, now 17, and John, 12, were dead. Mary believed that Andrew had poisoned them, but there was no way to prove Andrew did it, and he vigorously denied it.

On September 26, Mary's brother George was unwell, and she gladly sent Henry to assist in his uncle's farm work. Two days later, George's wife Rachel went to see her sister-in-law, and when she entered the door, she saw Andrew lying in bed in the front room, with his head, face, and clothing covered with blood. He told her that two nights earlier, two robbers had entered the house and beat him unconscious with a club. When he came to, he was lying on the bed, suffering too much to move. Rachel asked how Mary was; Andrew said he didn't know and told her to look in the back room. There, she found Mary's mangled corpse lying in a pool of blood with blood spattered all over the walls and ceiling.

A coroner's jury was hastily assembled in the house, and John Abel accused his brother-in-law of the murder. The jury, seeing Hellman lying prostrate on the bed, asked John what evidence he had. He said he had none but suggested that a physician examine Hellman's wounds. The examination was conducted, and the result was that no scratches, cuts, or bruises could be found anywhere on Hellman's body.

Mary's body, however, had six distinct cuts on the head, her hands and arms were dreadfully bruised, two of her fingers broken from warding off blows, and a large gash laid open the flesh of her right thigh as if inflicted by an axe; three separate gashes passed nearly through the neck in an attempt to sever the head.

Andrew had poured some of Mary's blood over his head to make his story more believable. This was evidence enough to charge him with murder.

Andrew was held in jail in Belfont, Ohio, as he awaited trial. He was held there for fourteen months, and during cold weather, he was confined to his cell only at night; during the day, he was allowed to occupy an upper room. One cold evening in November 1840, he was left upstairs longer than usual, and finding no fastenings on the door, he simply walked out. Though a reward of $300 was offered for Hellman's capture, all attempts to track him down in Ohio failed.

In April 1843, in Reisterstown, Baltimore County, Maryland, Catherine Hinkle was searching for her 17-year-old sister, Matilda Horn, wife of Adam Horn, aged 51. Catherine had not believed the story Horn had told her, that Matilda had left the house late one night two weeks earlier wearing just her night dress. It had snowed heavily that night, and she would not have gotten far if she had gone out. A search party was looking for any trace of her.

A quarter of a mile from the Horns' house, they found a coffee sack under two feet of ground in a ditch. Inside it was the torso of a young woman. Assuming it was the body of her sister, Catherine, the party went back to search around the house. Inside a building attached to the house, they found another coffee bag. This one contained the arms and legs severed from the trunk. Though the head was not found, Catherine could identify her sister's foot. They notified the police, who went to arrest Adam Horn for the murder of his wife, but Horn was nowhere to be found.

When the police circulated Horn's description – bald, German, about 50, speaks broken English – authorities in Ohio noted the similarity to that of Andrew Hellman, even down to details such as the third finger of the right hand was crooked. Horn was arrested in Philadelphia and extradited to Maryland. Sheriff Slicer of Logan County, Ohio, arrived in Baltimore soon after to get a look at the prisoner. When Slicer went to the jail, Hellman, alias Horn, recognized him immediately and greeted the sheriff as an old friend.

Sheriff Slicer was carrying a requisition from the Governor of Ohio to the Governor of Maryland asking for the delivery of the prisoner to Ohio to stand trial for the murder of his wife. Governor Thomas of Maryland denied the request, saying he must first stand trial in Maryland. If he escaped conviction, Maryland would hand him over to Ohio.

Trial: November 21, 1843

Adam Horn's trial generated excitement in Baltimore; a crowd assembled outside the courtroom twenty minutes before the trial began. The court had difficulty finding an impartial jury. It took two days and seventy-six potential jurors to find an acceptable jury of twelve.

Because of the mutilated condition of Matilda Horn's body, the cause of death was uncertain. To cover all possibilities, Horn was charged with nine counts of murder: by hatchet, knife, wooden club, a stone, his fist, dashed her against the ground, strangled with a cord, choked with his hands, and shot through the head.

The evidence against Horn was circumstantial. The only eyewitness, a man named Storic, who allegedly saw Horn dismember the body, committed suicide ten days before the trial. However, the circumstantial evidence was enough for the jury, and when they returned a guilty verdict, the crowd erupted with applause.

Verdict: Guilty of first-degree murder

Aftermath:

Ohio never got the opportunity to try Hellman/Horn. In November 1843, he was found guilty of the first-degree murder of Matilda Horn, and the following January, his hanging in the yard of the Baltimore Jail was witnessed by an estimated 10,000 spectators.

The New Hampshire Horror

After his wife left him in November 1883, Thomas Samon began a weekend of drunken debauchery in Laconia, New Hampshire, with the wife of his landlord. But when the beer ran out on Saturday morning, events turned unexpectedly violent, ending in a horrible triple murder.

The New Hampshire Horror
National Police Gazette, Dec. 15, 1883.

Date:	November 25, 1883
Location:	Laconia, New Hampshire
Victim:	Jane Ford, James Ruddy, Frank Ruddy
Cause of Death:	Beating, Blows from an ax
Accused:	Thomas Samon

Synopsis:

Stephen Andrews of Laconia, New Hampshire, suffering from insomnia, was still awake in the wee hours of Sunday, November 25, 1883. At 4.00 am, he heard screams coming from James and Rosa Ruddy's house across the street. He roused his son, and they hurried over and found Mrs. Ruddy lying on the ground beneath the front window, bleeding profusely. Shards of glass on the ground indicated that she had broken through the closed window.

In agony, Mrs. Ruddy said, "I am all cut to pieces; take me somewhere."

Her body truly was cut to pieces, but the men could see that it was not the broken glass that caused the wounds. It looked as if she had been chopped with an axe. Carefully, they carried her to the house of Mrs. Charles Filgate, who lived next door.

Soon after, they saw smoke rising from the Ruddy house. The *New York Tribune* reported that Andrews telephoned the police and the fire departments, then he and the neighbors went inside to try to douse the flames. They quickly extinguished the fire, but the men were sickened by what they saw. Mr. Ruddy and his 13-month-old son, Frank, lay with their bodies mutilated and charred under a partially burned feather bed. In the adjoining room, under a straw bed, were the charred remains of a woman, her legs nearly severed at the knees. They found a carpenter's hand axe covered with blood in a wood box in the kitchen.

The dead woman was not immediately recognized, but soon, John C. Ford, who lived nearby, came by to see what was happening and recognized her as his wife, Jane. Ford had a bad reputation and had recently been arrested for shooting at boys in the street. His wife had paid a $50 bond to the town to guarantee his good behavior. Thinking that Ford might be connected with this case, the officers took him into custody.

Ford was Jane's third husband. As a girl of seventeen in England, she married Clarence Chauncey, twice her age, who brought her to America and died soon after. She then married William Scales, a successful New York saloon-keeper. The couple did a considerable amount of traveling and lived in Cuba for a while. They moved to Laconia, New Hampshire, and William Scales died there. Jane remained in New Hampshire, eventually marrying Laconia carpenter John Ford. Fifty-nine-year-old Jane had a generally good reputation in Laconia – she belonged to the Ladies' Relief Corps and taught Sunday school at the Unitarian church – but she had lately been backsliding into drunkenness and promiscuity.

At the Filgate house, it looked as though Mrs. Ruddy was dying but, under doctors' care, she soon regained consciousness. By now, Sheriff D.B. Story had arrived with his deputies, the Laconia Selectmen, and other government officials. Realizing the importance of Mrs. Ruddy's testimony, they began questioning her as soon as she was conscious.

She told them that Thomas Samon had come to the house at about 1:00 p.m. the previous day, carrying a trunk in a wheelbarrow. He would not say what was in it but asked if he could leave it in their yard. Mrs. Ruddy agreed to let him leave it there until her husband came home. Samon left, saying that he would return for the trunk later. Samon and Mr. Ruddy both returned at about 5:00 p.m., and Samon asked if he could stay the night with them. Samon was their friend, and the Ruddys knew he had recently separated from his wife, so they had no objection. Ruddy helped Samon carry the trunk into the house. Samon said he would explain later what was inside.

Samon had trouble sleeping that night, and the Ruddys heard him walking around the house. They got up and got dressed, then went to find out what the matter was. Samon was too nervous to sleep; he thought he heard people trying to get into the house. Mrs. Ruddy went back to bed, leaving her husband quietly talking with him. Sometime later, she was awakened by a heavy thud from the kitchen. She went there and found her husband dead, in a chair with his head hanging over the back. Before she could touch him, Samon rushed her and struck her with an axe, nearly cutting off her hand. He hit her again, and she fell to the floor. The baby started crying, and Samon went to him. Mrs. Ruddy could hear the blow that struck the child. Samon returned with the boy's body and laid it beside Mr. Ruddy, then he took a feather bed and put it over the two bodies. Mrs. Ruddy pretended to be dead while Samon poured kerosene over the bed and over her. When he set the feather bed on fire, she sprang up screaming, ran into the front room, and jumped through the window, breaking the large pane of glass, to make her escape.

John Ford said he had not seen his wife since the preceding Friday evening. She had been in the company of Thomas Samon for two or three nights. The police believed his story and set him free. A hastily convened coroner's jury indicted Samon for three murders, and the search for him began. He had left town shortly after setting the fire, and it was believed he was heading for Plymouth, New Hampshire, where his wife worked.

Thomas Samon was about fifty years old at the time of the murders. He had come to America from Dublin when he was quite young, along with his brother, who opened a successful wholesale liquor dealership in Boston. Thomas was quiet and industrious, becoming a proficient hotel cook, well-known among the leading hotels in New Hampshire. In 1882, he married Johanna Welch, and they set up housekeeping in the Laconia tenement owned by the Fords, where the first murder took place. But Samon suffered from alcoholism and depression and had attempted suicide, at least once, by jumping off the South Boston bridge. At the time of the murders, Samon and his wife were living apart.

The Selectmen of Laconia offered a $500 reward for Samon's capture and telegraphed all of the nearby towns. At about 4:00 p.m., word arrived from Plymouth that Samon had been arrested there and would be taken back to Laconia on Monday.

Samon denied any knowledge of the crime. Believing that the fire had destroyed the evidence, he said that he intended to move his furniture to Plymouth and had moved his trunk full of household goods to the Ruddys' on Saturday in preparation. He returned to the Fords and slept until 5.00am, when he rose and started for Plymouth on foot, having no money for the train. It was not until Thursday, November 28, Thanksgiving Day, that Samon learned that the Ruddy house had not burned to the ground. Realizing that his story would not hold, Samon agreed to confess.

As John Ford had said, Thomas Samon and Jane had been sleeping together for several nights before the murders. They had also been drinking heavily. They drank whiskey and beer all night Friday, and on Saturday morning, Mrs. Ford asked if there was any more lager. When Samon said no, an argument ensued and quickly turned violent. Samon flung her to the floor and pressed down on her chest with his foot. When he lifted it, he found that Mrs. Ford was dead. In desperation, and considerably less than sober, he decided to pack her body into a trunk, chopping her legs at the knees to make her fit. He put the trunk in a wheelbarrow and wheeled it away to dispose of the body.

Samon had no idea what to do with the body; he ended up at the home of his friends, the Ruddys, and thought if he could sleep there, he would take it away in the morning and bury it somewhere else. From this point, Samon's story matched Mrs. Ruddy's. He brought the trunk into the house but did not tell them what was inside. That night, Samon could not sleep, believing the house was surrounded and he would be captured. Around three in the morning, the idea struck him that if he killed the Ruddys and burned down their house, all evidence of his crimes would be gone.

"The very moment that the thought came to me, I struck Ruddy," Samon told the police.

Arraignment: March 31, 1884

The courtroom in Laconia was packed when Thomas Samon was arraigned for murder, and at least 500 people stood outside. Samon's court-appointed attorneys complained to the judge that it was difficult to proceed when their client was determined to plead guilty to first-degree murder. Before the court would accept the plea, Samon was examined by Dr. J.P. Bancroft of Concord and Dr. George F. Jelly of Cambridge, Massachusetts, to determine his sanity. After examining Samon's current condition, his past, and his family lineage, the doctors concluded that there was no proof that he was insane presently or at any time in the past. His suicide attempts, they said, naturally followed from the debaucheries in which he indulged.

The court accepted Samon's guilty plea, and without a trial, he was sentenced to be hanged on April 17, 1885. When the sentence was read, Samon's wife threw her arms around him and started sobbing.

"It is all right," he said. "My sentence is just, I will go to the gallows like a man."

Verdict: Guilty of first-degree murder

Aftermath:

Thomas Samon had little sleep the night before the hanging; he was up past midnight drinking coffee and smoking cigars. He ate no breakfast that morning, and after receiving his last rights from Fathers Barry and Henry, he was led to the gallows. True to his word, Thomas Samon maintained his composure to the last and met his fate without flinching.

Arson To Hide a Worse Crime

After committing a violent robbery resulting in four deaths, Lee Heflin and George Dye thought they could escape justice by burning down the house. When the details of their atrocities became public, the legal justice system was the least of their problems.

Arson to Hide a Worse Crime
National Police Gazette, Dec. 5, 1891.

Date:	November 10, 1891
Location:	Calverton, Virginia
Victim:	Mrs. J.W. Kines, Lizzie Kines, Annie Kines, Gilbert Kines
Cause of Death:	Blows to the Head
Accused:	Lee Heflin, George Dye

Synopsis:
Lee Heflin ran to Thomas Robinson's farm near Calverton, Virginia, on November 10, 1891, to raise an alarm that a house on a neighboring farm was on fire. Heflin led Robinson and his son George to the burning house. When they arrived, other neighbors gathered, and the house was engulfed in flames.

The house belonged to Mrs. J.W. Kines, a widow who lived there with three of her children. It appeared that all four were still inside. The Robinsons went in and were able to pull out three bodies. Lizzie Kines, 8, lay near the door and was only slightly burned. Annie Kines, 10, was so badly burned as to be unrecognizable. Mrs. Kines's body was severely charred but not as badly as her daughter's. There was no trace of 4-year-old Gilbert.

Mrs. Kines had been having financial difficulties since her husband died and had told neighbors she did not know how she would take care of the children alone. But the coroner quickly ruled out murder-suicide; the victims had been killed before the fire started. Lizzie had deep wounds to her skull and between her eyes. Her jaw was broken as well. Mrs. Kines's skull had been crushed.

Lee Heflin had been shucking corn at the McMillan farm, about 40 yards from the burning house. When asked why he ran to Robinson's house a mile and a half away instead of trying to rescue those in the house, He responded, "I am a stranger here. I never saw a house on fire before and was afraid."

Heflin roomed with George Dye on the McMillan farm. Neither man could give a satisfactory account of their actions on the night of the murder, and they gave contradictory statements. However, the coroner's jury ruled that Mrs. Kines and her daughters were killed by a person or persons unknown, and the motive was believed to be robbery. The Governor offered a reward of $700 for the "detention, arrest, and conviction" of the murderer or murderers.

Heflin and Dye were arrested on suspicion in Warrenton and then taken to Alexandria for their own protection. A vigilance committee in Warrenton was formed to lynch the men. On the way to Alexandria, Heflin confessed to several witnesses that he committed the murders to secure some money. He also exonerated Dye.

Heflin said he had gone to the house at about 8:00 the night before the fire. He knocked on the door, and when Mrs. Kines answered, he asked her for some money. She told him she had none. He went into the house, picked up a heavy piece of firewood, and felled Mrs. Kines with one blow. He turned and saw Gilbert, then killed him with a blow to the back of the neck. Then he killed the other two children and secured what money he could find. He took between $25 and $75 and buried it. The next morning, he returned to the house, saturated the place with coal oil, and set it on fire. He said he needed the money because he was going to elope with the wife and daughter of a farmer who lived nearby. The police went to look for the money and planned to release Dye.

Trial: Lee Heflin, December 28, 1891

Joseph Dye was still in custody when Heflin went to trial in Warrenton that December. He had changed his story and now said that Dye had done the killing and he had done the burning. On December 29, Heflin was found guilty of first-degree murder. He was rushed from the courtroom and barely escaped an excited mob that had gathered there.

Verdict: Guilty of first-degree murder

Trial: Joseph Dye, January 7, 1892

In January, Heflin testified against Dye at his trial. Dye was found guilty as well, and both men were sentenced to be hanged on March 18.

Verdict: Guilty of first-degree murder

Aftermath:

The day before the hanging was to take place, the Governor granted them a 60-day stay of execution. Dye was appealing for a new trial, and Heflin would be a witness. Fearing violence, the authorities placed the men in a vehicle and started for the safety of Alexandria. A party of sixty men, worried that Dye and Heflin would escape justice on a technicality, overtook the vehicle near Gainesville. They overpowered the guard and then hanged the murderers from a tree. As they swung, the mob riddled their bodies with bullets.

The Northwood Murderer

When a senseless murder occurred with no apparent suspects, a community's worst fear was that some transient had drifted into town, done his dirty work, and left without a trace. The roads of rural America in the nineteenth century were filled with tramps; some were honest men looking for work in tough economic times, and others were aimless ne'er-do-wells, running from or heading toward trouble. Like today's serial killers, when these men turned to murder, they were likely to get away without capture and were prone to kill again. But occasionally, a wandering killer was caught, and his bloody itinerary was made public. Such was the case of Franklin B. Evans, known as the Northwood Murderer.

Franklin B. Evans

Dates:	October 30, 1850; October 25, 1872
Locations:	Derry, New Hampshire; Northwood, New Hampshire
Confessed Victims:	Georgianna Lovering, and the 5-yr-old daughter of Stephen Mills
Cause of Death:	Strangulation
Accused:	Franklin B. Evans

Synopsis:

On October 30, 1850, in the town of Derry, New Hampshire, the five-year-old daughter of Stephen Mills, one of a set of twins, was kidnapped from her home. The parents had left them alone, and someone had climbed through a window into the house and taken the girl. Mills offered what he could afford, a $100 reward for her return. The police had suspects but no evidence, and no trace of the missing girl was ever found.

Twelve years later, in the town of Strong, Maine, near Augusta, nine-year-old Lura Ville Libby walked to church alone on the morning of Sunday, September 14, 1862. She never returned. A search began at 4:00 p.m. and the next day her body was found buried under the turf in the woods about half a mile from her home. Her dress had been removed, and she had been raped; her head was cut and bruised, and her throat slashed, nearly severing the head.

The murder, of course, caused intense excitement in the town of Strong, and a citizen's committee promptly offered a $1,000 reward for the capture of the killer. Suspicion immediately fell on the Libbys' farmhand, Lawrence Doyle, who had behaved strangely that morning and had explicitly asked Mr. Libby if he would be accompanying Lura to church. At the coroner's inquest, a witness reported that Doyle had told him about a murder in Canada where the body was buried in the same way as Lura's. For these and other minor suspicions, Lawrence Doyle was held for trial.

The evidence presented at the trial was highly circumstantial, and the jury was deadlocked: seven for conviction and five for acquittal. At his second trial, Doyle was convicted and sentenced to hang.

Doyle's attorney, E.F. Pillsbury, was thoroughly convinced of his client's innocence and helped him persuade the Governor and Executive Council to commute his sentence to life in prison. When Doyle died in prison two years later, Pillsbury continued the fight to exonerate him and find the real killer.

In 1865, in the town of Roxbury, Massachusetts (which became part of Boston three years later), two children, John and Isabella Joyce, were found dead in Bussey's Woods. John, aged 12, and Isabella, aged 14, were staying with their grandmother in Boston. On Monday, June 12, they told her they would take a horse car to nearby May's Woods to make wreaths. They were not seen again until their bodies were found the following Sunday. They apparently had missed their stop and taken the car to the end of the line.

The murder scene was horrific. Isabella had been raped, and the condition of her clothing indicated that she had put up a fight before succumbing. She was stabbed twenty-seven times in the abdomen, possibly to hide the fact that she had been raped. John, frozen with fear over what was happening to his sister, did not run until it was too late. He was also stabbed to death.

There were no witnesses, of course, but one woman remembered seeing a frightening stranger with long, disheveled black hair near Bussey's woods that day. The first suspect in this murder was Thomas Ainsley, a painter who had some connection to the Joyce family, but Ainsley had an alibi and was soon released. Early in July, several tips pointed to a man named John Stewart, who had been a bounty jumper during the Civil War. He would join an army unit for the bounty they were paying, then desert soon after. He had done this in nine different places. But it turned out that John Stewart also had an alibi for June 12.

It wasn't until the following March that the police had another viable suspect. A tramp named Charles Aaron Dodge, alias 'Scratch Gravel', was being held in Fitchburg for housebreaking. He gave the impression of being something more than a burglar.

"I don't care a damn about being arrested for stealing that silver," Scratch Gravel told police, "but if you knew something I had done, it would be a feather in your cap. This little thing of three months don't amount to anything."

The police planted a detective in the Fitchburg jail who overheard enough loose talk from Scratch Gravel to charge him with the murder of the Joyce children. But he could prove that he was not even in Massachusetts that day.

In December 1866, the skeleton of a man was found in Needham Woods, not far from Boston, and a quantity of hair was found nearby that resembled the hair of the man seen in Bussey's woods the day of the murder. From this scant clue, the skeleton was postulated to be the man who killed the Joyce children. He had taken to the woods to elude capture and died there. While not everyone was satisfied with this conclusion, the case was closed.

There was nothing to connect these three heinous New England crimes until October 25, 1872, when 13-year-old Georgianna Lovering disappeared from her home in Northwood, New Hampshire. This time, there was little question of who was responsible – her 64-year-old great-uncle, Franklin Evans, who had previously made "improper advances" to Georgianna.

Evans had gray hair, wore a long gray beard, and had dark, piercing eyes, giving him a perpetually sinister expression. He had traveled extensively through New England and eastern Canada, sometimes as an Adventist preacher, sometimes as a self-styled 'botanic physician'. He married three times, had a son in Derry, New Hampshire, and a daughter in Lawrence, Massachusetts. Since the previous June, he had been living with his sister and her husband, Sylvester Day. Their granddaughter Georgianna was also staying with them while her widowed mother was away.

Evans set snares in the woods to catch partridges and showed them to Georgianna. On the day of her disappearance, Evans asked Georgianna to check his traps as he had to go to work. Georgianna went into the woods to check the traps and never came out. Evans did not go to work and was seen entering the woods that morning.

When Georgianna had not returned by 10:00 p.m., the family began searching for her. On the ground in the woods, they found her apron and a broken comb recognized as hers. News of the disappearance traveled fast, and by the end of the day, more than 100 people were in the woods searching for Georgianna Lovering.

Evans was immediately suspected of abducting his grandniece, and two days later, a warrant was issued for his arrest. At first, he denied any connection to the disappearance, but after prolonged questioning by Sheriff Henry A. Drew, he said she was alive and that he would tell where she was if the sheriff promised that he would not be harmed. Evans said he had agreed to help a man named Aaron Webster of Kingston kidnap Georgianna. The following day, Sheriff Drew took Evans to Kingston to look for Webster, but they found no trace of him. Evans said that maybe Webster had been from Kensington, so they traveled there. When the Kensington search also failed to pan out, Evans said perhaps it was Candia, but Sheriff Drew had lost all confidence in Evans and took him back to his own home in Stafford, New Hampshire.

Drew was determined to get to the truth, and late that night, in private conversation with his prisoner, he said, "In the hearing of no persons but us two and the Great Being above, I ask you this question: Is the body of the girl cold in death?"

After hesitating for several seconds, Evans turned pale and said, "It is, Mr. Drew. I have done wrong."

Believing his deal with the sheriff would protect him from prosecution, Evans agreed to take Drew to the body, and although it was nearly midnight, they left for the woods. Evans led Drew through the woods, then through a swamp, till they came to a fallen tree, and Evans showed him the body, hidden under a pile of leaves. By the light of his lantern, Sheriff Drew was shocked to see the mutilated body of Georgianna Lovering. The body was later examined by a doctor who found finger marks on her neck where she was strangled. But the most horrible discovery was that the killer had cut away her sexual organs as well as a portion of her bladder.

Trial: February 4, 1873

The town of Exeter, New Hampshire, where the trial was held, was inundated with spectators. Hotels were filled and many more people tried to get into the courtroom than the building could hold. But if they were expecting a long dramatic trial, they were sadly disappointed; the session lasted only two days.

The family testified to the circumstances of Georgianna's disappearance, several witnesses testified to seeing Evans enter the woods that morning, the sheriff told of Evans leading him to the body, and the examining doctor spoke of the body's condition. The only defense possible was insanity, and Evans's attorneys provided little beyond the crime itself to indicate that Evans was insane. His jailers testified that Evans was subject to fits of insanity, including attempted suicide, but it did not help his cause. The jury returned a verdict of guilty after only forty-five minutes of deliberation.

Verdict: Guilty of first-degree murder

Aftermath:

Evans was sentenced to hang on the third Tuesday of February 1874. In the year between his sentencing and his execution, he was visited by several lawmen and reporters attempting to connect Evans with other New England murders. He was known to have been in Derry at the time the Mills girl was kidnapped, and reportedly had been a suspect. Through his connection to the Adventists, they determined that Evans had been in Boston when the Joyce murders took place. E.F. Pillsbury, attorney to Lawrence Doyle, convicted of the murder of Lura Libby, believed he had evidence that Evans was her killer.

The Boston Daily Evening Traveler sent out a 'commissioner' to get to the bottom of all of these allegations and reported what he learned. Sheriff Drew had pressed Evans on his whereabouts during the years prior to the murder. Evans said he had spent much time in Derry, and when questioned about the Mills kidnapping, Evans admitted that he had taken the child, but her body would never be found. Everyone interviewed in Derry believed that Evans's confession was correct. He had the reputation of a man of low character, and he was quite familiar with the Mills house. It was also alleged that two years later he sold the skeleton of a child to a physician in Lawrence, Massachusetts.

Drew traced Evans's movements to Rhode Island, then to Roxbury, which brought to mind the unsolved Joyce murders. Evans admitted to being in Roxbury and seemed to know more about the case than Drew did. Evans, who had some knowledge of herbal medicine made a meager income by collecting herbs for pharmacists and was constantly walking in the woods around Boston. Drew continued to press Evans for information and Evans nearly confessed:

> E. *"Mr. Drew, I was right there when that boy and girl were killed."*
> D. *"Was he stabbed or not?"*
> E. *"Yes he was several times."*
> D. *"Did the girl make much ado?"*
> E. *"Yes."*
> D. *"More than the boy did?"*
> E. *"Yes."*
> D. *"Why did she?"*
> E. *"She was raped. Don't ask me any more I have now told you."*
> D. *"Was the act committed before she was killed?"*
> E. *"Yes. Mr. Drew, I won't say any more. I have told all about it now."*

The Libby murder was more difficult to pin on Evans. At one point, Evans asked Drew if anyone from Maine was looking for him. Drew asked what part of Maine and Evans said somewhere near Augusta. He said he knew of a little girl there in 1861 or '62 whose throat had been cut.

When he was told that no one from Maine was after him Evans said, "I won't say another word about it then."

Beyond the hints he gave Drew he would not admit to murdering the Libby girl. But attorney E.F. Pillsbury was convinced that Evans did it. He claimed that Evans had preached in Augusta and that the Libbys were Adventists who had entertained Evans in their house. This was verified by a "respectable lady" of Augusta who knew the Libbys. Pillsbury also said that aspects of the crime were not reported by the newspapers that implicated Evans.

Investigating the Joyce murders, the Traveler reporter talked to a young lady in Boston who was visiting friends in Roxbury in June 1865. She was surprised in the woods by the appearance of a wild, haggard-looking man of "horrible aspect." The man asked if there was any evergreen in the woods, and she "screamed at the very top of her voice." The reporter showed her a life-like picture of Evans among a group of pictures. Though it was over seven years prior, "she immediately, unhesitantly identified it as the portrait of the man who had so frightened her."

Franklin B. Evans was hanged at the New Hampshire State Prison in Concord on February 17, 1874. After the execution, his official written confession was released to the press. In it he admitted to the murder of Georgianna Lovering but attempted to mitigate the crime somewhat by describing the members of that household (with the exception of his sister, Deborah) as intemperate and immoral. His sister's husband Sylvester Day was often drunk and abusive, their daughter, Mrs. Lovering was a woman of loose morals, and even 13-year-old Georgianna was sometimes drunk and lewd, talking of her "shameful intercourse" with three young men. Evans's claimed that he, himself, had consensual sex with Georgianna, and she threatened to expose him. She caught him trying to alter a one-dollar bill to look like a ten-dollar bill and threatened to expose this crime as well. He found himself completely in Georgianna's power and decided that he must kill her. He strangled her in the woods and carried her to the swamp.

Evans explained why he cut away the organs. "I did this to gain some knowledge of the human system that might be of use to me as a doctor."

Evans also confessed to murdering the Mills child. He heard moaning from inside the house, climbed in the window and found her sitting on the floor, apparently very sick. He concluded that she would probably not live until morning, and he wanted a body to examine for "surgical purposes" so he took her to the woods and strangled her. He stopped his examination when he found she had a deformed hip and spine and buried the body in the woods under a chestnut stump, in a spot he was never again able to find.

These were the only two murders Evans confessed to. He admitted to theft, counterfeiting and attempted insurance fraud, but said he was entirely innocent of the murders he was accused of in Boston, Maine, and elsewhere.

The confession was dictated to the warden and chaplain of the prison. They wrote it down and read it back to him and he accepted it as correct and signed it. They explained that much of what Evans said was "too gross and indelicate to be written or read" and had to be rephrased.

Whether he committed only the two confessed murders or was the killer of five or more, as many believed, Franklin Evans was, as he was often described, a monster. In death the wandering Northwood Murderer finally found a home; in accordance with his lasts request Evans's body was sold to Dartmouth College for dissection, the proceeds of the sale going to his son. Franklin Evans's skeleton resided for many years in the college's anatomical museum.

Antoine Le Blanc

American opportunity lured thousands of European immigrants to the New World in search of fortune. But opportunity was not enough for French immigrant, Antoine Le Blanc, who became a farm worker in Morristown, New Jersey in 1833. After only two weeks on the job, Le Blanc realized that the fortune he sought would not be gained by hard work; it called for violent action. Le Blanc robbed and murdered his employers, the Sayre family, and their servant girl. He was quickly caught, speedily tried and executed at one of New Jersey's largest public hangings. Hatred for Le Blanc was so strong that after his death his body was desecrated – his skin was made into wallets and other leather products, some of which still exist nearly 200 years later.

Antoine Le Blanc

Date:	May 11, 1833
Location:	Morristown, New Jersey
Victim:	Samuel and Sarah Sayre, and their servant Phoebe
Cause of Death:	Clubbing
Accused:	Antoine Le Blanc

Synopsis:

Antoine Le Blanc came to America from the Moselle region of France leaving behind his sweetheart, Marie. They wanted to marry but Marie's parents rejected Le Blanc as too poor and low-bred. Le Blanc's plan was to attain wealth in the Americas and return to France a more acceptable suitor for Marie.

Within a few days of his arrival on April 26, 1833, Le Blanc was fortunate enough to find work at the farm of Samuel and Sarah Sayre. The Sayres were a prominent and well-to-do couple in their sixties, living with a servant named Phoebe, who may have been a slave. The Sayres had owned a young slave boy who ran off leaving them with no one to help with the spring planting.

The relationship was tense from the start; Le Blanc spoke no English and the Sayres spoke no French. In addition to communication problems, other workers on the farm complained of Le Blanc's cigar smoking and poor personal hygiene. For Le Blanc, resentment grew when the job he thought would be simple gardening turned out to be strenuous farm work and he would be working for room and board only.

On the night of May 11, 1833, Le Blanc drank hard cider at a local tavern, and returned to the farmhouse drunk. He found Samuel Sayre upstairs shaving. Gesturing excitedly, Le Blanc motioned for Sayre to follow him to the stable. There he killed Sayre with a single blow to the back of the head with a spade. He lured Sarah Sayre to the stable the same way. He knocked her down with the spade, but she did not die right away. He hit her again, then as she pleaded for her life, Le Blanc kicked her to death with his boot.

Le Blanc buried the bodies under a pile of manure and went back into the farmhouse. He sneaked into Phoebe's bedroom and murdered her in her sleep. Accounts differ on how he killed Phoebe; he may have clubbed her, split her skull with an axe, or rammed a pitchfork into her chest.

He then ransacked the place, prying open every box and drawer in the house and loading everything of value – coins and silverware down to thimbles and toothbrushes – into pillowcases. He changed his bloody clothing for one of Samuel Sayre's suits, stole a horse, and fled.

The plan was to pawn the valuables in New York and board a ship to Germany before the bodies were discovered. However, in his haste, Le Blanc had not secured the pillowcases and stolen items began to fall out as he rode. The next morning, someone found a piece of the Sayres' monogrammed silver on the road. When bodies were discovered, Sheriff George Ludlow led a posse who followed the trail of booty to the Mosquito Tavern in the Hackensack Meadows. They arrested Le Blanc and took him back to Morristown.

Trial: August 13, 1833

Le Blanc confessed to the murders in jail. His trial in the Morris County Courthouse was brief and the jury deliberated for only twenty minutes before finding Le Blanc guilty of murder. The next day Judge Gabriel Ford sentenced him to be hanged, and then his body would be delivered to Dr. Isaac Canfield, a surgeon, for dissection.

Verdict: Guilty of murder

Aftermath:

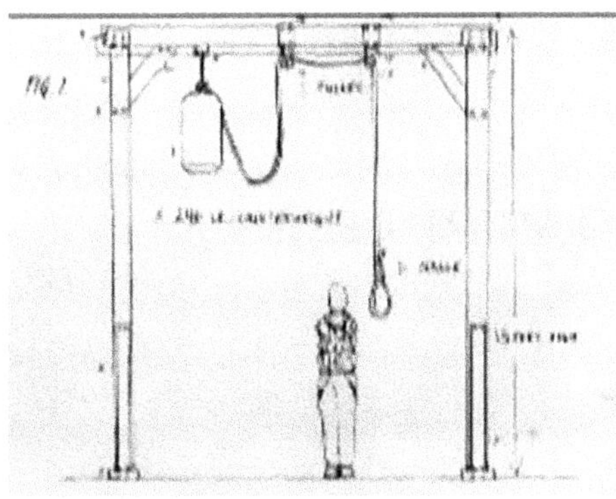

'Modern' Gallows

Twelve thousand people – more than five times the town's population – came to witness the hanging of Antoine Le Blanc on the Morristown village green on September 6. Observers noted that many of the spectators were women. Morristown would be using a 'modern' gallows, designed to jerk the prisoner upward, rather than drop through the floor as with a conventional gallows. When the weight was dropped, Le Blanc's body jerked eight feet into the air. Two minutes later the body stopped twitching and Le Blanc was dead.

It was not uncommon for doctors to dissect the bodies of executed men to advance their knowledge of anatomy. Often the bodies were obtained illegally by grave robbers. Judge Ford's order to deliver the body to Dr. Canfield may have officially sanctioned what would have happened anyway.

What was unusual in Le Blanc's case were the experiments then done on his body. Princeton professor, Joseph Henry - one of America's foremost scientists - used an electric battery to test a theory linking electrical current to muscle contraction. Reportedly, Henry was able to cause LeBlanc's limbs to tense, to make his eyes roll in their sockets, and to bring a slight grin to his lips.

When the professor was finished with his experiments, Le Blanc's ears were cut off and given away as souvenirs, and a plaster death mask was made of his face. They peeled the skin off his body and sent it to the Atno Tannery where it was tanned and made into wallets, purses, lampshades, and book jackets – each one dated and signed by Sheriff Ludlow. One of these wallets currently belongs to the New Jersey Historical Society. Allegedly, others are held in private collections.

CONNECTED MURDERS

With a Butcher's Keen Blade

Thomas Pallister made the mistake of picking a fight with some New York City policemen. Though he arguably won the fight, the result was murder. No matter how he spun the story, he could not save himself from a date with Sing Sing Prison's electric chair.

Thomas Pallister
Evening World, Oct.26, 1892.

Date:	April 30, 1892
Location:	New York, New York
Victims:	Adam Kane
Cause of Death:	Stabbing
Accused:	Thomas Pallister

Synopsis:

On the night of April 30, 1892, Policeman McGrath of the Prince Street Station, New York City, heard cries of pain coming from Grand Street, two blocks away from where he was patrolling. He ran to the source of the screams and found a man unconscious on the ground in a pool of blood and another bleeding man walking around as if in a daze. The policeman saw a third man throw a knife into a butcher shop and take off down the street. McGrath ran after him and subdued the man after a brief struggle and arrested him.

McGrath summoned an ambulance for the wounded men. Adam Kane, the man on the ground, was not expected to live. A policeman found the other bleeding man, Henry Kane, wandering near the corner of Charlton and Varick Streets. Both men had been stabbed with a long butcher knife. McGrath led Kane back to the scene, and an ambulance took the wounded men to St. Vincent's Hospital.

The police took the fugitive to the Prince Street Station. He said he was Thomas Kelly, a 28-year-old telegraph lineman. He gave his address but refused to make any other statement after his arrest.

Adam Kane was a new police officer, still on probation. Henry Kane – described variously as brother of, cousin of, or completely unrelated to Adam Kane – was also a policeman from the same precinct. There were quite a few witnesses on the street that night, but most of the early information on the crime came from Henry Kane.

The Kanes and three other men were walking down Grand Street when Kelly came along. Adam accidentally got in Kelly's way, and Kelly punched him. The two men clinched, and the others pulled them apart.

As Kelly left, he shook his fist at Adam and said, "I'll get even with you."

Kelly ran into the butcher shop and grabbed an 18-inch butcher knife from the counter. Five minutes later he ran toward the men brandishing the knife and "yelling like an Indian." Kelly plunged the knife into Adam's abdomen and twisted it. Henry tried to intervene, striking Kelly in the face.

Kelly said to him, "I'll stab you, too."

He made good on the remark, stabbing Henry in the side. Henry ran away, and Kelly followed him, stabbing him twice more. Then he threw the knife back into the butcher shop and ran away. Adam Kane died on May 2; Henry Kane survived.

The police soon learned that Thomas Kelly was not who he pretended to be. He had given them a false address. They first thought he was an ex-convict named Flaherty, who had recently finished a five-year term at Sing Sing for burglary. But by the time of his arraignment, he was known to be Thomas Pallister, of 30 Carmine Street, and had previously served 11 years in prison.

Pallister was housed in the Tombs while he awaited trial for the murder of Adam Kane. On the night of June 12, 1892, a guard noticed that the floor under Pallister's cot was wet. When he shone his lantern in the cell, he saw Pallister's left arm hanging down and a stream of blood running out of a gash in his wrist. He had attempted suicide by cutting himself with a piece of broken glass from a medicine bottle left in the cell by a former inmate. When he regained consciousness, he said he wanted to die. He was afraid there was enough evidence to convict him, and he wanted to avoid a long trial and the shame to his family of execution in the electric chair.

Trial: October 20, 1892

Pallister pleaded not guilty at his trial. In his opening statement, Pallister's attorney said his client should have been commended for bravery rather than indicted for murder. He risked his life to save that of his friend John Hammot that night on Grand Street.

Hammot testified that Adam Kane and his companions knocked him down and kicked him. Pallister interfered to save his life, and the five men attacked and beat him. He saw Pallister running away, pursued by the whole party. Two other witnesses testified to the same effect. Pallister testified that Kane and his party attacked him and his friends. He went into the store and got a butcher knife to defend himself. He struck with the knife after they knocked him down.

But the police and other witnesses corroborated Henry Kane's story and the evidence against Pallister was too strong. He was convicted of first-degree murder and sentenced to die in the electric chair the week of December 12, 1892. Pallister was taken to Sing Sing Prison along with three other convicted murderers – Frank Rohle, Michael Sliney, and John Osmond.

Verdict: Guilty of first-degree murder

Aftermath:

Pallister received a temporary stay of execution while his attorney appealed for a new trial. In April 1893, the Court of Appeals in Albany rejected the appeal and upheld the original verdict.

With no hope of avoiding the electric chair, Pallister plotted with fellow death-house inmate Frank Rohle to escape from Sing Sing. The end of Thomas Pallister's story would be tightly bound to Frank Rohle.

To be continued …

Murderer Quickly Caught

Frank Rohle brutally murdered Frank Paulson during a robbery. All he got were a couple of gold watches, some trinkets, and a death sentence. Although his murder trial was appealed on a technicality, he would not stay in prison long enough to learn the outcome.

Frank W. Rohle
The Evening World, May 10, 1893.

Date:	September 29, 1892
Location:	New York, New York
Victims:	Frank Paulson
Cause of Death:	Blows from an Axe
Accused:	Frank W. Rohle

Synopsis:
In 1892, Frank Paulson was a 55-year-old retired carpenter living off his Union Army pension. He lived alone in a rented room on Hester Street, New York City. Paulson was a man of frugal habits, leading some to believe he had a large sum of money hidden in his room.

On the night of September 29, Paulson's landlord, William S. Byrnes, saw a man enter Paulson's room. Twenty minutes later, he heard a door slam. Then, he and his wife saw a man run out of the house. Byrnes went to Paulson's room and found him sitting in a chair with his skull crushed. He had at least eight deep gashes in his head – blows from an axe.

Byrnes's wife, Anna, believed the man who ran was Charles Knoch, a former associate of Paulson who frequently visited him. The police arrested Knoch on suspicion of murder.

Meanwhile, in another precinct, Policeman Emanuel Meyers and Detective Sargent Lyman encountered a man trying to sell a watch and chain in front of a liquor store. When Meyers asked him where he got the watch, the man threw it into the street and started to run. Meyers chased the man and was about to catch him when he turned around and tried to strike Meyers with a hatchet. Meyers was able to deflect the blow with his billy club. When assistance arrived, the police disarmed the man and took him to the Fifth Street Police Station.

The prisoner was Frank W. Rohle, a Hoboken, New Jersey, marble polisher. He had two more gold watches in his pocket, along with a ring and some trinkets. When the police learned of the axe murder of Frank Paulson, they knew they had the killer. The next morning, Captains Cross and Dougherty took Rohle to headquarters. As they climbed the stairs, Captain Cross waved the bloody axe at the waiting reporters to signal they had captured Paulson's murderer.

Justice Hogan examined Rohle in his private room at the Essex Market Police Court. William Byrnes testified to finding the body and positively identified Rohle as the man he had seen going into Paulson's room. Anna Byrnes corroborated her husband's story and now identified Rohle as the man who ran from the building.

When she pointed him out as the man who entered Paulson's room, Rohle shouted, "That's a lie! You never saw me before in your life."

Frederick Mehrlbert, a barkeeper, identified Rohle as the man who was in his saloon shortly after the murder, exhibiting the gold chain and watches that the court showed him. Philip Kerker, proprietor of the Emblem Saloon, identified the chain he had sold Paulson. Rohle's landlord in Hoboken, Joseph Katain, testified that he had known Rohle for three years and had never seen him with the watches and chain. Katain said the ring was his own; Rohle had taken it from his bureau drawer. He also said an axe stolen from his house matched the description of the murder weapon

Trial: December 13, 1892

Frank Rohle was tried in December 1892 for the murder of Frank Paulson. The jury found him guilty and he was sentenced to die in the electric chair in the week beginning February 6, 1893. The police transported him to Sing Sing Prison to await execution.

Verdict: Guilty of first-degree murder

Aftermath:

Rohle's attorney requested a new trial on the ground that the District Attorney had made "undue use of the fact that the murdered man was a war veteran." The request was granted, and Rohle was given a stay of execution pending the outcome of his appeal.

The new trial was never held. On April 20, 1893, Frank Rohle and Thomas Pallister escaped from Sing Sing Prison.

To be continued…

Escape From the Death House

Sing Sing Death House
Evening World, May 16, 1893.

The death-house of Sing Sing Prison, which housed inmates awaiting execution, was under tight security. The inmates were under 24-hour surveillance, and the grounds outside were patrolled to prevent suicide or escape. But the keepers became complacent, and rules were not strictly followed. Frank Rohle and Thomas Pallister had little trouble escaping the death-house. What happened next is anybody's guess.

Date:	April 1893
Location:	Hudson River, New York
Victims:	Frank Rohle, Thomas Pallister
Cause of Death:	Gunshot
Accused:	Unknown

Synopsis:

The death-house of Sing Sing Prison, on the Hudson River in New York State, was a separate building attached to the south end of the main prison. It housed up to eight condemned men in 8x10 foot cells along the south wall in groups of four separated by a corridor. The cells were 8 feet high with iron bars on the front and brick partitions between the cells and on the top, with space between the top of the cell and the roof of the building.

At the south end of the corridor was a lean-to building called the death-cell, which housed the electric chair. Sing Sing installed the electric chair in 1891, and on July 7 of that year, four condemned murderers were electrocuted. The chair sat idle for nearly two years, but in April 1893, the death-house had five inmates awaiting execution – Carlyle W. Harris, John L. Osmond, Michael Geoghegan, Frank Rohle, and Thomas Pallister.

A 24-hour death watch was maintained in front of the cells to make sure there were no suicides or escapes. Keepers took shifts, so there was always at least one man on duty, and two more were stationed outside the death-house. At about 7:00 p.m. on April 20, 1893, Thomas Pallister told the man on duty, Keeper Hulse, that he had been sick and hadn't eaten all day. He asked Hulse to warm up a plate of meat and potatoes for him. Hulse complied and warmed the plate on the stove.

When Hulse opened the cell door to hand him the food, Pallister threw a handful of pepper into his eyes. He had saved the pepper, a pinch at a time, from his meals. Temporarily blinded, Hulse could not defend himself, and Pallister knocked him down. He took Hulse's keys and revolver, then locked him in the cell. He then unlocked Rohle's cell.

Pointing the revolver at Hulse's head, Pallister said, "It's your life or mine, and at the first sound from you, I will blow out your brains."

Pallister took Hulse's shoes and hat, tearing the word "Keeper" off the hat. Death-house prisoners wore dark clothes rather than the stripes worn by the rest of the prison population, so there was no need to change clothes.

They waited for the arrival of Keeper Murphy, the other death-watch guard, overpowered him and locked him in Rohle's cell. Then they unlocked the cells of Harris, Osmond, and Geoghegan, but they refused to leave. Carlyle Harris was especially adamant about staying. His case was still being appealed. He believed he would be proven innocent and saw no value in escaping.

Pallister and Rohle climbed to the top of the cells and broke the skylight in the roof with an iron bar. They climbed outside then jumped off the roof of the one-story building.

It had been a stormy night, with heavy winds and pounding rain, so no guards were on watch outside. The men stole a prison rowboat and rowed down the Hudson River.

The escape was not discovered until 5:40 a.m. when morning death-watch keepers arrived. They released Hulse and Murphy, then raised the alarm. When they briefed Warden Brown on what had happened, he ordered a massive search for the escaped murderers.

New York State Detective James Jackson was brought in to lead the search. He had twenty years' experience working for Sing Sing, capturing fugitives. Jackson telegraphed all the towns on both sides of the Hudson with detailed descriptions of the escaped prisoners. A reward of $250 for each man was offered for their capture. Jackson was optimistic that the men would be caught.

In New York City, where both Rohle and Pallister committed their murders, the police thought the escape story was "fishy." They questioned whether Pallister could save enough pepper from dinner to throw in a man's face, and whether it would still be potent after so much time. They pointed out that Rohle's brother had recently returned from Europe with $14,000 the brothers had inherited, and he had met with Rohle's attorney. The police implied that someone may have bribed the keepers.

Warden Brown and Principal Keeper Connaughton denied the possibility of any collusion between the prisoners and the keepers. However, rules were broken, so they suspended and later fired Hulse and Murphy, as well as keepers Glynn and Maher who were supposed to be stationed outside that night.

On April 22, two days after the escape, searchers found the stolen rowboat upturned on the shore near Tarrytown. Detective Jackson believed that the prisoners agreed to separate to prevent capture.

Warden Brown believed that the prisoners were still in the vicinity of the prison, but sightings of the fugitives were coming from all over. Two railroad workers saw three men board a train about 3 miles east of Sing Sing; they jumped off at Brewaters and disappeared. A "mysterious schooner" left her mooring near the prison the night of the escape and was seen speeding past Yonkers toward New York City. The Evening World reported that the prisoners had been captured in a freight car in Patterson, New Jersey. They were seen emerging from a barn in Mount Washington, New Hampshire. Men answering their descriptions were seen near the Hoosac Tunnel in Massachusetts. None of these sightings proved true.

The Warden received a post card on April 28, purporting to be from Rohle and Pallister:

> *Dear Warden Brown: -*
>
> *Dear, dear, dear Sir (you are very dear).*
>
> *I see you are trying to catch us, but you may as well give it up because you could never do it. Hulse and Murphy were not bribed as some people say, but some people say more than their prayers. I am going to Germany, Goodby, old sport. We will send you a New Year's card from Germany. You yourself know that no one can catch us.*
>
> *Yours,*
>
> *ROHLE, PALLISTER & CO*

The mystery took a new turn on May 10 when three fishermen found the body of Frank Rohle floating in the Hudson River near Rockland, directly opposite Sing Sing. His skull had been crushed, and he had been shot in the side of the head. The body was badly decomposed, but Detective Jackson was able to identify him as Rohle by a picture of Rohle's mother and other objects found in his pockets. He speculated that Rohle and Pallister had an altercation and Pallister shot Rohle and dumped his body overboard. Pallister's attorney, Ambrose H. Purdy, claimed that his client did not kill Rohle; river pirates shot him then took Pallister aboard their ship bound for some foreign port.

Rohle's attorney, E. Townsend Goldberg, stoutly maintained that the body found in the river was not Rohle. In any case, the prison officials thought Pallister got away safely and gave up the river search.

On May 16, fishermen found a second body floating in the Hudson. This body, too, was badly decomposed, but prison officials identified it as Thomas Pallister by distinctive tattoos on his arm and the contents of his pockets. He had been shot in the face, just under the left eye.

A coroner's jury determined that Pallister had been killed by a person or persons unknown, but outside the court, there were many theories as to what happened that stormy night. Jackson now believed that the men had decided that they could not get away and preferred death to capture. He believed that, by agreement, Rohle shot Pallister and then himself. The fracture of Rohle's skull happened after death when he struck the boat or a rock. Another theory said that the men were angry with each other and fired simultaneously, killing both. Or maybe they tried to board the "mysterious schooner" and were murdered by the crew.

Another school of thought said that the prison was hiding the truth. Prison guards had shot and killed both men. The most extreme conspiracy theory said that the prison had put two completely different bodies into the Hudson to hide the fact that the prisoners were still at large. The *New York Tribune* dismissed this theory by saying Sing Sing authorities were not that smart:

> *If there had been a deep conspiracy on the part of the prison authorities to hoodwink the public into believing that the two men were dead, it would have required a remarkable brain to engineer it all, and everyone who has had anything to do with Warden Brown or the two keepers, knows that they are not men of sufficient mental caliber to carry out a scheme which would require so much detail, such great shrewdness and executive ability.*

The most widely accepted theory said that Pallister crushed Rohle's skull with an iron rod, then shot him. Then Pallister, who had tried to kill himself while a prisoner in New York City, was seized again by "suicidal mania" and shot himself. In the end, though, the coroner's jury verdict was probably the most accurate – they were killed by a person or persons unknown.

Murder Among the Whyos, Part 1

The Whyos, in 1886, were the strongest and most brutal criminal gang New York City had ever known. Under the joint leadership of Dan Driscoll and Dan Lyons, the Whyos grew to control criminal activity throughout the city. But Driscoll and Lyons were too violent and reckless to rule for long and their mistakes led to the demise of the gang. The Whyos' downfall began when Driscoll stole Beezy Garrity from her pimp John McCarthy.

Daniel Driscoll
Defenders and Offenders, 1888.

Date:	June 26, 1886
Location:	New York, New York
Victim:	Bridget 'Beezy' Garrity
Cause of Death:	Gunshot
Accused:	Daniel Driscoll

Synopsis:
Street gangs have always been part of life in New York City. Before the Civil War, gangs with colorful names like, Dead Rabbits, Bowery Boys, Plug Uglies, Shirt Tails, Roach Guards, and Chichesters would battle over turf, primarily in the notorious Five Points neighborhood. At times they would unite behind the nativist Bowery Boys or the Irish Dead Rabbits and battle over national pride. Occasionally, all gangs would join together to battle a common enemy as in the Draft Riots or the Astor Place Riot.

By the 1880s, one gang, the Whyos, dominated New York and their central focus switched from fighting to crime. While still headquartered in the Five Points area, the Whyos' reach extended throughout Manhattan, as they engaged in pickpocketing, burglary, bank robbery, counterfeiting, and prostitution. They also provided violence for hire – when gang member Piker Ryan was arrested, he was carrying a menu of Whyo services:

Punching	$2
Both Eyes blacked	$4
Nose and jaw broke	$10
Jacked out	$15
Ear chawed off	$15
Leg or arm broke	$19
Shot in leg	$25
Stab	$25
Doing the big job	$100 and up

The Whyos were tough and ferocious. Legend says that a man could not become a full member of the Whyos until he committed murder.

Mike McGloin, a Whyo leader who was executed for murder, summed it up in one line, "A guy ain't tough until he has knocked his man out."

The Whyos' power peaked in the 1880s under the joint leadership of Dan Driscoll and Dan Lyons. They were successful leaders, but both had a weakness for strong, beautiful women, a trait which would lead to their ultimate downfall. The beginning of the end came when Driscoll met 18-year-old Bridget Garrity.

Bridget, better known as Beezy, was a prostitute working for gang member John 'Red' McCarthy but she had higher ambitions. Beezy aspired to be the queen of the Whyos and when Driscoll began paying attention to her, she was ready and willing to leave McCarthy and go with him. Though Driscoll was married with a young daughter, he began stepping out with Beezy Garrity. This devastated McCarthy; Beezy was not just one of his whores, she was his girl. Her desertion led to a bitter feud between Driscoll and McCarthy.

The feud escalated rapidly, and in early June 1886 McCarthy tried to kill Driscoll, firing two shots at him with his British bulldog revolver. On June 26, Driscoll decided to put an end to the matter. At 4.00am, Driscoll, carrying his own revolver, paid a visit to the Hester Street lodging house where McCarthy ran his brothel. Beezy came along with him, hoping to forestall any bloodshed.

Inside the building, Driscoll burst open McCarthy's door. Beezy went in first, then McCarthy pushed back on the door to prevent Driscoll from entering. As the two men pushed from opposite sides, Driscoll stuck the muzzle of his revolver through the crack in the door. McCarthy saw the gun and managed to stay clear. Driscoll fired. The bullet missed McCarthy but hit Beezy in the abdomen. McCarthy then ran down the back stairs followed by Driscoll who fired a second shot, missing McCarthy again.

A police officer heard the shots and after a hard chase captured Driscoll and put him under arrest. Beezy Garrity was taken to St. Vincent's Hospital where surgeons tried in vain to save her life. As she lay dying, the police questioned her about the incident, and she remained loyal to Driscoll. She told them

McCarthy had shot her, though the police had already confiscated McCarthy's revolver and saw that it had not recently been fired.

"Do you know that you probably are going to die?" the police captain asked.

"Well, I ain't going back on Dan, all the same," she answered, "'t'was McCarthy shot me."

Beezy's mother came in and tried to persuade her daughter not to die with a lie on her lips.

"I won't split on Dan," Beezy said, "McCarthy fired the pistol."

The coroner and a Catholic priest each tried to get her to tell the truth, but in each case she stuck to her story, murmuring in her dying breath that McCarthy had shot her.

The District Attorney was disappointed that Beezy Garrity's dying statement didn't condemn Driscoll but felt there was enough circumstantial evidence to charge him with her murder.

Trial: September 27, 1886

Driscoll was charged with first-degree murder for killing Beezy Garrity. Though Driscoll had not shot her intentionally, the District Attorney wanted to prosecute him for the highest charge possible because of his connection to the Whyos. Driscoll pled not guilty.

His defense attorney was William F. Howe, of the firm Howe and Hummel, the most successful criminal lawyers in the city. They had often defended members of the Whyos, as well as many other high-profile criminals such as notorious fence 'Marm' Mandelbaum. William Howe, who was noted for appearing in court wearing garish waistcoats and flashy jewelry, had in the course of his career defended more than 600 accused murderers.

Howe's defense was aggressive from the beginning. During jury selection, from a pool of fifty-seven prospective jurors, Howe found only nine acceptable. A second pool of twenty-five was questioned before Howe agreed to three more.

The first witness was a woman named Carrie Wilson who was at the Hester Street house the night of the murder who testified that she saw Driscoll force open McCarthy's door and heard the shot that killed Beezy. John McCarthy testified that Driscoll had fired the shot. In cross-examination, he was forced to admit that he had previously served eight years in State Prison for robbery and two weeks earlier had fired shots at Driscoll. He did not deny that he kept a house of ill-fame.

The most damaging testimony against Driscoll came from Mrs. Margaret Sullivan, Beezy's mother, who believed Driscoll and the Whyos had lured her daughter into a life of shame. On the witness stand she gave an account of her last conversation with Beezy which contradicted what had previously been reported:

Mother: Beezy, I knew something like this would happen to you for not doing as I told you.
Daughter: Mother, what's the use of you talking to me that way now; I'm going to die.
Mother: Who did it to you?
Daughter: 'Twas Danny Driscoll done the deed.

The trial lasted only three days, and the jury quickly returned a verdict of guilty.

Verdict: Guilty of first-degree murder

Aftermath:

Howe moved for a new trial on the grounds that evidence had been allowed relating to McCarthy handing the police a fully loaded pistol as proof of his innocence. He gave them the gun fifteen minutes after the shooting allowing McCarthy plenty of time to substitute another pistol. Recorder Smyth rejected the motion.

Driscoll was sentenced to hang on December 3 but the hanging was postponed due to appeals. An appeal to the General Term of the State Supreme Court was denied in June 1887. In November, Howe took the case to the Court of Appeals claiming to have evidence that eyewitness Carrie Wilson had not been at the Hester Street house that night. The court denied the appeal. Howe went directly to the Governor of New York asking for a pardon; this was denied as well.

While William Howe was attempting to free his client through legal means, Driscoll was looking for illegal ways out. During his trial, the warden of the Tombs made a routine inspection of Driscoll's cell and found a three-inch corkscrew with which the prisoner had removed three bricks from the cell wall.

In October 1887, convicted murderer Dan Lyons joined Driscoll on the Tombs' Murderer's Row. This was not the same Dan Lyons who had led the Whyos with Driscoll, but they were kindred spirits who were soon working together to escape. Along with a third convicted murderer, they began a hunger strike to protest conditions at the prison. At the same time, Driscoll and Lyons, who had been smuggled a saw blade, each cut an iron rod from his cot to use as a pry bar to break through the cell wall. The heavy bars would be used as weapons should they succeed in breaking through the wall. Warden Walsh uncovered the plan before they could finish.

For Driscoll's most audacious escape plan, one of his visitors had taken a soap impression of the lock and made a duplicate key. Someone smuggled in two bottles of kerosene and a false beard for Driscoll. The plan was to start a fire somewhere in the prison and in the confusion, Driscoll would unlock his cell and leave the prison in disguise. Walsh foiled this plan as well.

Driscoll made numerous death threats against the warden, whom he called 'Fatty' Walsh. Walsh decided he had had enough. He put Driscoll and Lyons in separate cells made of sheet iron – floor, walls, and ceiling. Within the cell, a woven iron fence separated visitors from the prisoner. Driscoll was allowed no visitors but his wife, Mary.

The hanging was now scheduled for January 20, 1888, but Howe, in his only victory for Driscoll, managed to get a respite of three days. Driscoll used the time to write a sentimental letter to Mary, which was reprinted in several newspapers. He also took the opportunity to publicly taunt Fatty Walsh. He continued to maintain his innocence of the crime but became resigned to his fate.

The day before the hanging Driscoll said goodbye to his weeping mother and to his devoted wife and child. He had a long conversation with Father Gelinas, who told the press, "Dan bears up bravely. He is reconciled to death and thinks that it will be his salvation. He is willing to die."

Dan Driscoll was hanged in the Tombs yard at 7:24 a.m. on January 23, 1888, in the presence of the Sheriff, the Sheriff's jury, a few jail officials and ten reporters. He died game.

Murder Among the Whyos, Part 2

Dan Driscoll and Dan Lyons were the successful leaders of New York City's Whyo gang in the early 1880s. After Driscoll's arrest for murder in 1886, Lyons became the sole leader, but his reign did not last long. Confusion surrounds the cause of the leader's downfall because in 1887, there were two Dan Lyons among the city's criminals, and most modern accounts combine the two. Dan Lyons, a petty thief executed for killing a popular athlete, was not Dan Lyons the Whyos leader who was shot to death by an angry saloonkeeper. Either way, murder led to the demise of the Whyos.

Daniel M. Lyons (burglar)
Defenders and Offenders, 1888.

Date:	July 5, 1887
Location:	New York, New York
Victim:	Joseph Francis Quinn
Cause of Death:	Gunshot
Accused:	Daniel M Lyons (burglar)

Date:	August 18, 1887
Location:	New York, New York
Victim:	Daniel Lyons (leader of the Whyos)
Cause of Death:	Gunshot
Accused:	Daniel Murphy

Synopsis:
On the evening of July 5, 1887, Joseph Quinn was sitting on the front steps of his home at 2nd Avenue and 38th Street in New York City, when a man named Dan Lyons walked up and, without provocation, shot him in the head. The men had been fighting over a woman named Kitty McGown, said Quinn's friends when the police arrived. Lyons had quickly fled the scene.

Quinn was a champion amateur catch-as-catch-can wrestler and a well-known all-around athlete who belonged to the New York Athletic Club and the Pastime Club. His day job was margin clerk of the New York Coffee Exchange. The murder caused quite a stir in the sporting community and on Wall Street as well. Thousands of people attended his funeral.

The city police were under pressure to make an arrest, but Lyons was a burglar, adept at eluding capture. The police first thought he had gone to Long Island, but they soon had reports that he had been seen in several dives in Philadelphia. Detectives Malarkey and Duncan were dispatched to that city, but on arrival, they learned that Lyons had gone to Pittsburg. As the detectives traveled west, so did Lyons and he was next seen in Chicago. Hoping to fool the police, Lyons doubled back to Pittsburg, and was arrested there for burglary. He may have deliberately let himself be caught to hide from his pursuers. When the detectives found him in the Pittsburg jail, Lyons agreed to return with them without formal extradition.

Back in New York, he told his version of the murder. The fight, he said, was not over a woman. The animosity between the men, which began with a petty disagreement, had been building for a year. The men had fought the day before the murder and Quinn had beaten Lyons badly. He did not want to be beaten again, so he made sure he was armed when he passed Quinn's house. Quinn had not been sitting on his steps the day of the shooting but had approached him on the street and threatened him with a "Chinese fan dagger."

Lyons told police, "I killed Quinn because if I hadn't done so, he would have killed me."

When the story broke that Joseph Quinn was killed by Dan Lyons, some speculated that the killer had to be Lyons, the infamous leader of the Whyos, New York's most dangerous criminal gang. Speculation ceased about a month later when Dan Lyons of the Whyos was murdered in a Five Points saloon while Dan Lyons, killer of Quinn, was safely behind bars in the Tombs.

The Whyos' Dan Lyons, who was described as having a lantern jaw and a head shaped like a bullet, had served time in Sing Sing Prison and on August 18, 1887, was out on bail after assaulting a policeman. Early that morning he entered Daniel Murphy's saloon on Worth Street, in the Five Points, with some friends. Lyons was already drunk and quickly became rowdy. When he threatened to kill everyone there, the bartender threw him out.

That afternoon Lyons went back to Murphy's, still extremely drunk, and demanded to be served. Reportedly, some kittens were running about on Murphy's floor. Lyons picked them up and bit off the ends of their tails. The bartender, Walter Butler, refused to serve him and told him to leave the saloon. Lyons got angry then and began throwing bottles of soda water at Butler. When the owner, Daniel Murphy, came in and saw what was happening he told Lyons to get out. Lyons threw a bottle of mineral water at Murphy, cutting a deep gash under his right eye. Murphy went behind the bar, grabbed his revolver from the shelf and pointed it at Lyons.

"Come now, you've got to go out." Murphy said.

Lyons reached for his revolver, but Murphy fired first, hitting him in the side of the head. Murphy, bleeding profusely, then ran from the saloon, straight to the Elizabeth Street Police Station and turned himself in. He feared the police less than he feared the Whyos. Dan Lyons died at the Chambers Street Hospital sometime after midnight.

His last words were, "I'm sorry, you can bet. I'd just like to have one more go at Murphy."

Trial for the Murder of Joseph Quinn: September 19, 1887

The trial of Daniel M. Lyons, the burglar, for the murder of Joseph Quinn lasted six days. The highlight of the trial was the testimony of the defendant who explained that Quinn harassed him every time he passed his house. He tried to avoid that corner as much as he could but sometimes, he could not. On July 5, he was carrying a revolver hoping to scare Quinn if he saw him. Lyons had believed the pistol was empty and when it went off, he was as surprised as anyone.

Lyons had no corroborating testimony to his assertion of self-defense. Mrs. Annie Bollinger testified that Lyons had not avoided the corner, she had often seen him loitering there. The jury found Lyons guilty of first-degree murder.

Coroner's Hearing for the Murder of Daniel Lyons of the Whyos: August 17, 1887

Dan Lyons's wake drew Whyos from across New York and Brooklyn, and while they mourned their lost leader, a coroner's jury met to determine the fate of his killer. Daniel Murphy was represented by William Howe. In his statement to the jury, Howe gave the Whyos a good raking, citing their violence and criminal activities, and said that the city was well rid of Danny Lyons. This was a bit disingenuous on Howe's part; the firm of Howe and Hummel were virtually on retainer with the Whyos, handling all of their major legal problems, and the previous year, Howe had defended Lyons's partner, Whyo leader Dan Driscoll in his murder trial. The jury in Murphy's case agreed with Howe, exonerating Murphy and calling the killing "entirely justifiable."

Aftermath:

Daniel M. Lyons, the killer of Joseph Quinn, was sentenced to hang, and while awaiting his execution, he was sent to murderer's row in the Tombs. There he met Driscoll, former leader of the Whyos and ex-partner of Lyons's namesake. The two became close friends and worked together on several failed escape attempts. Lyons's attempts to escape the gallows through legal appeals failed as well though they did manage to prolong his life until the following August. Lyons was hanged in the courtyard of the Tombs on August 21, 1888.

Most modern accounts erroneously state that Dan Lyons of the Whyos was executed for the murder of Joseph Quinn. This error first appeared in Herbert

Asbury's 1927 book, The Gangs of New York. Asbury was a great storyteller and chronicler of nineteenth-century crime, but he was known to embellish the facts for the sake of the story. In this case, he confused the two Dans, and in his version, Dan Lyons, the Whyo leader, shot Joseph Quinn in a gun battle across Paradise Square, over the affections of Pretty Kitty McGown. Asbury is so well respected that at least three serious authors retold Asbury's version in their books with very little variation.

The Whyos never again had leadership as strong as Dan Driscoll and Dan Lyons. The police came down hard on the Whyos and their numbers dwindled as members were sent to prison. By the end of the nineteenth century, though the Whyo gang still existed, it was no longer a major factor in New York City crime.

UNSOLVED

15 Corning Street

Scenes at 15 Corning St.
Boston Daily Globe, Nov. 6, 1897.

The strangulation of Alice Brown at 15 Corning Street in Boston's South End dominated the front page of the city's daily newspapers in the autumn of 1897. It was a sensational crime that seemed custom-made for the "yellow journalism" of the era, with a mysterious victim, a colorful cast of witnesses, no clear suspect, but several possibilities. The *Globe*, the *Herald*, the *Post*, the *Journal*, and other Boston dailies aggressively followed clues and gathered background, hoping to scoop each other and the police in their vivid reporting of the crime. In the end, they may have been too aggressive, adding more confusion than clarity.

Date:	November 4, 1897
Location:	Boston, Massachusetts
Victim:	Alice Brown
Cause of Death:	Strangulation
Accused:	William Leavitt

Synopsis:

Alice Brown, aged 25, was found dead in her room by another resident of the lodging house on the morning of November 4, 1897. The medical examiner performed an autopsy on the body and quickly determined that she had been strangled. There were seven finger marks on her throat, including cuts made by fingernails. The police brought in three house residents for questioning: two men who shared a basement room, John T. Stowell and Thomas Hughes, and the proprietor of the house, Edward Hurd. They were examined and released.

Very little was known about Alice Brown, who had moved to the lodging house at 15 Corning Street just two weeks before, and the search for her identity would become nearly as frantic as the search for her killer. Alice was known to keep late hours and was seen in the company of several different men. She had an ardent lover, over 60 years old, who visited night after night, pleading with her to marry him. She always refused. Around 11:30 p.m. the night of the murder, she was seen sitting on the front steps with another man. They spoke in earnest tones for about half an hour before he left.

The person who seemed to know her best at 15 Corning Street was William Leavitt, a blind man known as 'Blind Billy', who sold song sheets on the street on Tremont Row. Leavitt told police that he had been awake smoking in his room above Alice's around 3:00 a.m. the morning of the murder. His door was ajar, and he could hear Alice in the hallway talking to a man whose voice he did not recognize. It was a long conversation; the man tried to persuade Alice to marry him. Leavitt heard her say:

"No, I wouldn't marry the best man that ever lived."

He asked again, and she said emphatically, "No."

"Well, I suppose I might as well go then," he said.

"Yes," Alice replied.

Leavitt said he knew Alice's lover and said he was not the man she was talking to. It was believed that Alice was murdered sometime between 3:00 a.m. and 6:00am.

A magazine in Alice's room had the name Alice O'Brien scribbled on the cover. Alice O'Brien had previously lodged at 15 Corning. When the police found her at her new address, she said that she knew Alice Brown, but said she was somewhat reticent about her past. She grew up in a small town near Concord, New Hampshire. Her mother had died when she was 15, and within a year, she ran away, leaving the farm for the city where she hoped for a career on the stage. Lovers from her girlhood home had visited her in Boston.

She had left New Hampshire with her friend, Hattie Belmont. Alice, a brunette, and Hattie, a blonde, were the belles of their hometown. Romantic novels gave them the notion to run away, and they drifted between New York and Boston, working as shop girls but looking forward to a life on the stage. According to the *Boston Globe*, "The rouge on their cheeks told only too plainly after a while what sort of life they were living."

Alice and Hattie had been roommates at 15 Corning until Alice received a message that Hattie had been arrested and charged with undue intimacy with a married man. None of this information proved helpful to the police, and they could not find Alice's family in New Hampshire. Another resident of 15 Corning had seen letters postmarked Amherst, Massachusetts, addressed to Alice Brown, and they believed that was her home. Someone in Gloucester thought she had been in that city under the name Redmond and had been committed to an insane asylum.

On the night of the murder, two people living on Ohio Street, across from the rear of 15 Corning, reported hearing a muffled scream between 4:00 and 5:00 a.m. One woman who lived at 15 Corning also heard a scream, but no one else in the house did. This discrepancy made the police suspect that some of the residents were covering for the killer. There was no sign of forced entry, and the only way in through the front door was with a latchkey – Alice's was missing. The newspapers said the mystery was deeper than ever.

On November 6, a man from Lynn, Massachusetts, who was visiting Boston with his wife, reported that he had overheard a loud conversation on Tremont Row. He heard a blind song vendor say:

"She can't try that on me – she can't try that on me! I'll fix her!"

He was speaking with another man whose description matched that of James McMillan, Alice's 62-year-old suitor. The police scoured the city for McMillan and found him in Haymarket Square at about 1:30am. He was known to pursue Alice; in fact, it was said that his "mad infatuation" had caused her to leave her old residence and move to Corning St, hoping he would never find her again.

McMillan lived on Tremont Street with a woman named Sadie Hart, an intimate friend of Alice. McMillan told police that he and Hart had gone to Corning Street to call on Alice and ask her to join them for supper, but she was not there when they arrived. He said he had known Alice for about ten years by the name of Redmond. Alice stopped at his house the night of the murder but left before 10:00 p.m.. Both McMillan and Leavitt denied that the Tremont conversation ever happened.

The same day, several other witnesses came forward, and the newspapers printed their stories. A man claimed that he saw Alice at about midnight on the night of the murder, dining with a man at a café, and saw her leave with him. At Corning Street, a strange man came with a message for Alice Dewey, room 3. The landlady, Mrs. Hurd, told him there had been three Alices in the house. None was named Dewey, and the one in room 3 was dead. He said he had a message from Harris Gladwin, a waiter at the Parker House, but when the stranger realized he was in the murder house, he left without giving any more information. The Parker House denied ever having an employee named Harris Gladwin.

The former lover of Hattie Belmont, Alice's most intimate friend, said that Hattie's name was really Alice Ward, and the two Alices became friends when they were inmates of the same reformatory. Both were pretty girls, he said, but wayward. He believed they had left Boston for New Bedford, but police could find no trace of Hattie Belmont, Alice Ward, or Alice Brown there.

A man from Amherst, Massachusetts, came forward to say he believed the dead girl was his sister-in-law, Mary Retherham. She had lived in Amherst but was sent to a state reformatory. He would travel to Boston to identify the body.

The *Boston Globe* discovered that the man who overheard the conversation on Tremont Row was not a visitor from Lynn but was John Hy Kerrison, a reporter for a rival newspaper. Police said they trusted him and agreed to withhold his identity, but they also said their reasons for arresting McMillan had nothing to do with the alleged conversation. The following day, they released McMillan. Police investigations now focused on the unknown man who was seen leaving the South End restaurant with Alice around midnight the night of the murder. The *Boston Herald* made the truest statement yet, "It is expected that developments today will go a long way toward clearing the mystery, or else it will be darker than ever."

What happened next surprised everybody. The police arrested "Blind Billy" Leavitt for the murder of Alice Brown. Jack Whalen, a resident of 15 Corning, came forward with another story of the night of the murder. His room was directly above Alice's, and he could hear nearly everything that transpired in the room below as well as on his own floor. He was awake that night and, around 3:00am, heard a noise coming from Leavitt's room. He opened his door, looked out into the hallway, and saw Leavitt going down the stairs and through the hall toward Alice's room. All was quiet, and then he heard the muffled scream of a woman. Immediately after, Whalen saw the blind man coming up the stairs and heading for his room.

The police had been suspicious of Leavitt from the beginning. He was a little too eager to furnish them with information, and he seemed obsessed with the case, talking incessantly of it and continually providing them with new information. Some of his stories were contradictory. Alice O'Brien said Leavitt was among the men who would not leave Alice Brown alone. He made bold statements and entered her room uninvited. After driving Leavitt from her room, Alice Brown told Alice O'Brien that Leavitt was "a bad man."

Leavitt's record in New York and other cities bore this out; he had traveled extensively before coming to Boston and had served time at Blackwell Island for petty offenses. It was said that he was not as blind as he let on and had excellent hearing. Leavitt consorted with thieves and fallen women, and it was reported that he had previously spied for the police or anyone who would pay him.

The same day as Leavitt's arrest, the body of Alice Brown was positively identified as Mary Alice Ruderhan by Mrs. Lucy S. Brown of Cambridgeport, who had employed her as a domestic servant. When she saw the name 'Mary Rotherham' in the newspaper, she decided to see if the dead girl could be her former servant. Mary had said little about her past but told Mrs. Brown she had come from Rindge Center, New Hampshire, where she still had a brother. Mrs. Brown remembered Mary as a pleasant, trustworthy girl, but the family's attitude toward her changed after they caught her smoking cigarettes in her room. She moved out soon after, and Mrs. Brown said she had stolen a gold watch when she left. She also took their last name when she moved into Corning Street.

William 'Blind Billy' Leavitt took his arraignment as a joke. He declined counsel and waived examination but was still intent on explaining the situation. "I suppose I have to go through it. I might as well stand the pressure as anybody else. The statement is against me on account of the newspapers." He was still talking as he was led out of the courtroom.

Pending the grand jury hearing, Leavitt was held without bail. Seven fellow lodgers of 15 Corning Street, witnesses in the case, were also held on $500 bail, which none of them could raise.

Leavitt was well represented when he appeared before the grand jury. His attorney stressed that he had no motive for killing Mary Alice Ruderhan. While it was true that she repelled his advances, there was no evidence that he was strongly jealous. The marks on her neck were made by someone with long fingernails, and Leavitt bit his to the quick. Most importantly, the only witness against him was Jack Whalen, whose nickname at 15 Corning was 'Happy Jack' because his "mental force was said to be not of the strongest."

The grand jury concluded that there was insufficient evidence to indict William Leavitt. No one else was ever charged with the murder of Mary Alice Ruderhan, aka Alice Brown, and the case is sometimes cited as one of Boston's unsolved mysteries.

The Medford Mystery

Walter R. Debbins was shot twice in the back in broad daylight on Highland Street in Medford, Massachusetts, on the afternoon of Saturday, March 27, 1897. Though no one saw the murder or heard the gunshots, there was enough traffic on Highland Street that afternoon for the police to precisely pinpoint the time of the shooting to between 1:00 and 1:05 p.m.. But that was all they could identify; everything else about the crime was shrouded in mystery that grew denser with each new revelation.

Walter R. Debbins
Boston Daily Globe, Mar. 29, 1897.

Date:	March 27, 1897
Location:	Medford, Massachusetts
Victim:	Walter R. Debbins
Cause of Death:	Gunshot
Accused:	unknown

Synopsis:
Twenty-one-year-old Walter Debbins was on his way to the home of his friend, Franklin W. Wood. They had probably planned to spend the day walking in the woods near the Stoneham pumping station as they often did, sometimes accompanied by their friend, Charles Smith. This day, their signals were crossed; Woods went to Debbins's house, arriving there shortly after Debbins left for his house. He knew the route Debbins would take, and he hurried after. When he reached Highland Street, he saw several people gathered around a dead body lying on the ground. It was Walter Debbins; they believed he had died of heart failure. Two boys on bicycles rode off to tell the police. Woods took off his coat and ran back to Debbins's house to tell his mother.

When the coroner examined the body, he discovered that Walter Debbins had been shot twice in the back. He removed two .38 caliber slugs, one from the heart and one just below the shoulder blade. The police arrested Franklin Woods on suspicion. Though there was no evidence against him, they felt he had a connection to the murder and held him as a precaution.

It was well known that Debbins's sweetheart was Mary Hook, and the police first thought that Woods may have murdered his friend out of jealousy, but there was no evidence that Woods had any feelings for the girl. Debbins and Woods had been close friends since childhood and were not likely to let a girl come between them to the extent of murder. Both men were unemployed at the time of the murder and had been spending all of their free time together. Franklin's brother John told the *Boston Herald*, "My brother Frank could not possibly have any motive in killing his best and only chum." Franklin Woods was released from custody.

Finding a motive for the murder of Debbins was a daunting problem for the police. The killer had taken Debbins's gold watch and a signet ring but they ruled out robbery as a motive. Given the circumstances, revenge seemed more likely, but Debbins was an easy-going young man with no known enemies. If he had only been shot once, the police would likely have considered it an accident, a stray bullet from a hunter or target shooter, but two shots made it murder. Someone had intentionally killed Walter Debbins.

His romantic attachment to Mary Hook was the only controversy in Debbins's life; she was five years younger than he was and her family disapproved of the relationship. Several months earlier, her mother had forbidden them from seeing each other, and it appeared that Debbins had complied. Mary's brother, Frank, held a grudge over the relationship, but, like Wood, he had grown up with Debbins and still considered him a friend. Besides, it appeared that Mary was pursuing Debbins and was fonder of him than he was of her. The Boston Post reported, "Among Debbins's friends, he seems to have borne the reputation of being not a woman hater exactly, yet not especially fond of the company of ladies." The police rejected romance as a motive.

Debbins's friend Charles S. Smith, Jr. told the police about an incident involving Debbins and a group of Italian laborers working on repairs to the pumping station. Smith and Debbins had been drinking with the Italians in their camp near the waterworks, and Debbins accidentally broke an accordion belonging to one of them. The man threatened to kill Debbins. Another story surfaced involving Debbins and the Italians. A man named Vincent Salamone was arrested for illegally selling beer at the camp, and it was alleged that Debbins had informed the police about it. Salamone was not held for the crime, and the police had no record of Debbins as the informant. Both of these incidents occurred a year and a half before the shooting, and neither was deemed significant enough to incite murder. The Italian theory was rejected, though it did prompt the citizens of Medford to report sightings of suspicious Italians all over town.

The City Council of Medford offered a reward of $500 for information leading to the arrest of Debbins's killer, and the police received much new information. However, the case was growing cold, and at this point, it was hard to distinguish between real clues, coincidences, and totally irrelevant tips. A bloodhound was tried at the murder scene, but a week after the murder, there was no trail to follow. Two carpenters who had been working about a mile through the woods from the scene reported hearing gunshots around 1:00 p.m. on the day of the murder. The police experimented to see if it was possible to hear gunfire from that far away and concluded that it was not. Most likely, the men heard shots from a man who was seen doing target practice in the woods with a .42 caliber Winchester rifle – the bullets that killed Debbins were .38 caliber.

The police were now specifically looking for two persons of interest who were known to be near the murder scene that day. The first was an unidentified man who had been seen riding a bicycle down Highland Street about ten minutes before the body was found; the press referred to him as the "Lone Cyclist." He stopped to chat with the manager of the Longwood Hotel before continuing down the road. The timing was such that he would have seen the killer if he was not the killer himself.

The second suspect was a dark-haired stranger wearing a dark coat who had been seen by Johnny Doherty, a boy riding in a wagon with a peddler named Hugh Reynolds. Reynolds and Doherty were the first to see the body at about 1:10 p.m., and Doherty had seen the stranger on the road. A man who fit the description Doherty gave had been seen around 10:00 a.m. by A.W. Patterson, a fish store owner in Charlestown, a Boston neighborhood about 4 miles southeast of Medford. The man had dark hair and a sandy mustache, wore a black derby, and a black overcoat with a velvet collar. He said he needed money and tried to sell Patterson a .38 caliber revolver. When Patterson declined, the man asked for directions to the road to Stoneham, a town bordering Dedham.

The man – called the "Slick Stranger" by the *Boston Herald* – was next seen at about 11:45 a.m. by a stable owner in Dorchester. He had gone to several stables there to ask about employment. But if he was on his way to Stoneham, he was heading in the wrong direction; Dorchester is about eight miles south of Charlestown. He was seen again by Edwin Myers at about noon on Highland Street in Medford when he asked Myers how to get to Lawrence. Myers said he couldn't tell him how to get to Lawrence but told him he was on the road to Stoneham. The man thanked him and said he would know the way when he reached Stoneham. Myers said the man struck him as someone who had gone to Boston for a good time and had no money to get home.

On April 2, the police received an anonymous letter purporting to be from the Lone Cyclist. He said that on the day of the murder, he rode past two men who appeared to be wrestling for fun, and he stopped to watch the sport. When the man on top saw the Cyclist, he picked up a revolver from the ground, turned to him, and asked where in hell he came from. He was too frightened to respond. Then the man asked if the Cyclist knew what was wrong with the man on the ground.

"No," the man with the gun said. "You don't want to know either."

This was followed by a string of epithets too profane to print in the newspaper. The Lone Cyclist then rode away, chased by the man with the revolver, who fired one shot at him. He refused to give his name to the police for fear that he would be arrested for murder or that the real murderer would find him and kill him.

The first Friday evening after the murder, a man was seen in the woods near the murder scene, wearing nothing but a short undershirt. He had one foot on a stone from an old wall and an arm outstretched, index finger pointing to the sky. The police were notified, and fifteen officers were summoned to search the woods for the "lunatic or erratic stranger" who the *Boston Herald* was calling "the man in the 'altogether'." They had no luck.

The Slick Stranger was again seen in a Lowell, Massachusetts pawn shop. He matched the descriptions in the newspaper and was there to pawn his pistol, a .32 caliber revolver – once again, the wrong caliber. The following day, a man fitting the description of the Slick Stranger was arrested in Lawrence and held by the Medford authorities. Sergeant Wells took Edward Myers to Lawrence to see if this was the man he had seen the day of the murder. It turned out he was not the Slick Stranger but a man named Richard Donovan, who was well known by the Medford police and had already been rejected as a suspect. There were other sightings of the Slick Stranger in Lowell and Lawrence, but the Medford police were now convinced that he had fled in the other direction and returned to Boston.

As each new clue proved false, it became more apparent that the Debbins murder would probably never be solved, and gradually, the story disappeared from the newspapers. Then, on April 18, the body of an unknown black man, with two bullets in his head, was found in the woods in Winchester, near the Medford line, two and a half miles from where Debbins was killed. Rumors circulated in Medford that this murder was connected to Debbins's murder, but nothing was substantiated. It was never determined whether the two deaths were part of the same Medford mystery.

The murder of Walter Debbins faded into the shadows again until the following February when another death recalled it. Eleven months to the day after Debbins' murder, the body of Charles S. Smith, Jr., one of his closest friends, was found hanging from the limb of a tree about 500 yards from his house. He had committed suicide. Of course, a rumor began to circulate in Medford that Smith's death was connected to the Debbins murder. It was said that he had left a letter implicating himself and Frank Woods in the crime. The chief of police denied that any letter had been found either on Smith's person or in his house. He denied any connection between Smith's suicide and Debbins's murder, saying that Smith "suffered from mental trouble." The mystery endures.

In reading this case more than a hundred years later, one is left with the impression that more was going on in the lives of these young men than was being reported and that the woods off Highland Street were something more than a pleasant place to stroll. While it is fairly certain that the police never learned the identity of Walter Debbins's killer, it is possible that they did not tell all that they knew for the sake of those still alive. In any case, the motive for Walter Debbins's murder is still unknown, and the Medford Mystery will remain forever unsolved.

The Vanderpool-Field Tragedy

Though he was only twenty-one years old in 1869, Herbert Field had already faced death numerous times in a variety of exotic locations. He had lived an adventurous life and seemed to attract danger, but he never encountered a peril he could not overcome until he settled down in Michigan to become a banker.

George H. Vanderpool
History of the Trial of George Vanderpool, 1870.

Date:	September 5, 1869
Location:	Manistee, Michigan
Victim:	Herbert Field
Cause of Death:	Blows to the head
Accused:	George H. Vanderpool

Synopsis:
Herbert Field was born in 1848 in Lewiston, Maine. As a child, he was saved from drowning on three separate occasions, was nearly killed when a rifle he was loading discharged prematurely, and was severely burned and he almost suffocated when his house caught fire. At age 13, during the Civil War, he left home and joined a Maine army regiment encamped in Virginia, then joined the crew of a transport ship carrying supplies to the Union army in New Orleans.

At age fifteen, he sailed from Boston aboard the schooner John Tucker bound for South America. The men onboard were harshly treated and poorly fed and the ship was nearly destroyed in a storm. When Field left the ship at Cape Horn, he was arrested and held for three weeks in a Valparaiso jail. After returning to the States, he boarded an English ship bound for Liverpool and then to Russia. In the Baltic Sea, the ship was wrecked near Riga. While he managed to survive the shipwreck, he lost all his clothing and a large amount of gold.

Field returned to the United States bent on settling down and entering the business world. He studied at the Commercial College in Auburn, New York. Unable to find a position upon graduation, Field took to the lecture circuit, speaking of his travels in South America.

While speaking in Manistee, Michigan, Field met Rachel Hill, a fifty-five-year-old woman who was quite interested in the lecture and offered to help Field obtain a better education. He accepted her offer and began living in Miss Hill's house. She passed herself off as Field's aunt, and the people of Manistee accepted this, though it was rumored that their relationship was much more intimate.

Around the same time, another young man arrived in Manistee. George Vanderpool, who had experience in the lumber business, came with money borrowed from men in a neighboring town, intent on starting a bank. The bank opened in December 1868, and two months later, Herbert Field, investing $7,000 given to him by Miss Hill, became a partner in the new enterprise.

The partners had complementary skills – Vanderpool was the better businessman, while Field was the more affable – and the firm of Vanderpool and Field did quite well. But by September 1869, all was not well between the partners. Vanderpool believed that Field was drawing money without accounting for it. He changed the combination of the safe and began taking the petty cash home with him at night. According to Vanderpool, Field wanted out of the partnership by buying Vanderpool's share or selling his own. Vanderpool did not want to sell, so they decided to dissolve the partnership.

They drew up the necessary papers, and on Sunday, September 5, 1869, neighboring shopkeepers witnessed their signatures. The following day, Field could not be found in Manistee. He had many friends in town, and his absence was immediately noticed. Vanderpool speculated that Field had run away, gone off on another adventure. Field's friends were skeptical, especially Miss Hill, who knew that he had left behind $2,000 of his own money.

After Field had been gone several days, the people of Manistee began to speculate that he had been the victim of foul play. Suspicion fell upon his partner George Vanderpool. Though Field's body had not been found, and most believed that Vanderpool was incapable of murder, he was arrested on Wednesday, September 8, and held on suspicion. Meanwhile, the sheriff offered rewards for information on the whereabouts of Herbert Fields – $50 if alive and $300 for the body if dead. $300 was later raised to $500.

On September 17, a body was found on the shore of Lake Michigan, twenty-eight miles north of Manistee. It was brought by steamer back to the town, where it was positively identified as that of Herbert Field. He had not drowned; his skull had been crushed, and his body had been tied to a weight before being thrown into the water. The line had broken, setting the body free to be washed ashore.

Vanderpool's behavior before his arrest was now examined more closely by the sheriff and prosecutors. He had been seen mopping the floor of his office the morning of his arrest, cleaning up what appeared to be a large amount of blood. A section had been cut out of the middle of the carpet, and investigators could tell from the ashes in the stove that the piece of carpet had been burned there. A pair of Vanderpool's trousers had also been burned in the stove, and witnesses remembered seeing Vanderpool wearing Field's clothes on September 5. Witnesses also remembered sounds of a scuffle coming from the bank that morning.

The explanations that Vanderpool gave for these events were far from satisfying. The blood, he said, had come from a bloody nose. He had bled into the spittoon and later filled it with water, preparing to clean it. He accidentally knocked over the spittoon and the contents spilled on the floor, the water augmenting the size of the resulting blood stains. He had cut out the section of carpet because it was worn and dirty. He said that on September 5, he had a bad case of diarrhea and had soiled his pants so badly that he decided to burn them and wear a pair that Field had kept in the office. The sounds witnesses thought were from a scuffle were merely Field playing with his dog.

On September 18, the coroner's jury indicted George Vanderpool for the murder of Herbert Field

First Trial: 1. December 21, 1869

The courtroom was filled to capacity on December 21, 1869, the opening day of the trial, as more than five hundred people came to get a look at the accused murderer. A quick look was all they got because after pleading "not guilty," Vanderpool was removed from the courtroom, and the trial was held over until the next term due to the absence of some material witnesses for the defense.

The trial commenced again on February 1, 1870. The prosecution presented all the now familiar circumstantial evidence against Vanderpool, along with testimony from medical experts that the wounds on Field's head were consistent with the blunt end of a hatchet kept in the bank office.

The defense countered with the explanations Vanderpool had previously given, along with the assertion that had he murdered Field, Vanderpool would have immediately cleaned his office and not waited until the following Wednesday. The prosecution asserted that there was too much blood to be accounted for by the spittoon story; the defense said there was not enough blood in the office if Field was killed there by a blow to the head. But most importantly, several witnesses testified that they had seen Herbert Field alive at 2:00 p.m. on September 5. All of Vanderpool's time was accounted for that afternoon, so if Field was alive at 2:00, he could not have been murdered by Vanderpool.

The testimony took thirteen days, and closing arguments lasted six days. Then Vanderpool himself spoke directly to the jury for three hours, asserting his innocence. The jury deliberated for six hours and then returned a verdict of guilty of first-degree murder. George Vanderpool was sentenced to life in solitary confinement at Jackson Prison.

As Vanderpool was beginning his sentence, a growing sentiment in Michigan said that he had not received an impartial trial in Manistee. His supporters raised money to meet the expenses of seeking a new trial and a retrial was secured, with the venue changed to Kalamazoo. This trial was called "a battle of giants" because attorneys on both sides included some of the greatest lawyers in Michigan.

Second Trial: 2. October 23, 1870

This followed much the same lines as the first, with the additional assertion by the defense – including a minute-by-minute breakdown – that even if the murder had been committed the morning of September 5, Vanderpool would not have had time to dispose of the body and return home by the time witnesses saw him there. The trial ended in a hung jury – nine for conviction, three for acquittal.

Third trial: 3. August 8, 1871

This was held in Barry, Michigan. The most dramatic feature of this trial was the appearance of Herbert Field's mother, who, on the first day, confronted a man she incorrectly thought was George Vanderpool and exclaimed,

"Where is my son; where is Herbert Field? Oh, wretched man!"

This time, the defense challenged the identification of the body, claiming it was not conclusively proven to be that of Herbert Field. They also introduced evidence of a strange man in a rowboat rescued in Lake Michigan near the Manistee River around the time of Field's disappearance. He was carrying a large sum of money and later fled to Canada. The defense speculated that he could have been the murderer.

This time the jury deliberated for six hours and returned a verdict of not guilty.

Verdicts: 1. Guilty of first-degree murder,
2. Hung jury,
3. Not guilty.

Aftermath:

As Vanderpool's attorneys were entering a carriage to take them to the train depot, Herbert Field's mother stepped up and exclaimed, "The blood of my son is in Michigan, and will yet be avenged upon Vanderpool and his defenders! You will have your share of the punishment, and I shall meet you at the judgment!"

After leaving prison, Vanderpool did not return to banking. He tried his hand on the lecture circuit for a time but found less interest in his case than he anticipated. Following that, he did his best to escape the notoriety of the Michigan murder by working as a traveling salesman for an Ohio shoe company.

The Boston Barrel Tragedy

1872 was an eventful year for Boston, Massachusetts. That year, the city hosted the World's Peace Jubilee and International Musical Festival, which lasted 18 days and drew thousands of visitors. The Boston Red Stockings won the National Association of Professional Base Ball Players Championship. The Great Boston Fire devastated 65 acres of downtown real estate. And the dismembered body of Abijah Ellis was found stuffed inside two barrels, floating in the Charles River.

Washington St. and Water St., Boston

Date:	November 5, 1872
Location:	Boston, Massachusetts
Victim:	Abijah Ellis
Cause of Death:	Blows from an axe
Accused:	Leavitt Alley

Synopsis:

On the afternoon of Wednesday, November 6, 1872, two barrels were seen floating in the Charles River near the gas works in Cambridge. Some employees pulled them ashore, opened them, and were horrified at what they found. In one barrel, packed with wood shavings and horse manure, was a man's headless, limbless torso. In the other, similarly packed, were his arms, legs, and head. They went for the police and the coroner who determined that the man had been killed by three or four blows to the head from an axe. On close examination of the barrels' contents, they found a piece of brown paper among the wood shavings, upon which was written, "P. Schouller, No. 1049, Washington Street."

Boston police went to the Washington Street address where Mr. Schouller manufactured billiard and bagatelle tables. There, they learned that Leavitt Alley, who ran a delivery business, was in the habit of taking wood shavings from the factory for use in his stable. The previous Monday, Mr. Alley had taken three barrels of shavings to his stable on Hunneman Street.

Sometime between midnight and 1:00 a.m., Boston Police Chief Edward Savage went, with officers Skelton and Dearborn, to the home of Leavitt Alley.

Alley took them to the stable, where he kept four horses. The policemen saw the wood shavings and piles of manure but found nothing unusual that night. The following day, they took Alley to Cambridge to look at the body and the barrels. Alley said that he recognized one of the barrels and that it had been in his stable; he was not sure about the other.

The body had been identified as that of Abijah Ellis, an elderly Boston real estate broker. Alley had purchased a house from Ellis and had fallen behind in his payments. He said he had been with Ellis the previous Saturday and made a small payment to his account. Alley promised to meet him on Tuesday and pay some more, but Alley said they did not meet that day. The police searched the stable in the daylight, and under the manure, the police found blood spatters on the floorboards. They also found blood stains on Alley's clothing. That Saturday, they arrested Leavitt Alley for the murder of Abijah Ellis.

Trial: February 3, 1873

The Great Boston Fire, which started the night of his arrest and raged for twelve hours, destroying 776 buildings in Boston's downtown and financial district, delayed Alley's trial. From his jail cell, Alley was heard lamenting the business he had lost by being imprisoned during the fire, "I should have such a mighty good chance to clear half a thousand dollars if I only had my team."

When the trial began, Massachusetts Attorney General Charles R. Train presented the government's case. The prosecution contended that Leavitt Alley had murdered Abijah Ellis on the night of November 5 during an argument about money Alley owed Ellis. Ellis was known to carry large sums of money, which the prosecution contended was stolen by Alley. They would endeavor to prove that Alley had dismembered the body in his stable and packed it in barrels. The following morning, he pushed the barrels down the sluiceway of the Milldam into the Charles River.

The prosecution called witnesses who had seen an express wagon near the Mill dam in Boston carrying two barrels covered with a piece of old carpet. One man recognized Alley as the driver; others said a very sick horse pulled the wagon. An epidemic of horse distemper was spreading through Boston in 1872 – it was known that one of Alley's horses had the disease.

Ellen Kelley, who lived nearby, testified that on Tuesday night, she heard voices coming from the stable. It was a loud argument, but she could not make out the words until someone shouted, "God damn you." Several witnesses said that on November 6, Alley had paid the money he owed; one man saw him pull bills for a large roll in his pocket.

Regarding the bloodstains in the stable and on Alley's clothing, Alley claimed that a veterinarian had been bleeding one of his horses, treating it for distemper. The blood stains were horse blood, not human. In 1872, it was impossible to prove, with certainty, that a blood stain was human blood; however, in the universities and hospitals of Boston and Cambridge were several experts who did a microscopic analysis of the stains and contended that the blood was human, not horse. The size of the corpuscles determined it – according to the testimony, a human corpuscle is 1/3200 in., and a horse corpuscle is 1/4200 in.

Leavitt Alley's defense attorneys, Lewis S. Dabney and Gustav A. Somerby, challenged the circumstantial evidence against their client. Some witnesses who saw Alley the morning of the 6th gave contradictory testimony. One witness saw him at the Mill dam at half-past eight; another saw him between seven and eight, on Charles Street, driving the other way. They could not both be right.

Several witnesses had seen the barrels floating near the mill dam at various times during the day. If they had all seen the same barrels, the barrels would have had to travel faster than could be accounted for by the tidal flow of the river to be found at the Cambridge gasworks.

The attorneys questioned the motive, saying Ellis's death would not end their client's debt on the house. They also attempted to prove that Alley's financial position was healthy, and he did not need to kill for money.

They also pointed out that the blood analysis had been done on dried blood. To measure the corpuscles, the blood had to be rehydrated. The resulting size of the corpuscles would depend on the quantity and nature of the solution used. The measurement could not be accurate.

The trial lasted for nine days. The jury retired to deliberate shortly before 6:00 p.m., the evening of February 12, 1873. Shortly before 10:00 p.m., they returned with a verdict of not guilty.

Verdict: Not guilty

Aftermath:

The prosecution of the case had been lackluster. There were too many gaps, too many suppositions, and too many leaps of faith. They were unable to present an unbroken chain of evidence against Alley.

Many years later, Ira Nay, a juror in the case, told the *Boston Globe* that Attorney General Train had appeared 'logy' and that the jury referred to him as the 'mud-turtle'. Nay said that he and several other jurymen believed that Alley was guilty but that the Commonwealth had not proven it, so they voted to acquit.

Leavitt Alley died two years after the trial at the age of fifty-nine. It has never been determined who killed Abijah Ellis.

The Maggie Hourigan Mystery

The body of Maggie Hourigan was found floating face down in a small pool of water outside Greenwich, New York. Dr. S. Walter Scott performed a hasty autopsy and concluded that Maggie had committed suicide by drowning. No one who knew Maggie believed she had killed herself, and a second autopsy proved them right. Maggie had been struck on the head before entering the water. Dr. Scott was accused of deliberately hiding this information. Whether true or not, it ruined his reputation.

Maggie Hourigan
National Police Gazette, Nov. 30, 1889.

Date: October 20, 1889
Location: Greenwich, New York
Victim: Maggie Hourigan
Cause of Death: Blows to the head, drowning
Accused: Dr. S. Walter Scott, Lawton Wilber

Synopsis:
Two children playing near their house in Greenwich, New York, on the morning of Saturday, October 20, 1889, found a woman's hat and jacket lying on a log and reported them to a group of men working on a nearby road. Reuben Stewart, Superintendent of Streets, who was also President of the Village, thought the circumstances were suspicious and went down to take a look for himself. It was a secluded spot about halfway between two villages with a small pool of water near the road. Stewart found the owner of the hat and jacket floating face down in the pool.

The woman was soon identified as Maggie Hourigan. The autopsy conducted by Dr. S. Walter Scott and several other physicians determined that she had drowned, and a coroner's jury concluded that it had been suicide.

Maggie's friends did not believe that she had taken her own life. She was a healthy, attractive 19-year-old woman who worked as a servant for the family of

Herbert Reynolds. Her employers described her as "competent, industrious, tidy, cheerful, and an agreeable person to have in the house." Her habits and manners were exemplary; she was naturally timid and not known to have a boyfriend. Maggie's friends said she was happy and lively when they were last together. She was a devout Catholic, and her pastor, Father Fields, spoke of her in glowing terms and did not think it possible that she had committed suicide.

District Attorney Hull ordered a second autopsy, fearing that the autopsy had not been thorough enough. This time, a different team of doctors found a wound on the side of her head that was made before death and was sufficient to produce death or at least unconsciousness. Dr. Montgomery Jones testified that he believed she was alive but unconscious when she entered the water, and the final direct cause of death was drowning. Two other doctors agreed that the wound was inflicted before death, and she was either dead or unconscious when she entered the water. This time, the coroner's jury said they were unable to determine the means or causes of Maggie Hourigan's death.

She had left the Reynolds's house around 7:00 p.m. on October 19. She was to meet three of her friends, Ella and Bertha Obenauer, and Julia Nolan, in front of the Post Office. They were planning to spend the evening with Mrs. Sprague, the wife of the Postmaster. Mrs. Sprague was an excellent musician; the girls had spent Wednesday evening listening to her and were anxious to do it again. When Maggie didn't show up at the Post Office, Julia and the Obenauer sisters called at the Reynolds's to look for her, but no one knew where she had gone.

Maggie's body was found about a mile away from where she lived but in the opposite direction from the Post Office. Rumors were circulating surrounding the death – two strange men were seen on a bridge near the pool where the body was found; a farmer said he heard men's voices and the sound of a struggle nearby, but it was too dark to see; a man's gold watch and chain were found in a stream near the pool. But there were no solid clues. The county offered a reward of $1,500 for information leading to the arrest and conviction of Maggie Hourigan's killer, and District Attorney Hull hired the Pinkerton Detective Agency to investigate.

After the second autopsy, an article in the *New York Sun* implied that Dr. Scott may have come to a false conclusion in the first autopsy because of a conflict of interest in the case. His name came up numerous times in the investigation that followed. In January 1890, it was reported that Dr. Scott admitted to knowing more about the death than he first revealed. He said that on the night of Maggie's death, he was called by a man said to be Howard Bailey to attend an injured girl. He found her in a field with three men who said she had fallen and struck her head. She appeared to be dead, and Scott told the men "they were in a bad scrape" and refused to advise them what to do.

Either the report of Scott's admission was untrue, or it was not taken at face value because soon after, the police brought in a man named Edward Scully for questioning after he told a different story. While drunk, Scully told someone he had been sleeping in a barn near the bridge, and two men came in carrying Maggie's body. They said they had been riding in a carriage when the driver thought he recognized Maggie walking down the road. He tried to snap his whip and give her a start, but the carriage lurched, and he hit her head with the butt of the whip. They sent for a doctor, but she was dead by the time he arrived. The men offered the doctor $500 to keep quiet.

The police knew Scully by reputation and had reason to believe he knew about the murder. Though a young man, he had already served time for horse stealing and burglary. In custody, Scully denied any knowledge of the case. He said he may have spoken of the murder but never told the story that the police had heard. Scully was able to prove that he was not in Greenwich on the night of October 19.

About a month later, Scully and his father told the police that a man named Lawton Wilber had come to their house and talked about the murder. The police arrested Wilber on suspicion of murder, but he was not held. With little progress being made on the case, the Governor of New York offered another $1,000 reward for the capture of her killer.

The following July, an inmate at Dannemora Prison named Merrit Schuler claimed to have information on the murder. District Attorney Hull went to Dannemora to interview Schuler, who was serving five years for forgery. He had been living near Greenwich at the time of the murder and had seen Scott pick up Maggie in his carriage and drive away with her. Schuler said he would provide the whole story if granted a full pardon from the Governor. Hull said he was favorably impressed with the story and would swear Schuler in at the next session of the grand jury. However, it does not appear that he took Schuler up on his offer.

Allegations of his connection to Maggie's death had hurt Scott's practice to such an extent that in May 1892, he sued the *New York Sun* for $20,000 damages for a libelous article in October 1889 regarding his autopsy. In the court case, Scott presented evidence from the coroner and other doctors that Maggie had, in fact, died of drowning as his autopsy concluded. District Attorney Hull, arguing in favor of the Sun, said that if he had not ordered a second autopsy, it would not be known that Maggie was foully murdered.

The jury awarded Dr. Scott $10,000 in damages. The *Sun* appealed the verdict, and in December 1893, a settlement was reached, awarding him $6,000.

The true circumstances of Maggie Hourigan's death remain a mystery.

The Rogers Murder

The morning stillness on East 12th Street, New York City, was shattered on December 31, 1869, by cries of "Murder!" Charles M. Rogers lay bleeding on the sidewalk in front of his house as two men were seen running from the scene. Trying to identify the men would prove daunting.

The Rogers Murder
Frank Leslie's Illustrated Newspaper, Feb. 13, 1869

Dates:	December 31, 1869
Locations:	New York, New York
Victims:	Charles M. Rogers
Cause of Death:	Stabbing
Accused:	James Tallent, James Logan

Synopsis:

Charles M. Rogers, a 60-year-old boardinghouse proprietor, was sweeping the sidewalk in front of the house that morning. The servant who usually swept was sick in bed, so Rogers did the job himself. Around 7:00 a.m., two strangers approached, and one of them, without provocation, accosted Rogers. In the fight that followed, the stranger stabbed Rogers in the abdomen and fled. Rogers, severely wounded, was carried into his house.

Charles Rogers clung to life, but he was clearly on his deathbed. Coroner Flynn was summoned to take Rogers's dying declaration:

> *I am proprietor of the boarding house No. 42 East twelfth street; about 7 o'clock I went out to sweep the sidewalk; while sweeping two strange men came along; one of them took off his coat and handed it to the other when the other said, "Don't Jim," and went across the street; the short man then returned and attacked me brandishing a large knife; he made several strokes of the knife at my head which cut my hat through; I then clinched with him; while struggling he seized my watch and chain and my wallet from my pantaloon*

> *pockets; while he was robbing me I cried "Murder!" and then he stabbed me in the left side and went across the street and got his coat; he then ran away, and I saw him throw something away at the time.*

With Rogers still in critical condition, the police began their investigation. They had very little to go on; the killer had fled, leaving behind his hat, the leather sheaf of his knife, and the tail of his suit coat torn off in the scuffle. And they knew his name was Jim. One witness, a boy named William Gloucester, had seen the fight but could not say who the men were. The police began looking for known criminals in the area; particularly members of the Nineteenth Street Gang named Jim.

Around 1.00 a.m., on January 1, James Tallent. a member of the Nineteenth Street Gang went to the Fifteenth Ward Station House and told the desk sergeant that he understood that the detectives were looking for him on suspicion of murder. He said he was innocent, and he wanted to clear his name. They took him before Charles Rogers, who was clinging to life but still in full possession of his faculties. Rogers confirmed that Tolland was not the man who assaulted him. However, the witness, William Gloucester, identified Tallent as one of Rogers's assailants. The police held Tallent in custody to await further developments.

Charles Rogers died soon after seeing Tallent. The crime became murder, and the police offered a $500 reward – raised at the mayor's request to $1,000 – for the apprehension of the killer. A coroner's inquest commenced on January 6.

Tallent was still in custody, and the police were looking for a different Jim. Inside the torn piece of coat found at the scene was an empty envelope addressed "Jim Logan, city," followed by "This will be delivered to you by Tom."

When it was reported in newspapers, another man came to the police station and said, "This 'ere article in this newspaper was shown to me this evening, and as that is my name and description, I came to give myself up. It is a very serious matter to have one's name in the newspaper."

Jim Logan denied any knowledge of the murder but thought the letter might have been intended for him. He had been in Sing Sing prison, and the letter looked like the kind they would sneak out of the prison through canal boats, visitors, or released prisoners. But he had not received the letter and had no idea who Tom was. The police kept Jim Logan in custody.

On January 11, the police arrested George "Butch" Johnson, another Nineteenth Street gang member, in the St. Bernard Hotel's barroom where he was drinking with a group of men. The police believed that Butch was in possession of certain undisclosed facts regarding the murder, but he had nothing important to tell them and was released after a night in jail.

The following day, the police arrested another Jim Logan along with his brother Michael. The brothers had been absent from their home since the murder, raising suspicion. The killer's hat fit Jim, but beyond that, there was no evidence to connect Jim or his brother to the murder. Nevertheless, Jim was locked up in the police station, and Michael was held as a witness in the House of Detention.

Coroner Flynn traveled to Sing Sing Prison, 30 miles north of New York City on the Hudson River. After consulting with the warden, Flynn believed that the killer was an escaped convict (name withheld "for prudential reasons") who was an associate of the first Jim Logan. He had intended to hand the letter to someone on the sloop docked at Sing Sing but saw an opportunity to escape on board the boat. He tore up the letter but, for some reason, kept the envelope.

Not everyone in the police or the public accepted this theory. A private citizen in the Fifteenth Ward learned that yet another James Logan was living in Hoboken, New Jersey. He took the information to the police, who rushed to New Jersey, grabbed the man, and brought him to New York. The third James Logan proved to be an honest man with no criminal record or connection to the crime. He was released after spending a miserable night in a stationhouse cell.

Another theory, floated by a police detective, said the murder was committed by "…some lawless boatman or river pirate, returning from a debauch with his companion…his bad passions inflamed by the effects of the previous night's frolic."

Meanwhile, the escaped prisoner (name still withheld) sent word, through his friends, that he was innocent of the murder. Had he been guilty, he was sure one of his companions would have sold him out for the reward. He offered to give himself up and prove his innocence, provided he was not sent back to Sing Sing. The police did not accept the offer.

The mayor issued a proclamation that was posted in all parts of the city. It included a facsimile of the envelope.

Below the picture, it asked for information about the writer of the letter, the carrier, the handwriting, or Tom's identity, offering a reward of $250 to $1,000, depending on the value of the information.

The people of New York were horrified by the coldblooded murder and were appalled by the ineptitude of the police – a sentiment echoed in the press:

"The search for the murderers of Charles M. Rogers is still prosecuted by the police with unrelenting vigor, but with rather indifferent success," said the New York World. "The police evidently will not rest satisfied until every person bearing the fatal name James Logan has been arrested and examined."

"The history of the case is made up, thus far, of doubts, suspicions, speculations, vague reports, and contradictory statements, leaving the public mind in a feverish condition of suspense and excitement," said *Frank Leslie's Illustrated Newspaper*.

"Have the police caught the murderer of Mr. Rogers, or have they not?" asked the *Journal of Commerce*. "They act as if they wanted to make people think they have the murderer locked up; and yet we understand that the detectives are pushing fresh scents in every direction."

The investigation was stalled until mid-March when William C. Cunningham, a prisoner in jail for bigamy in Westchester County, claimed to have information on the murder. His long and rambling story essentially said that James Logan (No. 2) and James Tallent plotted to murder Charles Rogers because he testified against Logan in an 1859 robbery case in Patterson, New Jersey. Cunningham offered to provide evidence against Logan if he was assured immunity from prosecution. The story proved false; no James Logan was tried in Patterson that year and Logan No. 2 would have been 12 years old then. It was considered a hoax, either contrived by a reporter to excite attention or by the Nineteenth Street Gang to further muddy the waters.

Though Cunningham's story was discredited, suspicion around Logan No. 2 continued to grow. It was reported that the police were ready to take Logan to the Grand Jury, but there was no movement until Logan's attorney, William Howe, filed a petition with the Supreme Court to either indict his client or set him free. On March 19, the District Attorney filed papers to indict James Logan No. 2 for the murder of Charles Rogers. The Grand Jury failed to find an indictment, and on March 31, James Logan No. 2 was released.

The investigation of the Rogers murder was effectively over. In April, the remaining prisoners and witnesses were released.

The case remained dormant until January 1870, when James Logan No. 2 was shot in an affray on Houston Street. As Logan lay dying in Bellevue Hospital, Coroner Flynn and his deputy hurried to his bedside to take his antemortem statement in which they hoped he would confess the murder. Logan dictated this statement:

> *I, James Logan, believing that I am about to die this night, and having no hopes of recovery from the injuries I have received, do hereby declare that the charge that was made against me last year, of murdering Mr. Charles M. Rogers, on December 21, 1869, in Twelfth street, was false, and that I am entirely innocent; I did not know the party who committed the deed, nor have I any knowledge whatsoever of it.*
>
> *his*
> *"James (X) Logan."*
> *mark*

James Logan died five minutes after making his mark on the statement. The murder of Charles M. Rogers will remain forever unsolved.

Chloroformed to Death

A terrible crime occurred at the home of Dr. Arthur Kniffin in Trenton, New Jersey, on the night of January 2, 1890. While he was out of town, someone entered the house and chloroformed his wife Myra and her cousin Emma Purcell. Myra died as a result, but Emma recovered and told of burglars charging through the door and subduing them both. Friends and family accepted this story, but Emma had a history of crying wolf, and rumors afloat in Trenton said that Dr. Kniffin's relations with his wife's cousin "were not what they should have been."

How Miss Purcell Was Found
National Police Gazette, Jan. 15, 1890

Date:	January 2, 1890
Location:	Trenton, New Jersey
Victim:	Myra Kniffin
Cause of Death:	Chloroform
Accused:	Arthur Kniffin & Emma Purcell

Synopsis:
Early on the morning of January 2, 1890, Dr. Arthur Kniffin left to catch a train to the town of Broadway, New Jersey, to look at a piece of property he was planning to buy. Broadway was the home of his wife's cousin, Emma Purcell, who lived with the Kniffins in Trenton in 1890. She worked there as a typist for the Empire Rubber Works. Dr. Kniffin had seen Miss Purcell at the train depot when he arrived on Broadway – she had been home for the holidays and would be returning to Trenton that afternoon.

Dr. Kniffin had also been away from home on the night of November 30. That night, three burglars climbed a ladder and broke into the house through a third-story window. They entered the room where Emma and Myra were sleeping, and while one man held Emma in bed at knifepoint, the other two went through the house, opening drawers and examining jewelry. They left with $16 cash and nothing else. Mrs. Kniffin, in the same bed, managed to sleep through the entire incident. The police were notified, and an investigation was begun, but after several days with no clues, they gave it up. The case was entered in their books as "mysterious."

Though little was taken, the burglary upset the household, and the Kniffins' ten-year-old son, Lennie, began sleeping at the home of Mrs. James Murphy, his grandmother. On January 2, with Kniffin away again, Mrs. Murphy asked her daughter and Emma to stay with her as well. Myra declined, saying she was not afraid; she kept a loaded seven-shot revolver under her pillow.

The following morning, Kniffin's partner, Dr. William Shannon, arrived at 7:30 a.m. to open the office. He found the furniture in disarray, burned matches on the floor, and other evidence of burglary. He called for Mrs. Kniffin and, receiving no reply, went upstairs to her bedroom. He found her lying in bed and Emma Purcell lying on the floor. Thinking they were both dead, Shannon hurried downstairs for help. When he returned with two men from the drugstore, he found that Miss Purcell was partly conscious.

When touched, she exclaimed, "Oh, the burglars! Run, Myra, run!"

Myra was dead. A corner of a quilt had been saturated with chloroform and held over her face. The odor still lingered in the room.

Later that afternoon, when Emma Purcell was sufficiently revived to make a statement, she said she was not unconscious when they found her on the floor but felt as though she was paralyzed, unable to move her hands and feet. Emma told the police she and Mrs. Kniffin had gone to bed at the same time. Both were cheerful and stayed awake talking for a time. Then she nodded off. She couldn't say how long she had slept but was awakened by a touch from Mrs. Kniffin, who screamed that a burglar was pushing open the door. Miss Purcell heard the noise, sprang out of bed, and, running to the front window, called loudly for help. One of the burglars seized her, then threw her to the floor and pressed a wet cloth over her face. That was all she remembered. When she was told that Myra was dead, Emma became hysterical.

Kniffin was summoned home by telegraph but not told of his wife's death until he arrived at 8:30 p.m. He was taken to Police Headquarters and extensively questioned about his movements the previous day, then brought to his house to determine if anything had been stolen. Nothing appeared to be missing, but the furniture had been disturbed in the dental office. The day's receipts were usually kept in a drawer there, but Dr. Shannon had taken the cash home the night before for safekeeping.

While relatives of Mrs. Kniffin, including her mother, believed Emma Purcell's story of the burglary, the police and the press did not. In a story dated January 3, 1890, the *New York Times* put the word "robbery" in quotes while describing Miss Purcell's account. The house had been locked, there was no evidence of a break-in, and nothing was taken.

Kniffin was known to be a sporting man who would bet $500 or more on a horse race. That would explain why burglars might target his house but not why the burglaries always occurred when he was away. To the chagrin of the Kniffin family and their friends, the police were doing nothing to investigate the alleged robbery.

The murder became the talk of the town, and the rumor mills of Trenton were churning out their own opinions of the case. Kniffin was a lifelong resident of Trenton, prominent and well-known; many in town had stories about the family. It was said that relations between him and his wife had deteriorated, and he was known to hit her on occasion. He would often walk Emma Purcell home from the Rubber Works where she worked, and the two had been seen "in secluded localities together, conducting themselves as lovers usually do." Many believed that the burglary story was a ruse and that Emma Purcell had conspired with Dr. Kniffin to murder his wife.

Coroner's Inquest: January 6, 1890

As the coroner's inquest into the cause of Mrs. Kniffen's death began, events outside the courtroom took another sensational turn. Around 3:30 a.m. on January 7, Dr. Kniffin attempted suicide. Emma's brother, David Purcell, was staying at the house, and he and Dr. Kiffin had been up after 1:00 a.m. to say goodbye to another relative. Kniffin told Purcell that he wanted to take a bath before bed. Around 3:30am, Purcell heard him stumbling to bed and went to see what was wrong. He found Dr. him vomiting and realized that he had taken poison; he was also bleeding from his wrist and throat. Purcell gave him an emetic and ran to get help. He brought two physicians back to the house, saving Kniffin's life.

The family said that Kniffin had acted out of grief over the death of his wife, but once again, the police and the press were unconvinced. Though Kniffin had ingested a large amount of the poison aconite, he would have known that the effect would be nausea, with the result of eliminating the poison. On his wrist was a slight cut, "a feeble attempt to sever the radial artery," and on the right side of his neck was "another weak attack on the carotid artery." Both cuts were only deep enough to penetrate the skin. If he had been intent on suicide, he had plenty of uninterrupted time to do so.

As the inquest proceeded, with more than sixty witnesses scheduled to testify, Kniffin and David Purcell hired the Pinkertons and a local private detective to do what the Trenton police refused: find the burglars. The people of Trenton were divided in their opinion, though most were against Kniffin. As the story became national news, the police received letters from around the country expressing opinions on how to proceed.

The inquest into Mrs. Kniffin's murder went on until January 28, with the courtroom filled to capacity every day. Kniffin and Emma were considered suspects, and by the end, Dr. Shannon, Kniffin's partner, was also considered. However, James Murphy, Mrs. Kniffin's father, and other members of her family did not believe that anyone in the household or Shannan was involved. There was some attempt to identify the alleged burglars, but, in the end, the jury found that Myra Kniffin was murdered by the hand of "some person unknown to the jury." But the jury had their suspicions and recommended that the Grand Jury take up the case. This was done in February, but to the consternation of the Trenton Police, the Grand Jury did not hand down any incitements.

Verdict: No indictments

Aftermath:

With no one indicted, the Trenton Police's interest in the case was effectively over, but the press would have one more go-round. The following December, the *Washington Critic-Record* printed an unsubstantiated rumor that Kniffin had married Emma Purcell and the two were living together in New Brunswick, New Jersey. When confronted, Dr. Kniffin accused the newspapers of persecuting him but did not deny the rumor.

Conclusion

The bloody nineteenth century, in many ways, set the stage for an even bloodier twentieth. The per capita murder rate rose steadily throughout the nineteenth century and continued rising, with some fluctuation through the twentieth. But the numbers are only part of the story. As the century progressed, immigration, industrialization, and the growth of cities led to heightened social tension. Increased mobility made murderers' escape easier but was offset by modern investigation methods.

Murder weapons changed over time. In the nineteenth century, knives and axes, found in every home, were weapons of convenience, often used in domestic murders. Clubs, hammers, rocks, and other blunt instruments were always handy when disputes turned violent. Poisons, especially arsenic, were readily available for more premeditated homicides. Firearm technology increased rapidly and, following the Civil War, a surprising number of men regularly carried pistols, even in eastern cities. Handguns were increasingly prevalent and in the twentieth century became the most common murder weapon.

Changes in law enforcement were the most dramatic. In the nineteenth century, forensic analysis was rudimentary. Chemists could not distinguish human blood from that of other animals, examination of bullets revealed little beyond the caliber, poison deaths were often misdiagnosed, and fingerprinting was unknown. Criminal prosecution relied on eyewitness testimony and circumstantial evidence. In the twentieth century, scientific analysis would dominate the courtroom.

Crime-related murders have increased, but beyond that, motives for murder have not significantly changed. Financial gain, passion and jealousy, revenge, domestic violence, and mental illness remain ever-present motives. Times may change, and technology improve, but the murderous impulse endures.

Notes

CRIME

The Long Island Murders

"The Alleged Murderer." *New Haven Register.* November 20. 1883.
"Another Long Island Tragedy." *Cincinnati Commercial Tribune.* January 9, 1884.
"Brookville's Horror." *Truth.* November 21, 1883.
"Charles Rugg Escapes." *New York Herald.* February 18, 1884.
"Clamoring for the Reward." *New York Herald.* April 27, 1885.
"A Horrible Confession." *Boston Journal.* January 18, 1884.
"Garrett Maybee Testifies." *New York Herald.* April 24, 1884.
"How Rugg Was Recaptured." *New Haven Register.* February 21, 1884.
"The Long Island Murders." *New York Herald.* January 29, 1884.
"The Long Island Tragedy-the Murder Probably Caught." *Boston Journal.* November 20, 1883.
"Long Island's Strange Crimes Extraordinary Conflict of Evidence in the Maybee and Townsend Cases." *New York Herald.* February 3, 1884.
"Mason Tappan Arrested The Owner of the Hammer and Overalls Charged with the Townsend "Outrage." *New York Herald.* January 16, 1884.
"Maybee." *Truth.* December 1, 1883
"The Maybee Murders." *New York Herald.* January 25, 1884.
"The Maybee Tragedy." *Philadelphia Inquirer.* November 22, 1883.
"Murder Most Foul." *National Police Gazette.* December 8, 1883.
"Points for the Tramp." *New York Herald.* November 23, 1883.
"Robbery the Only Motive." *New York Herald.* January 9, 1884.
"Rugg Guilty of Murder." *New York Herald.* April 26, 1884.
"Rugg's Neck Broken." *New York Herald.* May 16, 1885.
"Strangled to Death." *New York Herald.* November 18, 1883.
"The Strangled Victims." *New York Herald.* November 20, 1883.
"Struck down in His Barn." *New York Herald.* January 26, 1884.
"The Tappan Brothers." *New York Herald.* January 21, 1884.
"Tappan Cries in Court." *New Haven Register.* January 28, 1884.
"Wife And Daughter Killed." *New York Tribune.* November 19, 1883.

Professional Poisoners

"Charged with Many Murders," *Daily Inter Ocean,* Jul. 14, 1893.
"Dr. Meyer in Sing Sing," *New York Herald,* June 9, 1894.
"Dr. Meyer Killed His Partner in Crime for His Life Insurance," *Cincinnati Tribune,* February 16, 1896.
"An Expert Murderer," *Daily Inter Ocean,* Jul. 14, 1893.
"The Insurance Swindle," *Worcester Daily Spy,* Dec. 9, 1893.

"Juryman Low's Mind Unbalanced," *New York Herald,* Dec. 19, 1893.
"Long-Sought Murderer Arrested," *Fitchburg Sentinel,* Jul. 13, 1893.
"Meyer Gets A New Trial," *New York Tribune,* Dec. 22, 1893.
"Meyer May Break Down To-morrow," *New York Herald,* Dec. 17, 1893.
"Meyer's Defense Was Soon Closed," *New York Herald,* Dec. 16, 1893.
"Poisoned For Insurance," *Syracuse Evening Herald,* Jul. 13, 1893.
"A Poisoner's Crimes," *New York World,* Jul. 16, 1893.
"Professional Poisoners," *Owyhee Avalanche,* Jan. 6, 1894.
"A Sigh of Relief," *Worcester Daily Spy,* May 19, 1894.
"The Trial Of Dr. Meyer Postponed," *New York Tribune,* Dec. 20, 1893.

A Harum-Scarum Creature

"A Beautiful Murderess on Trial," *Wheeling Register,* Jan. 20, 1885.
"A Beautiful Woman Held for Murder," *Cleveland Leader,* Nov. 2, 1883.
"Divorce Wanted," *Plain Dealer,* Nov. 5, 1883.
Mary E. Jackson, *The Life of Nellie C. Bailey* (Topeka: R. E. Martin & Co., 1885).
"Naughty Nellie," *Daily Register,* Jan. 26, 1885.
"Nellie Bailey," *Daily Gazette,* Nov. 9, 1883.
"Nellie Bailey," *Rockford Weekly Gazette,* Nov. 14, 1883.
"A Noted Woman Acquitted on the Charge of Murder," *Boston Journal,* Jan. 21, 1885.
"A Pretty Woman in Trouble," *National Police Gazette,* Dec. 1, 1883.
"Suspicious Death," *Statesman,* Oct. 25, 1883.
"A Wicked Beauty," *Wheeling Register,* Nov. 10, 1883.

The Minneapolis Svengali

Goodsell Edward H, *Harry Hayward: Life, crimes, dying confession and execution of the Celebrated Minneapolis Criminal,* (Minneapolis: Calhoun, 1896).
"Harry Hayward Hung at Night," *New York Times,* Dec. 12, 1895.
"Hayward Has Confessed," *New York Times,* Dec. 11, 1895.
Tim and Allen S. Koenigsberg, "The Last Words Of Harry Hayward (A True Record Mystery)," *The Antique Phonograph Monthly,* June-July 1973.
"The Notorious Harry Hayward," MOST NOTORIOUS! Jun. 4, 2016, https://www.mostnotorious.com/2012/11/07/the-notorious-harry-hayward/.
John-Ivan Palmer, "The Origin of Mesmeric Death," Whistling Shade, 2009, http://www.whistlingshade.com/0901/mesmerism.html.
Walter N. Trenerry, Murder *in Minnesota: A collection of true cases,* (St, Paul: Minnesota Historical Society, 1985).
Stuart Charles Wade, *Lured to death, or, The Minneapolis murder,* (E. A. Weeks, 1895).

He Knew Too Much

Mark E. Dixon, "In 1874 Chester County, photography was enough to hang a man," Main Line Today. March 24, 2009.
https://mainlinetoday.com/uncategorized/picture-perfect-2/
Headsman. "1874: William Udderzook, because a picture is worth a thousand words," Executed Today. November 12, 2008,
https://www.executedtoday.com/2008/11/12/1874-william-udderzook-because-a-picture-is-worth-a-thousand-words/
John B. Lewis and Charles C. Bombaugh. *Strategems and Conspiracies to Defraud Life Insurance Companies: An Authentic Record of Remarkable Cases. 2nd ed.* (Baltimore: Office of the Baltimore Underwriter, 1896).
William E. Udderzook and George L. Barclay. *The Udderzook Mystery! Containing a Detailed and Accurate Account of The Life of The Murderer, His Trial and Sentence, The Disappearance of W.S. Goss, ... Closely Bearing upon this Great Case,* (Philadelphia: Published by Barclay & Co., 1873.

The Nicely Brothers

"Accused of Murder," *Patriot.* Mar. 5, 1889.
"An Atrocious Murder," *Daily Illinois State Journal,* Mar. 1, 1889.
"Board Of Pardons," *Patriot,* Nov. 12, 1890.
"Dave Nicely Confessed," *Patriot,* Apr. 10, 1891.
"General News Two Murderers Escape from Jail but Are Captured after a Lively Chase," *Bismarck Tribune,* Sept. 17, 1889.
"Held for Trial," *Cincinnati Commercial Tribune,* Mar. 7, 1889.
"Murderer Nicely Insane," *Patriot,* Mar. 13, 1891.
"Murder Of Herman Umberger," *Plain Dealer,* Mar. 2, 1889.
"Nicely Recaptured," *Jackson Citizen,* Dec. 9, 1890
"A Prison Mystery," *Jackson Citizen Patriot,* Mar. 9, 1891.
"Slid Down a Rope," *Cleveland Leader,* Nov 30, 1890.
"A Startling Conspiracy," *Evening Star,* May 7, 1889.
"The Murderers Found," *Philadelphia Inquirer,* Mar. 7, 1889.
"The Nicely Case," *Patriot,* Jan. 10, 1891.
"The Nicelys Hanged!," *Somerset Herald,* Apr. 2, 1891.
"The Nicelys May be Guiltless," *Philadelphia Inquirer,* Mar. 29, 1891.
Edward H. Werner, *The Umberger Tragedy*, (Somerset: The Highland Farmer, 1890).
"What the Pardon Board Did," *Patriot,* May 3, 1890.
"A Winter Night's Terrible Crime," *New York Herald,* Aug. 4, 1889.

The Blue Eyed Six

Edna J. Carmean, The *Blue Eyed Six*, (Lebanon, PA: Sowers Printing Company, 1974).
Gary Ludwig, *The Blue Eyed Six: A Historical Narrative.* (Lebanon, PA: Hodge Podge USA. 1979).

"The Infamous Blue-Eyed Six of Lebanon Co., Pa." *users*.nbn.net. http://users.nbn.net/charo/blueeyed6.html
"The Trial of The Blue Eyed Six For The Murder Of Joseph Raber." *Sgtmajor*.net. https://www.sgtmajor.net/blueyed.htm

The Cannibal of Austerlitz

"1888: The Last Hanging in New York State," Cornell University Law School, https://forum.lawschool.cornell.edu/Vol36_No1/Feature-3.cfm.html
"The Alford Tragedy Hudson, New York," *New York Herald,* Jan. 15, 1882.
"An American Cannibal," *Jackson Citizen,* Feb. 7, 1882.
"Another Hill-Town Tragedy," *Springfield Republican,* Jan. 13, 1882.
"The Austerlitz Horror," *Boston Herald,* Jan. 14, 1882.
"Berkshire County," *Springfield Republican,* Jan. 17, 1882.
"The Cannibal Caught," *Wheeling Register,* Feb 13, 1882.
"Crazed by a Murder," *Jersey Journal,* Jan. 27, 1882.
"A Hermit Savaged," *Jersey Journal,* Jan. 13, 1882.
"Local Intelligence Local Notices," *Springfield Republican,* Feb. 8, 1882.
"Local Matters," *Times,* Jan. 19, 1882.
"The Man-Eater Captured," *Chicago Daily News,* Feb. 7, 1882.
"On the Gallows," *Boston Globe,* Mar. 1, 1888.
"Roasting a Corpse," *National Police Gazette,* Jan. 28, 1882.

The Brooklyn Barber

"The Death Penalty." *New York Times.* Apr. 11, 1874.
Allan McLane Hamilton and Lawrence Godkin. *A system of legal medicine.* (New York: E.B. Treat, 1900).
Emil Lowenstein, *Trial of Emil Lowenstein for the Murder of John D. Weston, at West Albany, August 5, 1873, Commenced at the Albany Oyer and Terminer, Monday, January ... Arguments of Counsel, Charge of the Court.* (Albany: William Gould & Son, 1874).

The Notorious Mrs. Clem

"A Murder Trial," *Elkhart Weekly Review,* Dec. 24, 1868.
"Another Chance," *Indianapolis Sentinel,* Jun. 14, 1873.
"Arrested for Murder," *Cleveland Leader,* Sep. 17, 1868.
"Confession and Suicide," *Sun,* Mar. 1869.
"Criminal Circuit Court," *Indianapolis Journal,* Jul. 12, 1871.
"Free," *Indianapolis Sentinel,* 30 Apr. 1874.
"From Indianapolis," *Cincinnati Daily Gazette,* Dec. 9, 1868.
Wendy Gamber, "'The Notorious Mrs. Clem': Gender, Class, and Criminality in Gilded Age America," *The Journal of the Gilded Age and Progressive Era,* 2012.
"Indiana," *New York Herald,* Sep. 14, 1868.

"Indianapolis," *Cincinnati Commercial Tribune,* Feb. 9, 1869.
"Letter from Indianapolis," *Muncie Telegraph,* Jun. 17, 1871.
"Marion County Criminal Court," *Indianapolis Journal,* Apr. 7, 1869.
"Nancy E, Clem Dead," *Evening Star,* Jun. 9. 1897.
"Nancy E, Clem!" *Indianapolis People*, Mar. 20, 1880.
"The Abrams Trial," *Indianapolis Journal,* Sep. 1, 1869.
"The Abrams Trial," *New Albany Daily Ledger,* Sep. 3, 1869.
"The Cold Spring Tragedy," *Indianapolis Journal,* 8 Oct. 8, 1868.
The Cold Spring Tragedy: Trial and Conviction of Mrs. Nancy E, Clem, (Indianapolis: A, C, Roach, 1869).
"The Cold Spring Horror," *Indianapolis People.* Jun. 16, 1872.
"The Notorious Mrs. Clem Arrested for Larceny," *Cincinnati Daily Gazette,* Jun. 14, 1878.
"The Prather Case," *Indianapolis Journal,* Jun. 7, 1871.
"The Spring Trial," *Indianapolis Evening Journal,* May. 31, 1872.
"The Trial of Mrs. Clem," *New Albany Daily Ledger,* Jun. 28, 1872.
"The Young Murder," *New Albany Daily Ledger,* Dec. 2, 1868.
"The Young Murder," *Indianapolis Daily Journal,* Dec. 3, 1868.
"The Young Murder Case," *Cincinnati Daily Enquirer,* Mar. 7, 1869.
"The Young Murder Trial," *New Albany Daily Commercial,* Dec. 3, 1868.
"The Young Murder Trial," *Indianapolis Journal,* Feb. 24, 1869.

ROMANCE

A Crime of Passion

Joel Clough and Christian Brown, *Trial, Sentence, Confession and Execution of Joel Clough: Who Was Executed on the 26th July, for the Willful Murder of Mrs. Mary Hamilton, at Bordentown, N. Jersey on the 6th of April, 1833.: Also an Account of His Escape from Prison a Few Days Previous to His Execution* (New-York: Printed and sold wholesale and retail by Christian Brown, no. 211 Water near Fulton Street, 1833).

Joel Clough, *The authentic confession of Joel Clough: The murderer of Mrs. Mary W. Hamilton. With an extract of a letter to his mother. Chief Justice Hornblowers charge ... by order of the Sheriff of Burlington County.* (Philadelphia, Pa.: By order of the Sheriff of Burlington County, 1833).

Confessions, Trials, and Biographical Sketches of the Most Cold Blooded Murderers, Who Have Been Executed in This Country from Its First Settlement Down to the Present Time, (Boston: William H. Hill, 1843).

The Six Capsules

Carlyle W. Harris, *The Trial Of Carlyle W. Harris For Poisoning His Wife, Helen Potts, At New York: For The People: Francis L. Wellman. Charles E. Simms, Jr. For The ... A Taylor. Wm. T. Jerome. Chas. E. Davison...* (New York: [s.n.], 1892).

H.M. Snively, "The Six Capsules," *Pearson's Magazine.* Jan. 17-22, 1919.

"Carlyle W. Harris is Dead." *The New York Times, May 9, 1893*

The Bessie Little Mystery

"A Bullet in Her Head," Philadelphia Inquirer, Sep. 6, 1896.

"The Death Penalty," *Dayton Herald,* Nov. 19, 1897.

"Devil's Deed," *Kentucky Post,* Sep. 7, 1896.

"Frantz's Fight For His Life," *Kentucky Post,* Dec. 14, 1896.

"Frantz's Revolver," *Dayton Herald,* Dec. 18, 1896.

"Franz has Another Story," *Plain Dealer,* Sep. 11, 1896.

"His Love for Another," *Kentucky Post,* Sep. 10, 1896.

"Is it Murder?" *Kentucky Post,* Sep. 5, 1896.

"Located," *Kentucky Post,* Sep. 12, 1896.

"Murder or Suicide?" *National Police Gazette,* Jan. 16, 1897.6.

"One Link," *Kentucky Post,* Sep. 5, 1896.

"Sentenced Frantz," *Aberdeen Daily News,* Jan. 27, 1897.

"She Was Murdered," *Plain Dealer,* Sep. 6, 1896.

"Two Stories Of A Crime," *Plain Dealer,* Dec. 17, 1896.

"A Woman's Death," *Cleveland Leader,* Sep. 4, 1896

Kissing Cousins

"The Murder of Lillian Madison, 1885," The *Shockoe Examiner*, Jun 18, 2019, https://theshockoeexaminer.blogspot.com/2010/06/murder-of-lillian-madison-1885.html.
Cluverius, Thomas J. *Cluverius: My life, trial, and conviction,* (Richmond, Va.: S.J. Dudley, 1887).
Ezekiel, Herbert T. *The Recollections of a Virginia Newspaper Man,* (Richmond, Va.: H.T. Ezekiel, 1920).
"Fannie Madison's Death," *New York Times*, Mar. 20, 1885
"Lilian Madison Buried," *New York Times,* Mar. 21, 1885
Michael Ayers Trotti, *The Body in the Reservoir: Murder and Sensationalism in the South.* (Chapel Hill: University of North Carolina, 2008).

The Kentucky Tragedy

The Avenger's Doom, (Louisville: E. E. Barclay, A. R. Orton & Co., 1851).
The Beauchamp Tragedy in Kentucky. (New York: Dinsmore & Co., 1858).
Steve Dunn, "Jereboam Orville Beauchamp." *Find a Grave, May 17, 2003, https://www.*findagrave.com/memorial/7456387/jereboam-orville-beauchamp.
"Jereboam Orville Beauchamp." *Murderpedia.* https://murderpedia.org/male.B/b/beauchamp-jereboam.htm
Matthew G. Schoenbachler, *Murder & Madness, The Myth of the Kentucky Tragedy.* (Lexington: University Press of Kentucky, 2009).
L. J. Sharp, *Vindication of the Character of the Late Col. Solomon P. Sharp.* (Frankfort: Amos Kendall and Co., 1827).

JEALOUSY

Murder by Mail

"Botkin Defense Maligns Living and Dead to Account for Poison," *San Francisco Chronicle,* Mar. 24, 1904.
"Botkin Extradition Papers," *Oregonian,* Oct. 2, 1898.
"Botkin Trial Ends in a Sensational Manner," *Bisbee Daily Review, Mar.* 31, 1904.
"Contrary to Expectation Jury in Botkin Case Will Continue," *San Francisco call,* Apr. 1, 1904.
"Death in Candy," *Middletown Transcript,* Aug. 13, 1898.
"Death of Mrs. J. P. Dunning," *Wilmington Daily Republican,* Aug. 13, 1898.
"The Dover Case," *Evening Journal,* Aug. 22, 1898.
"Family Poisoned by Candy," *Evening Journal,* Aug. 12, 1898.
"Grand Jury Acts in Botkin Case," *St, Louis Republic,* Oct. 29, 1898,
"Imprisoned for Life," *Evening Bulletin,* Aug. 23, 1904,
"Law's Net for Two Women," *Wilmington Daily Republican,* Aug. 23, 1898,
"Life Imprisonment," *Paducah Sun,* Apr. 8, 1904,
"Mr. Dunning Gives No Clue," *The Wilmington Daily Republican,* Aug. 22, 1898.
"Mrs. Botkin, Charged with Murder, Asks for Justice," *San Francisco Call,* Aug. 30, 1898.
"Mrs. Botkin is Buried," *Los Angeles Examiner,* Mar. 20, 1910.
"Mrs. Botkin Plans a Desperate Defense," *San Francisco Chronicle,* Aug. 26, 1898,
"Mrs. Botkin Will fight for Liberty," *Oakland Tribune,* Aug. 26, 1898.
"Mrs. Botkins' Arrest," *Evening Journal,* Aug. 24, 1898.
"Mrs. Dunning Dead," *Evening Journal,* Aug. 13, 1898.
"A Mysterious Letter," *Evening Journal,* Aug. 18, 1898.
"New Trial for Mrs. Botkin," *Jersey Journal,* Aug. 17, 1900.
"Reward For Poisoner," *Evening Journal,* Aug. 19, 1898.
"Sentenced for Life," *Daily Ardmoreite,* February 7, 1899.
"State Has a Clue," *Wilmington Daily Republican,* Aug. 20, 1898.
"Women are Watched," *Wilmington Daily Republican,* Aug. 24, 1898.

The Webster Mystery

"Alice Hoyle Recants," *Boston Herald,* Oct. 10, 1888.
"Confessed," *National Police Gazette,* May 26, 1888.
"Cruelly Murdered," *New York Herald,* Sep. 22, 1887.
"Fair Lillie Hoyle," *Worcester Daily Spy,* Sep. 22, 1887.
"For the Lilla Hoyle Murder," *Boston Herald,* May 6, 1888.
"A Foul Murder," *Boston Daily Advertiser,* Sep. 21, 1887.
"Lilla Hoyle's Death," *Boston Herald,* March 19, 1891.
"Lillian Hoyle's Slayer," *New York Herald,* Oct. 15, 1887.
"Lillie at Camp White," *New York Herald,* Sep. 23, 1887.
"Lillie Hoyle," *National Police Gazette,* Oct. 8, 1887.

"Lillie Hoyle," *National Police Gazette,* Oct. 15, 1887.
"The Lillie Hoyle Case," *New Haven Register,* Sep. 26, 1887.
"Lillie Hoyle's Fate," *National Police Gazette,* Oct. 8, 1887.
"Lillie Hoyle's Murder," *Boston Daily Advertiser,* Nov. 1, 1887.
"Lillie Hoyle's Murder," *Worcester Daily Spy,* Oct. 2, 1888.
"Lillie Hoyle's Sad Fate," *New York Herald,* Oct. 11, 1887.
"Lillie's Uncle Arrested," *New York Herald,* May 6, 1888.
"Murder Mystery at Webster," *Boston Herald,* Sep. 21, 1887.
"She Was Not Murdered," *Trenton Evening Times,* Oct. 15, 1888.
"Stranger than Fiction," *Boston Herald,* Nov. 16, 1888.

Cain and Abel

Anonymous, "The Modern Cain and Abel."
"Dying in Cell," Boston Daily Globe, Dec. 26, 1891.
"Found Guilty," *Boston Daily Globe*, Dec. 26, 1890.
"He was Foully Murdered," *New York Times*, Feb. 15, 1890.
"Headless in the Woods," *Sun*, Feb. 15, 1890.
"Hiram Sawtelle's Skull Found," *New York Times*, Dec. 7, 1891.
"In Isaac's Defense," *Boston Herald*, Dec. 24, 1890.
"Isaac's Cry," *Boston Daily Globe*, Dec. 1, 1891.
"Issac's Fate," *Boston Daily Globe*, Dec. 7, 1891.
"His Brother's Blood Found Upon Him," *New York Herald*, Feb. 15, 1890.
"Lone Grave," *Boston Daily Globe*, Dec. 23, 1890.
"Most on the Mystery," *Lake George News*, Feb. 20, 1890.
"The Sawtell Murder," *Boston Evening Transcript*, Dec. 1, 1891.
"Sawtelle Must Hang," *Day*, Dec. 26, 1890.
"State Opens," *Boston Daily Globe*, Dec. 17, 1890.
"'Twas Apoplexy," *Boston Daily Globe*, Dec. 28, 1891.
"A Very Macabre Christmas Greeting," *Portsmouth Herald*, Dec. 11, 1958.
"Was it Opium?," *Boston Daily Globe*, Dec. 27, 1891.

FAMILY

Married at 15; Dead at 20

"Benham Arrested," *Buffalo Evening News.* Jan. 9. 1897.
"Benham Behind The Bars," *Buffalo Courier.* Jan. 10. 1897.
"The Benham Case," *Evening Tribune.* Jun. 1. 1900.
"Benham Found Guilty," *The Buffalo Enquirer.* Jul. 29. 1897.
"Benham Held for Murder," *New York Times.* Feb. 13. 1897.
"Benham is at the Bar," *Democrat and Chronicle.* Jan. 21. 1897.
"Benham Murder Trial," *Watertown Daily Times.* Jul. 17. 1897.
"Benham Now A Catholic," *Buffalo Times.* Jan. 17. 1900.
"Chemist and Coroner," *Democrat and Chronicle.* Feb. 1. 1897.
"Conference of Benham Lawyers," *Buffalo Evening News.* Feb. 11. 1897.
"Death of Mrs. Howard Benham," *Buffalo Evening News.* Jan. 4. 1897.
"Found Much Morphine," *The Buffalo Commercial.* Jan. 16. 1897.
"Genesee," *Democrat and Chronicle.* Jan. 8. 1897.
"Hardly a Trace," *Buffalo Courier.* Jul. 10. 1897.
"Married at 15. Died at 20," *Buffalo Times.* Jan. 4. 1897.
"Not Guilty," *Evening Tribune.* Jun. 21. 1900.
"Search Begun," *Buffalo Enquirer.* Jan. 11. 1897.
"The Testimony Very Damaging," *Democrat and Chronicle.* Jan. 13. 1897.
"Wild Excitement in Batavia," *Buffalo Courier.* Jan. 7. 1897.

Little Conestoga Creek

"Arrest of the Husband," *Philadelphia Inquirer,* Oct. 8, 1888.
Israel Smith Clare, A *Brief History of Lancaster County*, (Lancaster, PA: 1892).
"Dellinger Found Guilty," *Reading Times,* Mar. 15, 1889.
"Dellinger Re-arrested," *Patriot,* November 1, 1888.
"Did He Kill His Young Wife?" *Patriot,* Oct. 8, 1888.
"Feared Wife Murderer," *Daily Times,* February 27, 1897.
"Ten Years for Killing his Wife," *Belvidere Standard,* Apr. 3, 1889.
"The Conestoga Mystery.," *Patriot,* Mar. 8, 1889.
"The Dellinger Murder," *Lancaster Daily Intelligencer,* Mar. 9, 1889.
"The Supposed Wife Murderer Released," *Evening Star,* Oct. 18, 1888.
"Very Dramatic," *National Police Gazette*, November 3, 1888.
"Was She Murdered?" *Lancaster Weekly Examiner,* Oct. 10, 1888.
"Woman Found Murdered," *Philadelphia Inquirer,* Oct. 6, 1888.

Thrown Out of the Window

John Davison Lawson, American *State Trials: a collection of the important and interesting criminal trials which have taken place in the United States from the beginning of our government to the present day.* (St. Louis: Thomas Law Books, 1916).

S. U. Pinney, *Reports of cases argued and determined in the Supreme Court of the territory of Wisconsin.* (Chicago: Callaghan, 1874).
George S. Twitchell and F. Carroll Brewster, *The Trial and Conviction of George S. Twitchell, Jr for The Murder of Mrs. Mary E. Hill, His Mother-In-Law, With The Eloquent Speeches of Counsel on ... Judge Brewster's Charge to The Jury, in Full,* (Philadelphia: Barclay & Co., 1869).

The Talbotts

"Paying The Last Penalty; Two Brothers Hanged For The Murder Of Their Father." *New York Times.* Jul. 23, 1881.
"Perry Hoshor Talbott and Belle (McFarland) Talbott." *Our Family Gallery.* http://www.shoreheritage.com/gallery04.html
Kerry Segrave, *Parricide in the United States, 1840-1899,* (Jefferson, NC: McFarland & Co., 2009).
Albert P. Talbott and Charles E. Talbott. *History of The Assassination of Dr. P.H. Talbott and The Trial of His Two Sons.* (Maryville, Mo.: Printed by the Republican Steam Job and Book Office, 1880).

An Unfortunate Organization

Reuben A. Dunbar, *Life and Confession of Reuben A. Dunbar, Convicted and Executed for The Murder of Stephen V. and David L. Lester, (Aged 8 and 10 Years,) in Westerlo, Albany County, September 28, 1850, Second ed.* (Albany: Published by John D. Parsons. Weed, Parsons & Co., Printers., 1851).
"Wickham Farm Burying Ground," Helderberg Hilltowns of Albany County, NY, https://albanyhilltowns.com/Wickham_Farm_Burying_Ground.
William Henry Paddock, *History of the police service of Albany from 1609 to 1902: from ancient and modern authoritative records ... with reminiscences of the past, ... of leading criminal cases and trials.* (Albany, N.Y.: Police Beneficiary Association of Albany, N.Y., 1902).
Alvin V. Sellers, *Classics of the Bar.* (Baxley, Ga.: Classic Pub. Co., 1909).
The Columbian speaker: readings and recitations for young people, with handsome illustrations. (Chicago: W.B. Conkey, 1903).
Margaret Thompson, *Phrenological Character Of Reuben Dunbar, With A Short Treatise On the Causes And Prevention Of Crime.* (Albany: P. L. Gilbert Museum Building, 1851).

The Walton-Matthews Tragedy

"Accidents and Offences," *Frank Leslie's Illustrated Newspaper,* May 21, 1864.
"An Atrocious Double Murder," *Boston Herald,* Jul. 2, 1860.
"Another Chapter in Metropolitan Crime," *New York Herald,* Jul. 2, 1860.
"Conviction of Charles M, Jefferds," *New-York Observer,* Jan. 2, 1862.

"The Eighteenth Ward Murders," *New-York Daily Tribune*, Jul. 4, 1860.
"From New York," Sun, March 9, 1863.
"Horrible Tragedy," *Commercial Advertiser*, Jul. 2, 1860.
"Investigation of the Murder in Sing Sing Prison," *New-York Tribune*, May 18, 1868.
"Jefferds Gone to State Prison," *New York Dispatch*, May 8, 1864.
"The Jefferds Murder," *World*, May 25, 1868.
"Mayor's Office, New York, Jul.," *Evening Post*, Jul. 13, 1860.
"Murder in Sing Sing State Prison," *Evening Post.*, May 15, 1868.
"News Article," *Frank Leslie's Illustrated Newspaper*, Jun. 6, 1868.
"Supreme Court," *Journal of Commerce, Jr*, November 8, 1862.
"Trial of Charles M, Jefferds," *World*, Jul. 11, 1861.
"Verdict in the Walton Matthews Murder," *Philadelphia Inquirer*, Jul. 20, 1860.
"The Walton and Matthews Tragedy," *Frank Leslie's Illustrated Newspaper*, Jul. 14, 1860.
"The Walton Tragedy," *New York Atlas*, Jul. 8, 1860.
"The Walton-Mathews Murder," *New York Herald*, February 24, 1861.
"The Walton-Mathews Murder," *New York Herald*, Jul. 12, 1861.
"The Walton-Mathews Murder," *Evening Post*, Apr. 8, 1864.
"The Walton-Mathews Murder," *Evening Post*, Dec. 19, 1861.
"Will Of The Late John Walton," *Boston Courier*, Jul. 9, 1860.

REVENGE

Tragedy at Vineland

"The Death of Uri Carruth," *New York Tribune,* Oct. 25, 1875.
"Death of Uri Carruth," *Vineland Advertiser,* Oct. 30, 1875.
"The Landis Trial," *Massachusetts Spy,* Feb. 11, 1876.
"The Landis-Carruth Trial," *West-Jersey Pioneer,* Jan. 13, 1876.
"Mr. Landis' Statement," *Vineland Weekly,* Mar. 27, 1875.
"The Natural Result of Personalities," *Caledonian,* Mar. 26, 1875.
"Terrible Tragedy," *Vineland Advertiser,* Mar. 20, 1875.
"The Tragedy at Vineland Last Spring," *Daily Graphic,* Jan. 26, 1876.
"The Vineland Tragedy," *Albany Evening Journal,* Mar. 22, 1875.
"The Vineland Tragedy," *West Jersey Press,* Mar. 24, 1875.
"The Vineland Tragedy," *West-Jersey Pioneer,* Mar. 25, 1875.

A Weight of Grief

"The Case of Mrs. Hyde," *New York Times,* April 23, 1872.
"The Fate of a Seducer," *Illustrated Police News,* February 8, 1872.
Fanny Windley Hyde and William Hemstreet, *Official Report of the Trial of Fanny Hyde, for the Murder of Geo, W, Watson, Including the Testimony, the Arguments of Counsel, and the Charge of the, Portraits of the Defendant and the Deceased,* (New York: J.R, McDivitt, 1872).
Ann, Jones, *Women Who Kill: Profiles of Female Serial Killers,* (New York: Holt, Rinehart, and Winston, 1980).

Dark Kentucky Politics

"Brave to His Death," *Pittsburg Dispatch,* Nov. 11, 1889.
"Dark Kentucky Tragedy," *New Haven Register,* Nov. 9, 1889.
"A Double Murder," *National Police Gazette,* Nov. 23, 1889.
"Hot Southern Blood," *Milwaukee Journal-Sentinel,* Nov. 8, 1889.
"The Kentucky Code," *Daily Nebraska State Journal,* Nov. 12, 1889.
"A Kentucky Tragedy," *Evening Star,* Nov. 9, 1889.
"Slain by Goodloe," *Daily Gazette,* Nov. 9, 1889.
Albert P. Talbott, and Charles E. Talbott, *The Talbots, History of The Assassination of Dr, P.H, Talbott,* (Maryville, Mo, Republican Steam Job and Book Office, 1881).

ADULTERY

The Guttenberg Murder

"The Guttenberg Murder," *New York Tribune,* June 10, 2024.
"Kinkowski Found Guilty Of Murder," *New York Tribune,* Oct. 22, 1881.
"Kinkowski Led to the Gallows," *National Police Gazette,* Jan 21, 1882.
"Kinkowski Sentenced to Death," *New York Herald,* Nov. 6, 1881.
"Kinkowski's Confession," *New York Herald,* Dec. 15, 1881.
"Kinkowski's Defence," *New York Herald,* Oct. 15, 1881.
"Kinkowski's Defense Begging to be Allowed to Visit the Place Where He Last Saw Mina Muller," *Cincinnati Commercial Tribune,* Oct. 8, 1881.
"Kinkowski's Farewell," *New York Herald,* Jan. 2, 1882.
"Kinkowski's Fate," *New York Herald,* Dec. 4, 1881.
"Martin Kinkowskis Trial Damaging Testimony Against Kinkowski Identified by a Lady," *New York Herald,* Oct. 8, 1881.
"Mena Muller's Murder," *New York Herald,* Oct. 6, 1881.
"Nearing the Gallows," *New York Herald,* Jan. 4, 1882.
"Paying The Death Penalty," *New York Tribune,* Jan. 7, 1882.
"The Weehawken Murder," *National Police Gazette,* Oct. 22, 1881.
Wedded and murdered within an hour! (Philadelphia: Barclay & Co., 1881).

Love and Law

Peyton Boyle, James Wells Goodwin, and Robert Desty. *The Federal Reporter, with key-number annotations., Vol. 185.* (St. Paul: West Pub. Co., 1880).
"Crime and Criminals." *Perry Chief.* May 4, 1883.
Hazard, W.B. *St. Louis Criminal Record, Vol. 6.* (St. Louis: W. B. Hazard Md & C.A.S. Harris, 1880).
Charles F. Kring and D. C. J. Broemser. *Love & law.* (St. Louis: author, 1882).
"Kring v. Missouri, 107 U.S. 221 (1883)." *Justia US Supreme Court Center, https://supreme.*justia.com/cases/federal/us/107/221/

The Cuban Con Artist

Linda Wolf, The *Murder of Dr. Chapman: The Legendary Trials of Lucretia Chapman and Her Lover.* (New York: Harper Collins, 2004).
Du Bois, William E., *Trial of Lucretia Chapman: otherwise called Lucretia Espos y Mina, who was jointly indicted with Lino Amalia Espos y Mina, for the murder of William Chapman.* (Philadelphia: G.W. Mentz & Son, 1882).

Illicit Infatuation

"Crozier Respited," *New York Herald,* Apr. 23, 1876.
"Crozier to be Hanged," Auburn Daily Bulletin, Mar. 17, 1876.

"Death of George C, Crozier, Wife Murderer, in Auburn Prison," *Geneva Gazette,* August 28, 1896.
"George E, Crozier (1833-1896)," Find a Grave, Sep. 4, 1833, https://www.findagrave.com/memorial/124337576/george-e-crozier.
'Minerva Dutcher Calhoon (1857-1915)," Find a Grave, Mar. 1, 1857, https://www.findagrave.com/memorial/121833912/dutcher.
New York (State) Legislature Assembly, *Documents of the Assembly of the State of New York: Volume 8,* (Albany: Jerome B, Parmenter, State Printer, 1877).
The Trial of Geo, E, Crozier, (Penn Yan: Cleveland & Cornell, 1876).
"Uxoricide," *New York Herald,* Mar. 19, 1876.

Thus She Passed Away

"A Most Horrible Crime," *Cincinnati Daily Gazette,* Oct. 23, 1880.
"A Singular Murder," *Cincinnati Daily Gazette,* Oct. 22, 1880.
"A Strangler Hanged," *Cincinnati Commercial Tribune,* Jan. 24, 1884
"Another Juror Obtained," *San Francisco Chronicle,* Jan. 28, 1881.
"Found Guilty of Murder," *New York Herald,* Sep. 15, 1882
"George A, Wheeler" San Francisco Bulletin, Jun. 21, 1882.
"George A, Wheeler's Defense," *San Francisco, Bulletin Feb.* 4, 1881.
""Thus She Passed Away," National Police Gazette, Nov. 6, 1880.
"The Wheeler Murder Case," *San Francisco Bulletin,* Feb. 3, 1881.
"Wheeler's Atrocious Crime," *San Francisco Bulletin,* Oct. 22, 1880.

INSANITY

A Woman Scorned

Leonard Benardo and Jennifer Weiss. *Brooklyn by Name: How the Neighborhoods. Streets. Parks. Bridges and More Got Their Names.* (New York: New York University Press. 2006).
Wesley Bradshaw, *The Goodrich horror: being the full confession of Kate Stoddart. or Lizzie King: Why She Killed Charles Goodrich. Showing a Deserted Woman's Vengeance.* (Philadelphia: Old Franklin Pub. House. 1873).
"The Goodrich Murder. The Detectives Working in the Dark," *New York Times.* Apr. 1, 1873.
"The Goodrich Murder; Latest Details. Arrest of the supposed murderess," *New York Times.* Jul. 11, 1873.
"The Goodrich Murder; The Inquest," *New York Times.* Jul. 13, 1873.
"Kate Stoddard Finally Disposed Of." *New York Times.* Jul. 16, 1874.
"Kate Stoddard, the Goodrich Murderess." *Canadian Illustrated News.* Jul. 26, 1873.
George W. Walling and A. Kaufmann. *Recollections Of A New York Chief Of Police: An Official Record Of Thirty-Eight Years As Patrolman. Detective. Captain. Inspector. And Chief Of The ... Of The Denver Police.* (Denver: Specially issued for the benefit of the Denver Police Mutual Aid Fund. 1887).

Murdered at Prayer

"Arraigned for Murder," *The Boston Globe,* Jan. 2, 1879.
"Arraignment of the Byfield Murderess," *Boston Evening Journal,* Jan. 2, 1879.
"The Byfield Murder," *Boston Globe,* Jan. 1, 1879.
"The Byfield Murderess," *Boston Evening Transcript,* Jan. 14, 1879.
"The Byfield Murderess Seat to the Insane Asylum," *Boston Evening Transcript,* February 5, 1879.
"The Byfield Tragedy," *Boston Globe,* Jan. 1, 1879.
"The Byfield Tragedy," *Boston Post,* Jan. 2, 1879.
"Eastern Massachusetts," *Springfield Daily Republican,* Jan. 1, 1879.
"Murdered at Prayer," *Illustrated Police News,* Jan. 11, 1879.
"A Shocking Tragedy," *Boston Post,* Jan. 1, 1879.
"Suburban Short Notes," *Boston Post,* February 4, 1879.
"Terrible Deed of an Insane Wife," *Evening Post,* Jan. 3, 1879.

The Veiled Murderess

"The 'Veiled Murderess'; Her Life and History," *New York Times,* July 31, 1855.
"Veiled Murderess Dies with 50 Years' Secret," *New York Times.* May 15, 1905.
D. Wilson, *Henrietta Robinson,* (New York: Miller, Orton & Mulligan, 1855).

The Worst Woman on Earth

"The Burlingham Murder," *New Haven Register*, Sep. 7, 1893.
"Crimes That Only a Fiend Could Commit," *New York Herald*, Sep. 6, 1893.
"Exciting War Play Produced By The Insane Inmates Of Mattawan Asylum," *Kalamazoo Gazette*, Nov. 1, 1898.
"Halliday's Bullet Riddled Body Found," *New York Herald*, Sep. 8, 1893.
"Insane Woman Kills Nurse She Loved," *Boston Herald*, Sep. 28, 1906.
"Lizzie Halliday Dead," *New York Times,* Jun. 29, 1918.
"Lizzie Halliday's Past," *New York Tribune*, Sep. 9, 1893.
"Lizzie Halliday's Trial," *New York Herald*, June 18, 1894
"Mother And Daughter Both Met Their Death on the Halliday Farm," *Trenton Evening Times*, Sep. 7, 1893.
"Mrs. Halliday Anxious to Die," *New York Herald*, Dec. 12, 1893.
"Mrs. Halliday to Plead," *New York Herald*, Jun. 19, 1894.
"Murdered By a Woman," *National Police Gazette*, Sep. 23, 1893.
"Murdered Women Found in a Barn," *New York Herald*, Sep. 5, 1893.
"She is a Murderer," *New York Herald,* June 22, 1894.
"Was a Triple Murder," *New Haven Register,* Sep. 7, 1893.
"Whitechapel Murders," *Kalamazoo Gazette,* December 3, 1893.
"Will Not Execute Her," *New York Herald*, July 17, 1894.

Horrible Murder in Twelfth Street

"The Appalling Murder in Twelfth Street," *Frank Leslie's Illustrated Newspaper, Dec. 22, 1860.*
"Arrest of the Murderer of Mrs," *Albany Evening Journal,* Dec. 11, 1860.
"Court of Oyer and Terminer," *New York Herald, Dec. 23, 1860.*
"Horrible Murder in Twelfth Street," *New York Herald,* Dec. 8, 1860.
"Murder in New York," *Boston Post,* Dec. 10, 1860.
"Mysterious Murder a Woman Butchered in Broad-Day No Clue to the Murderer," *New York Tribune,* Dec. 8, 1860.
"News Article," *Herald,* Dec. 13, 1860.
"News Article," *World,* Jan. 28, 1861.
"The Twelfth Street Murder," *New-York Atlas,* Dec. 16, 1860.
"The Twelfth Street Murder," *New York Herald,* Dec. 12, 1860.
"The Twelfth Street Tragedy," *New York Herald,* Dec. 11, 1860.
"The Twelfth Street Tragedy," *New York Herald,* Dec. 14, 1860.

Salvation Army Tragedy

"Bloody Deed at Omaha," *Chicago Tribune,* Nov. 16, 1891.
"The Motive Was Jealousy," *National Police Gazette,* Dec. 5, 1891.
"Salvation Army Tragedy," *Sioux City Journal,* Nov. 16, 1891.
"Shot by a Salvationist," *Saint Paul Globe,* Nov. 16, 1891.

"Was it Jealousy?" *Champaign Daily Gazette,* Nov. 16, 1891.

RANDOM VIOLENCE

Rum and the Knife

"Cowardly Murder of a Young Woman in South Boston," *Boston Daily Advertiser,* Nov. 15, 1877.
"A Drunken Passion," *New York Herald,* Nov. 18, 1877.
"A Life Sentence," *Lowell Daily Citizen and News,* Mar.19, 1878.
"Massachusetts," *Woonsocket Patriot and Rhode Island State Register,* Nov. 29, 1877.
"Rum and the Knife," *Illustrated Police News,* Nov. 24, 1877.

Little Mary Mohrman

"Execution of Hanlon," *Sun,* Feb. 2, 1871.
John Davidson Lawson, *American State Trials*, (St. Louis: P.H. Thomas Law Book Co., 1915).
"Legal Intelligence," *Philadelphia Inquirer,* Nov. 16, 1870.
Life, Trial, Confession and Conviction of John Hanlon, (Philadelphia: Barclay & Co., 1870).
"The Barbarous Murder of a Little Girl." *Public Ledger, Sep.* 10, 1868,
"The Mary Mohrman Murder." *Philadelphia Inquirer, Nov.* 18, 1870.

The Car-Hook Tragedy

Headsman, "1873: William Foster." *Executed Today.* March 21, 2011. https://www.executedtoday.com/2011/03/21/1873-william-foster/
J. Edwards Renault, The *"Car-Hook" Tragedy. The Life, Trial, Conviction and Execution of William Foster for the Murder of Avery D. Putnam.* (Philadelphia: Barclay & Co., 1873).
Charles Sutton, James B. Mix, and Samuel Anderson Mackeever. *New York Tombs, Its Secrets and Mysteries (Patterson Smith Series in Criminology, Law Enforcement & Social Problems.* Publication No. 178). (New York: United States Pub. Co., 1873).
George W. Walling, Recollections *of a New York Chief of Police.* (New York: Caxton Book Concern, 1887.)

Queen of the Demimonde

Herbert Asbury, French *Quarter.* (New York: A.A. Knopf, 1936).
Robert Tallant, *Ready to Hang*, (New York: Harper, 1952).
"A Jealous Pimp." *National Police Gazette, Nov.* 24, 1883.
"Kate Townsend's Will." *Times-Picayune.* Nov. 9, 1883.
"Murder of the Queen of the Southern Demi Monde." *Plain Dealer.* Nov. 8, 1883.

"Sykes Addresses the Jury." *Patriot.* Feb 2, 1884.
"The Kate Townsend Succession." *Times-Picayune.* Jan. 30, 1884.

MULTIPLE MURDERS

Horror!

Anton Probst, *The Life, Confession, and Atrocious Crimes of Antoine Probst, The Murderer of The Deering Family, To which is Added a Graphic Account of Many of the .., Murders Committed in this and other Countries,* (Philadelphia: Barclay, 1866).
Howard O. Sprogle, The *Philadelphia Police, Past and Present*, pp, xxiv, 671, (Philadelphia: [The Author] 1887).
Daniel Rubin, "Daniel Rubin: After the Massacre Of All But A Boy, Family Lives To Tell The Tale." *Inquirer [Philadelphia], Apr.* 12, 2009.

Andrew Hellman, alias Adam Horn

"Adam Horn," *Baltimore Sun,* April 24, 1843.
"Adam Horn Alias Andrew Hellman - Requisition from the Governor of Ohio," *Sun,* May 4, 1843.
"Andrew Hellman, Alias Adam Horn," *Baltimore Sun,* Dec. 2, 1843.
"Arrival of Adam Horn in Custody," *Baltimore Sun,* May 1, 1843.
"Conviction of Adam Horm," *Philadelphia Inquirer,* Nov. 29, 1843.
"Horrible Murder," *American and Commercial Daily Advertiser,* Apr.19, 1843.
"Horrible Murder," *Carroll Free Press,* Apr. 28, 1843.
"Horrible Murder in Baltimore County," *Baltimore Sun,* Apr. 19, 1843.
Serious Almanac, (New York: 1845)
"Suicide Of A Witness In The Case Of Adam Horn," *Commercial Advertiser,* Nov. 15, 1843.
"Supposed Murderer Arrested," *Sunbury American and Shamokin Journal,* Apr. 29, 1843.
"Trial of Adam Horn, For Murder," *Baltimore Sun*, Nov. 23, 1843.
"Trial of Horn," *Baltimore Sun*, Nov. 22, 1843.
"Trial of Horn," *Dollar Newspaper*, Nov. 29, 1843.

The New Hampshire Horror

"An Almost Incredible Crime," *New York Herald,* Nov. 26, 1883.
"New Hampshire Horror," *National Police Gazette,* Dec. 15, 1883.
Particulars of the New Hampshire Horror, (Laconia: J, Lane & Co, 1883).
"Samon Confesses," *New York Tribune,* Dec. 4, 1883.
"Samon Refuses To Confess," *New York Tribune,* Dec. 3, 1883.
"Samon, The Triple Murderer," *Truth,* Dec. 4, 1883.
"Samon's Neck Broken," *New Haven Register,* Apr. 17, 1885.
"The Leconia Tragedy," *Daily Evening Bulletin,* Apr. 1, 1884.
"Triple Murder at Laconia, N.H," *Springfield Republican,* Nov. 26, 1883.

Arson to Hide a Worse Crime

"Arson to Hide a Worse Crime," *National Police Gazette,* Dec. 5, 1891.
"A Family Murdered," *Evening Star,* Nov. 28, 1891.
"The Fauquier Tragedy," *Alexandria Gazette,* Nov. 12, 1891.
"The Fauquier Tragedy," *Alexandria Gazette,* Nov. 14, 1891.
"Fired to Conceal Murders," *Morning News,* Nov. 11, 1891.
"Guarded in Court," *Roanoke Times,* Dec. 30, 1891.
"Hanged on the Day Appointed," *Watertown Daily Times,* Mar. 18, 1892.
"Heflin Respited," *Shenandoah Herald,* Mar. 18, 1892.
"Joseph Dye on trial," *Washington Post,* Jan. 8, 1892.
"A Murderer Confesses," *News and Observer,* Nov. 27, 1891.
"Murderers Lynched," *Evening Star,* Mar. 18, 1892.
"South and West," *Boston Herald,* Nov. 11, 1891.
"To Swing for Their Crimes," *Atlanta Journal,* Jan. 14, 1892.
"Virginia," *Weekly Union Times,* Nov. 20, 1891.

The Northwood Murderer

"A Terrible Tragedy In Roxbury," *Providence Evening Press,* Jun. 18, 1865.
"B, Franklin Evans," *Boston Traveler,* Feb. 18, 1873.
"Bussey's Woods," *Boston Traveler,* Feb.7, 1873.
"The Case of 'Scratch Gravel' Investigation by the Legislature," *Boston Daily Advertiser,* Apr. 26, 1866.
"Child Lost," *New Hampshire Patriot and State Gazette,* Nov. 14, 1850.
"Concord and Vicinity Franklin B," *New Hampshire Patriot and State Gazette,* Feb. 18, 1874.
"Confession of Franklin B, Evans," *New Hampshire Sentinel,* Feb. 26, 1874.
"Discovery of the Skeleton: The Supposed Murder of the Joyce Children," *Cincinnati Daily Enquirer,* Dec. 21, 1866.
Alonzo J, Fogg, *The Statistics and Gazetteer of New-Hampshire,* (Concord: D, L, Guernsey Bookseller and Publisher, 1874).
"Franklin B. Evans," Wikipedia, Apr. 17, 2024, https://en.wikipedia.org/wiki/Franklin_B._Evans
"Franklin County," *Portland Daily Press,* Feb. 12, 1873.
"Girl Outraged and Murdered by her Uncle," *Springfield Republican,* Nov. 5, 1872.
William N. Hobbs, "*Georgiana Lovering, 12 years old murdered,*" Luminous-Lint, https://luminous-lint.com/app/image/5085483405021889325917637 42/.
"Horrible Murder And Outrage," *Hartford Daily Courant,* Jun. 20, 1865.
Milli S. Knudsen, *Hard Time in Concord, New Hampshire,* (Westminster: Heritage Boos, 2008).
"The Murder of the Joyce Children," *Age,* Apr. 24, 1866.
"The Murder Trials at Farmington.," *Daily Eastern Argus,* Oct. 31, 1863.
"The New Hampshire Horror.," *New York Herald,* Nov. 5, 1872.

"Trial of the Northwood Murderer," *New Hampshire Patriot and State Gazette,* Feb. 5, 1873.
"The Trial of the Northwood Murderer," *Boston Globe*, Feb. 5, 1873.
"The West Roxbury Tragedy," *Saturday Evening Gazette,* Jul. 8, 1865.
"The West Roxbury Tragedy the Murderer Discovered," *Boston Journal,* Mar. 9, 1866.

Antoine Le Blanc

"Antoin LeBlanc." *New Jersey Hall of Shame, http://www.*njhallofshame.com/NomineesPages/Nominee_AntoineLeBlanc.html
L'Aura Muller, "The Haunted Restaurant of Morristown." *Cromwell Hills On-line, 2000, http://cromwellcrew.*com/WedgewoodInn.html
Jon Blackwell, *Notorious New Jersey: 100 True Tales of Murders and Mobsters, Scandals and Scoundrels*, (New York: Rivergate Books, 2007).
Sayre family; lineage of Thomas Sayre, a founder of Southampton (Toronto: Nabu Press, 2010).

CONNECTED MURDERS

With a Butcher's Keen Blade

"Arraigned for Murder," *Evening Post,* May 27, 1892.
"Attempts at Suicide," *Evening Post,* Jun. 11, 1892.
"Carved Two Men with a Butcher's Keen Blade," *New York Herald,* May 1, 1892.
"Doomed to the Electrical Chair," *Muskegon Daily Chronicle*, Apr. 13, 1893.
"Guilty of Murder, First Degree," *Kingston Daily Freeman*, Oct. 27, 1892.
"He Will Soon Know His Fate," *Evening World,* Oct. 26, 1892.
"Killed With a Cheese Knife," *Evening World,* May 2, 1892.
"Pallister Has Hope," *Evening World,* Oct. 27, 1892.
"Pallister Murder Trial," *Evening World,* Oct. 20, 1892.
"Pallister Sentenced to Death," *New York Herald,* Nov. 5, 1892.
"The Prisoner's Story of The Killing," *New-York Tribune,* Oct. 26, 1892.
"Saw Him Commit Murder," *New York Herald,* Oct. 25, 1892.
"Says He Was Protecting A Friend," *Sun,* Oct. 26, 1892.
"Tried to Follow Woffel," *New York Herald,* Jun. 11, 1892.
"Will Soon Know His Fate," *New York Herald,* Oct. 26, 1892.

Murderer Quickly Caught

"Forging Frank Rohle's Chain," *Evening World,* Dec. 13, 1892.
"Gotham by 'Phone," *Philadelphia Inquirer,* Dec. 24, 1892.
"The Murderer of Paulsen Caught," *New-York Tribune,* Oct. 1, 1892.
"Murderer Quickly Caught," *Jersey City news,* Sep. 30, 1892.
"The New York Murder," *Evening Bulletin,* Sep. 30, 1892.
"A New York Murder Mystery," *Evening Journal,* Sep. 30, 1892.
"Paulsen's Slayer," *Evening World,* Sep. 30, 1892.
"Roehl, The Murderer Sentenced," *New York Tribune,* Dec. 24, 1892.
"Rohle May Die Monday," *Evening World,* Feb. 1, 1893.
"Rohle Slain," *Evening World,* May 10, 1893.
"Sentenced to Die," *The Daily Times,* Jan. 20, 1893.
"Stay for Murderer Rohle," *The New York Times,* Feb. 2, 1893.
"Sure it Was Rohle," *Evening World,* Oct. 1, 1892.

Escape from the Death-House

"Both Taken," *Evening World,* Apr. 22, 1893.
"Condemned Convicts Escape," *Evening capital journal,* Apr. 21, 1893.
"Doomed Men Escape," *Evening World,* Apr. 21, 1893.
"Escaped," *Buffalo Evening News,* Apr. 21, 1893.

Noah Sheidlower, "Explore the History of the Notable Sing Sing Prison," Untapped New York, https://untappedcities.com/2021/05/25/sing-sing-prison/.
"Give Up the Search," *Evening World,* May 12, 1893.
"List of People Executed in New York," Wikipedia, May 20, 2024, https://en.wikipedia.org/wiki/List_of_people_executed_in_New_York.
"Murder the Only Plausible Theory," *New York Herald,* May 18, 1893.
"Murderer Roehle Found," *Buffalo Evening News,* May 10, 1893.
"Murderers May Be in the Mountains," *New York Herald,* Apr. 28, 1893.
"Murders Escape," *Evening Bulletin,* Apr. 22, 1893.
"Pallister," *Evening World,* May 16, 1893.
"Pallister Fake Now," *Jersey City news,* May 16, 1893.
"Pallister Is Dead, Too," *New-York Tribune,* May 17, 1893.
"Rohle Slain," *The Evening World,* May 10, 1893.
"Will Not Find Pallister's Body," *New York Herald,* May 13, 1893.

Murder Among the Whyos, Part1

Herbert Asbury, *The Gangs of New York*, (New York: A, A, Knopf, 1928).
Defenders and Offenders, (New York: Buchner & Co, 1888).
"An Amateur Athlete Murdered," *Daily Register,* Jul. 6, 1887.
"Dan Lyons Found Guilty," *Plain Dealer,* Sep. 27, 1887.
"Dan Lyons Hanged," *Daily Critic,* Aug. 21, 1888.
"Dan Lyons Homeward Bound," *New York Herald,* Jul. 29, 1887.
"Dan Lyons in the Tombs," *New York Sun,* Jul. 30, 1887.
"'Dan' Lyons Laid Low," *New York Herald,* Aug. 14, 1887.
"Dan Lyons Tells His Story," *New York Sun,* Sep. 24, 1888.
"Dan Lyons Wake," *New York Herald,* Aug. 16, 1887.
Anthony M. Destefano, *Gangland New York*, (New York: LP, 2015).
"Execution of Dan Lyons for the Murder of Joseph Quinn," *Evening News,* Aug. 21, 1888.
"Lyons in the Tombs," *New York Herald,* Jul. 30, 1887.
"Lyons Pleads Self-Defense," *New York Herald,* Sep. 21, 1887.
"Lyons Tells How He Killed Quinn," *New York Tribune,* Sep. 24, 1887.
"Lyons to Be Hanged," *New York Herald,* Sep. 24, 1887.
"Murphy Got First Shot," *New York Sun,* Aug. 14, 1887.
"Planting a Tough," *New York Herald,* Aug. 17, 1887.
"Quinn's Murderer in Court," *New York Sun,* Aug. 4, 1887.
"Shot By a Saloon Keeper," *Brooklyn Daily Eagle,* Aug. 14, 1887.
"The Shot Whyo is Dead," *New York Sun,* Aug. 15, 1887.
"Was it a Conspiracy?" *New York Herald,* Jul. 24, 1887.
"Whyos Leaderless Again," *New York Sun,* Sep. 22, 1887.
"'Whyo' Lyons Dead," *New York Herald,* Aug. 15, 1887.

Murder Among the Whyos, Part 2

Herbert Asbury, The *Gangs of New York*, (New York: A, A, Knopf, 1928).
"Awaiting the Rope," *New York Herald,* Jan. 20, 1888.
"Beezy Garrity's Murder," *New York World,* Jan. 23, 1888.
"Dan Driscoll Indicted for Murder," *Cleveland Leader,* Jul. 9, 1886.
"Dan Driscoll Must Hang," *New York Herald,* Jun. 19, 1887.
"Dan Driscoll's Bold Plot.," *New Haven Register,* Jan. 10, 1888.
Defenders and offenders, (New York: Buchner & Co, 1888).
"Driscoll in a Surly Mood," *New York World,* Dec. 3, 1887.
"Driscoll's Last Hope Gone," *New York Herald,* Nov. 30, 1887.
"Driscoll's Pistol Shot," *New York Tribune,* Sep. 29, 1886.
"Driscoll's Short Respite," *New York Herald,* Jan. 19, 1888.
"Iron Cages for Desperadoes," *New York Herald,* Jan. 5, 1888.
"Murderers Baffled," *New York Herald,* Dec. 3, 1887.
"The Queen of the Whyo Gang," *Times,* Jul. 4, 1886.
Jacob August Riis, *The Making of an American,* (New York: The Macmillan Company, 1901).
Luc Sante, *Low Life: Lures and Snares of Old New York,* (New York: Farrar, Straus and Giroux, 2003).
"Summary of the News," *New York Herald,* Oct. 2, 1886.
"Who Killed Bridget Garrity," *New York Herald,* Sep. 28, 1886.
"The Whyo Chief to be Hanged," *New York Herald,* Oct. 9, 1886.
"'Whyo Dan' is Hanged," *Daily Critic,* Jan. 23, 1888.
"The Whyo Exults," *New York World,* Jan. 21, 1888.

UNSOLVED

15 Corning Street

"'Blind Bill' Free," *Globe,* Dec. 11, 1897.
"Alice Ruderhan's Career," *Post,* Nov. 14, 1897.
"Boy Lovers," *Globe,* Nov. 6, 1897.
"Crime Bared," *Globe,* Nov. 9, 1897.
"Foul Murder," *Globe,* Nov. 5, 1897.
"Is Believed," *Globe,* Nov. 8, 1897.
"Is Leavitt the Murderer?" *Boston Daily Advertiser,* Nov. 15, 1897.
"Leavitt Defense," *Post,* Nov. 12, 1897.
"Leavitt In Court," *Boston Herald,* Nov. 10, 1897.
"McMillan Found," *Globe,* Nov. 7, 1897.
"Murdered Alice Brown," *Post,* Nov. 6, 1897.
"A Mystery," *Boston Daily Advertiser,* Nov. 6, 1897.
"Perhaps Murder," *Boston Journal,* Nov. 4, 1897.
"Scenes at 15 Corning St.," *Globe,* Nov. 6, 1897.
"Unavenged Women Victims of Unsolved New England Murder Mysteries," *Post,* Oct. 3, 1905.
"Who Killed These Men and Women?" *Post,* Oct. 17, 1909.

The Medford Mystery

"A Mystery to Unravel," *Boston Herald,* Mar. 29, 1897.
"Another Clew," *Boston Herald,* Apr. 9, 1897.
"A Poor Witness," *Boston Herald,* Apr. 3, 1897.
"Hard to Solve," *Boston Herald,* Apr. 7, 1897.
"Man on Bicycle," *Boston Herald,* Mar. 30, 1897.
"Medford Mystery Solved," *Boston Herald,* Feb. 28, 1898.
"Medford's Mystery," *Boston Post,* Mar. 29, 1897.
"Murderer of Debbins," *Boston Herald,* Apr. 6, 1897.
"Slick Stranger Traced.," *Boston Herald,* Apr. 5, 1897.
"The Mystery Deepens," *Boston Post,* Mar. 31, 1897.
"Tried to Sell Revolver," *Boston Herald,* Apr. 4, 1897.
"Two Bullets in his head," *Boston Herald,* Apr. 19, 1897.
"Vain Search for Clues," *Boston Post,* Mar. 30, 1897.
"Was Murdered," *Boston Post,* Mar. 20, 1897.
"Woods is Free," *Boston Journal,* Mar. 29, 1897.

The Vanderpool-Field Tragedy

Joseph Wesley Donovan, *Modern Jury Trials and Advocates Containing Condensed Cases. With Sketches and Speeches of American Advocates: The Art Of Winning Cases And Manner Of Counsel Described: With Notes And Rules Of Practice.* (New York: G.A. Jennings Co.. 1881).

"The Northwest," *Daily Inter Ocean [Chicago]*, April 25, 1874.
"Personal Points," *Cincinnati Daily Times,* October 22. 1872.
"The Vanderpool-Field Tragedy," *Plain Dealer [Cleveland*, November 19, 1870.
George Vanderpool, *History Of The Trial Of George Vanderpool For The Murder Of Herbert Field, Including A Brief Sketch Of The Life Of Both Parties. The Judge and Attorneys In The Case,* (Detroit: Printed by the Tunis Steam Print. Co., 1870).

The Boston Barrel Tragedy

"Washington St. and Water St. Boston," Wikimedia Commons. August 28, 2010. File:1860 WashingtonSt WaterSt Boston 2.png - Wikimedia Commons
Leavitt Alley and Franklin Fiske Heard. *Report Of The Trial Of Leavitt Alley. Indicted For The Murder Of Abijah Ellis. In The Supreme Judicial Court Of Massachusetts.* (Boston: Little. Brown, 1875).
"The Boston Fire," *Otago Witness,* January 25, 1873.
"Death of Leavitt Alley," *The Boston Daily Globe,* July 25, 1876.
"How Leavitt Alley was Saved," *The Boston Sunday Globe,* January 29, 1905
"The Unsolved Barrel Tragedy," *The Boston Daily Globe,* May 16, 1892

The Maggie Hourigan Mystery

"$1.000 Reward for a Murderer," *Waterbury Evening Democrat,* Mar. 20, 1890.
"Another Scully Story," *Post-Star,* Mar. 22, 1890.
"For Alleged Libel," *Democrat and Chronicle,* May 14, 1892.
"For Maggie Hourigan's Murder," *New York Herald,* Feb. 5, 1890.
"Gets Ten Thousand Dollars," *Times,* May 19, 1892.
"A Girl's Strange Death," *Times,* Jul. 21, 1890.
"The Governor Offers a Reward," *Brooklyn Daily Eagle,* Mar. 19, 1890.
"The Greenwich Mystery," *Scranton Republican,* Feb. 7, 1890.
"The Hourigan Murder," *Democrat and Chronicle,* Mar. 21, 1890.
"The Hourigan Murder," *Buffalo Courier,* Feb. 7, 1890.
"The Hourigan Murder Mystery," *Erie Times-News,* Mar. 20, 1890.
"Hourigan's Assassin is Liberated," *New York Herald,* Jul. 20, 1890.
"Libel Suit Settled," *Post-Star,* Dec. 5, 1893.
"Maggie Hourigan's Death," *Sun and New York Press,* Nov. 6, 1889.
"Maggie Hourigan's Murderer," *Waterbury Evening Democrat,* Mar. 22, 1890.
"Poor Pretty Maggie!" *National Police Gazette,* Nov. 30, 1889.
"A Mystery Cleared Up," *Sun and the Erie County Independent,* January 3, 1890.
"News Article," *Waterbury Evening Democrat,* Oct. 21, 1889.
"Verdict Against the 'Sun'," *Buffalo Morning Express,* May 15, 1892.

The Rogers Murder

"Another Cold Blooded Murder," *Boston Herald, Jan. 1, 1869.*
"City Intelligence," *New York Journal of Commerce, Jan. 2, 1869.*
"Crimes and Casualties," *Times, Dec. 4, 1869.*

"Death of James Logan," *Evening Post, Jan. 7, 1870.*
"Local Items," *World, Jan. 6, 1869.*
"The Murder Of Charles M. Rogers," *Evening Post, Mar. 11, 1869.*
"News Article," *New-York Atlas, Jan. 9, 1869.*
"Release of Logan No," *New York Tribune, Mar. 31, 1869.*
"The Rogers Murder," *New York Herald, Jan. 4, 1869.*
"The Rogers Murder," *New York Tribune, Jan. 6, 1869.*
"The Rogers Murder," *Boston Herald, Jan. 11, 1869.*
"The Rogers Murder," *World, Jan. 13, 1869.*
"The Rogers Murder," *New York Journal of Commerce, Jan. 14, 1869.*
"The Rogers Murder," *Evening Post, Jan. 15, 1869.*
"The Rogers Murder," *World, Jan. 15, 1869.*
"The Rogers Murder," *Frank Leslie's Illustrated Newspaper, Feb. 13, 1869.*
"The Rogers Murder," *New York Tribune, Jan. 18, 1869.*
"The Rogers Murder," *Herald, Mar. 11, 1869.*
"The Rogers Murder," *New York Herald, Mar. 19, 1869.*
"The Rogers Murder-Another Logan Arrested," *New York Tribune, Feb. 7, 1870.*
"The Rogers Outrage," *New York Herald, Jan. 2, 1869.*
"The Sequel to the Rogers Murder," *Herald, Jan. 6, 1870.*
"The Twelfth Street Murder," *Evening Post, Jan. 5, 1869.*
"Will Murder Out?" *Daily National Republican, Apr. 26, 1869.*

Chloroformed to Death

"Chloroformed To Death!" *Trenton Evening Times*, Jan. 3, 1890.
"A Very Peculiar Case," *New York Times,* Jan. 4, 1890.
"Chloroformed To Death," *New York Tribune,* Jan. 4, 1890.
"A Case of Many Theories," *New York Times,* Jan. 6, 1890.
"Kniffin Tries Suicide," *Philadelphia Enquirer,* Jan. 7, 1890.
"Murdered in Bed!" *National Police Gazette*, Jan. 18, 1890.
"The Kniffin Murder," *National Police Gazette,* Jan. 15, 1890.
"End of the Kniffin Inquest," *Philadelphia Enquirer,* Jan. 29, 1890.
"Freed by The Grand Jury," *Philadelphia Enquirer,* Feb. 14, 1890.
"Kniffin, Pursell and Cupid," *Critic-Record,* Dec. 11, 1890.
Charles Webster, IV, "Bygone Murder and Intrigue," *Trentonian,* Mar. 13, 2012.

About the Author

Robert Wilhelm is a true crime author with a particular interest in nineteenth-century American murders. His 2014 book, The *Bloody Century* (Night Stick Press), summarizes 50 of the most intriguing murder cases from the archives of American crime. In *So Far from Home* (Night Stick Press, 2021), he examines unanswered questions surrounding the 1896 murder of Pearl Bryan. *Wicked Victorian Boston* (History Press, 2017) and *Murder and Mayhem in Essex County* (History Press, 2011) chronicle vice and crime in old Massachusetts. Robert's blog Murder by Gaslight (murderbygaslight.com), has been running continuously since 2009.

www.ingramcontent.com/pod-product-compliance
Lightning Source LLC
Chambersburg PA
CBHW051414090426
42737CB00014B/2667

* 9 7 9 8 9 9 0 7 8 8 1 0 7 *